FRAMED

DIGITALCULTURE**BOOKS**
is a collaborative imprint of the
University of Michigan Press and the
University of Michigan Library.

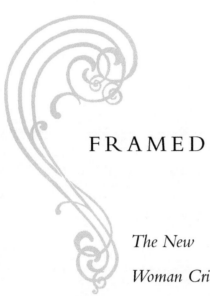

FRAMED

The New
Woman Criminal
in British Culture
at the Fin de Siècle

ELIZABETH CAROLYN MILLER

The University of Michigan Press AND
The University of Michigan Library
ANN ARBOR

Copyright © 2008 by Elizabeth Carolyn Miller
All rights reserved
Published in the United States of America
by The University of Michigan Press and
the University of Michigan Library
Printed and bound by CPI Group (UK) Ltd, Croydon, CR0 4YY

2011   2010   2009   2008   4   3   2   1

A CIP catalog record for this book is available from the British Library.

Library of Congress Cataloging-in-Publication Data

Miller, Elizabeth Carolyn, 1974–
    Framed : the new woman criminal in British culture at the fin de
siècle / Elizabeth Carolyn Miller.
        p.   cm.
    Includes bibliographical references and index.
    ISBN-13: 978-0-472-07044-2
    ISBN-13: 978-0-472-05044-4 (pbk.)
    1. Detective and mystery stories, English—History and criticism.
2. English fiction—19th century—History and criticism.   3. Female
offenders in literature.   4. Terrorism in literature.   5.
Consumption (Economics) in literature.   6. Feminism and literature—
Great Britain—History—19th century.   7. Literature and society—
Great Britain—History—19th century.   8. Detective and mystery
films—Great Britain—History and criticism.   9. Women in popular
culture—Great Britain—History—19th century.   I. Title.
PR878.D4M55   2008
823'.087209—dc22   2008015026

    ISBN-13 978-0-472-02446-9 (electronic)

ACKNOWLEDGMENTS

It is the keenest of pleasures to have the opportunity to thank—with all the authority of print—the many people who have helped me write this book. *Framed* began as my doctoral dissertation at the University of Wisconsin–Madison, and my first and foremost thanks go to Susan David Bernstein, Caroline Levine, and Rebecca Walkowitz; they have been the most generous and stalwart of mentors, and their support was only beginning on the day I submitted my dissertation. I would also like to thank Anne McClintock and Kelley Conway, who served on my dissertation committee and offered brilliant advice. At Madison, I owe thanks to more people than I could possibly enumerate, but I am especially grateful to Jacques Lezra and Susanne Wofford, for their inspiration and encouragement; to Bob Baker and Joseph Wiesenfarth, for initiating me into the study of Victorian literature; to David Bordwell, whose film theory class opened my eyes to a whole new way of thinking about visuality; and to Theresa Kelley and Mario Ortiz-Robles. Support from the Department of English helped me complete my dissertation, and Wisconsin's International Institute provided me with a crucial yearlong fellowship to the University of Warwick, which allowed access to key archival materials in England. Thanks to Jacqueline Labbe for directing my work during my year at Warwick.

I wrote most of this book while I was a postdoctoral fellow at the University of Michigan, and I would like to thank the Public Goods Council, Francis X. Blouin, and the Mellon Foundation for the precious time this fellowship gave me. I am eternally grateful to John Kucich, Jonathan Freedman, and Adela Pinch for their expert feedback on my book manuscript, and for their much-appreciated encouragement. I would also like to thank Martha Vicinus for her wise and generous guidance, Robert Aguirre for his friendship and advice, and the Nineteenth-Century Forum at Michigan. My colleagues at Ohio University offered friendship and support in the final stretch of this project. Special thanks to Johnnie Wilcox, for helping me format images for the book, and to Josie Bloomfield, Andrew Escobedo, George Hartley, Paul Jones, Joseph McLaughlin, Beth Quitsland, Nicole Reynolds, Catherine Taylor, and Jeremy Webster. The National Endowment for the Humanties seminar "The Oscar Wilde Archive," held at the Clark Library at UCLA, came as an unexpected boon in the summer of 2007. Thanks to Joe Bristow and my fellow seminar participants, who enriched my understanding of Wilde and indulged my passion for *Vera.* By the time this book is published, I will have begun a new position at the University of California, Davis, and I would like to thank my new colleagues in the English Department for their insights and ideas as I completed the book manuscript.

An early version of chapter 2 was published in *Victorian Literature and Culture,* and some parts of chapter 4 appeared in the *Henry James Review.* Librarians at a wide range of institutions have offered assistance: thanks especially to the Bodleian Library, the British Film Institute, the British Library, the Colindale Newspaper Library, the Special Collections Library at the University of Michigan, and the Library of Congress. The VICTORIA listserve has provided an online scholarly community and many good leads. I am grateful to everyone at the University of Michigan Press, especially Alison MacKeen for her enthusiastic editorial stewardship, and Marcia LaBrenz.

Numerous friends and colleagues have directly or indirectly helped me finish this book. My friends Laura Vroomen, Lucy Frank, Margaret Ann, and Henry Escudero offered hospitality during various underfunded research trips to England, for which I thank them. Among my graduate school friends, I learned a great deal from Thomas Crofts, Christine Devine, Deirdre Egan, Melissa Huggins, Matt Hussey, Mike LeMahieu, Kristin Matthews, Jack Opel, Elizabeth Rivlin, John Tiedemann, Janine Tobeck, and Laura Voracek. Rich Hamerla, Cathy Kelly, and Todd Shepard extended their friendship and camaraderie during my year at the University of Oklahoma, as did Michael Alexander, Kathy Gudis, and Ronald Schleifer. Other dear friends to whom I owe thanks include Meredith Alt, Angie and Scott Berkley, Lawrence Daly, Chris

Frederick, Julie Gardner and Ashley Stockstill, Gretchen Larsen, Laura Larson, Alison O'Byrne, Ji-Hyae Park, Marina Peterson, Jane Poyner, and Jenny Terry.

Finally, I come to my family. I owe more than I can say to my parents, sisters, and grandparents: Jim and Phyllis Ghiardi, Cathy Miller, Cristina Miller, Frank Miller and Ellen Powers, Rhea Miller, and Sarah Miller and Jon Konrath. Thanks also to Mary and Rich Merlie, Vickie Simpson, Stephanie Beltz, and the Stratton clan. This book is dedicated to Matthew Stratton, whom I met on the first day of graduate school, and who has challenged and enriched my thinking ever since. I am deeply grateful for his love and companionship (not to mention his many meticulous readings of the following chapters).

CONTENTS

ILLUSTRATIONS

INTRODUCTION

In 1901, R. W. Paul, one of Britain's first filmmakers, released *The Countryman and the Cinematograph,* a film that reflexively "explains" cinema just five years into this new narrative form. It depicts a countryman at the movies, who mistakes cinematic illusion for real-world phenomena: he attempts to dance with a lovely on-screen dancing girl (figure 1) and flees a filmic train seemingly moving in his direction (figure 2). Bewildered by these images, he tears down the film screen, only to find the projector and operator behind it.[1] Movies that mocked the ignorant or uninitiated film viewer were common at the turn of the century; they served as elementary primers on cinema spectatorship, disseminating a culture and ethics of audience behavior for a new form of narrative entertainment. *The Countryman* taught filmgoers that savvy spectatorship is a necessary condition of modern subjectivity, that only a "bumpkin" or "yokel" would be taken in by film's illusion, and that sophisticated film viewers are not distressed by what they see on screen. The message of the film is that to be a "modern" rather than a "primitive" subject, one must adjust to the shock of modern narrative forms.

At the same cultural moment, however, many critics were arguing that shocking fiction and film were not tests of one's poise, but symptoms of cultural degeneration, part of that "strange disease of modern life" that Matthew Arnold had diagnosed nearly fifty years earlier. In 1904, for example, Arnold Smith complained in the *Westminster Review* about the public fascination with "crime and criminals" in fiction: "The

I

Fig. 1. *The Countryman and the Cinematograph* (1901)

increasing mass of sensational literature which appears daily is a serious symptom of mental debility in the country at large. The cause of the demand for this fiction is not far to seek. It lies in the nerve-shattering conditions of modern life; in the ceaseless strain and sorrow which must be escaped from somehow . . . in the jaded state of the mind which craves a stimulus" (190).[2] Here, in echo of earlier reactions against sensation fiction and penny dreadfuls, shocking stories are a symptom of "modern life," and modernity itself is a "ceaseless" and destructive juggernaut, not unlike a moving train.[3] As *The Countryman* illustrates, however, popular sensationalism both produced and diffused shock; it sought new ways to affect audiences while simultaneously rewarding audience members who learned not to be moved. Popular sensationalism, as this film shows, often worked to naturalize change.

This book argues that crime narratives of the fin de siècle use the shocking figure of the female criminal to naturalize change: the fictional female criminal, a ubiquitous persona in turn-of-the-century crime narrative, was a herald of changing political and social conditions, changing

Fig. 2. *The Countryman and the Cinematograph* (1901)

gender roles, and changing definitions of "private" and "public." While
the figure of the female criminal has a long and rich literary history, this
book considers her unique role in three new crime genres that emerged
in the 1880s and 1890s: the detective series, the crime film, and the "dynamite narrative" (a popular genre focused on political terrorism). Along
with the era's other new, and not so new, symbols of the modern—cinema, dynamite, bombs, violent crime, cosmetics, lurid posters, vivid advertising—these immensely popular crime genres represented "newness"
for a culture obsessed with modernity, and they employed the female
criminal to embody and explain the shock of modern life.

The new crime genres of the fin de siècle engendered a character that
I call the "New Woman Criminal." Like the figurative "New Woman"
who emerged in 1890s cultural discourse, the New Woman Criminal
represents a specifically *public* form of femininity for a culture that was
redefining and redistricting "public" and "private" amid modern social
change. The New Woman Criminals populating crime narrative have
very little to do with real, historical female criminals of the period. Most

women convicted of crimes at this time were poor and desperate; they did not represent new choices available to women, as New Women did, but often were victims of abuse or of desolate circumstances. Far from representing women's new public influence, as fictional New Woman Criminals did, they tended to commit domestic crimes: the vast majority of Victorian murderesses, for example, killed their own children, husbands, or parents.[4]

The New Woman Criminal's distinction from "real" female criminals indicates that she was a figure of fantasy rather than a reproduction of the headlines. She was not a realistic representation of a subject in her society, but an imaginative creation within a wildly expanding popular culture of crime narrative. The disjunction between real and fictional female criminals raises key questions: Why did authors write about New Woman Criminals? Why did audiences enjoy them? Unlike most male criminals of the period, fictional female criminals tend to be attractive, successful, and alluring. Unlike Mr. Hyde or imaginative depictions of Jack the Ripper in the late-Victorian press, fictional female criminals cannot be classified or labeled within the criminological taxonomy that social scientists of the era had invented. The figure of the female criminal was in many ways a contradictory fictional persona: in a culture increasingly fixated on detectives and policing, she seems to represent not the new circumscriptions of modern society, but its new freedoms.

In this way, the New Woman Criminal offers insight into the development of both modern crime narrative and the modern women's movement. Critics such as Rita Felski, Elaine Showalter, and Judith Walkowitz have described the rich history of feminist social reform in Britain between 1880 and 1913; these years were also exceptionally fertile for new representations of criminality. Many of our current narrative sensibilities regarding crime and criminality can be traced to this epoch, which saw the birth of Sherlock Holmes, the invention of crime film, the first modern serial killer (Jack the Ripper), and the first dynamite campaigns for revolutionary causes like Irish nationalism. In recent years, crime and criminality have been pervasive topics in studies of late-Victorian literature, but these studies have failed to recognize the distinctiveness of the female criminal as a narrative figure, often overlooking her altogether. There is a simple explanation for this omission: female criminals do not suit the dominant critical models and methodologies that have been brought to bear on crime narrative of the period. In the wake of Michel Foucault's profound impact on literary studies, narrative depictions of criminality have been understood to discipline readers to omnipresent surveillance and power extending beyond the modern state apparatus, and to celebrate the containment of the criminal "other."[5] Recent critics have contested this reading of Foucault within Victorian studies, and Lauren Goodlad in particular has argued that Foucault's later work on governmentality (as in "Omnes et Singulatim") seriously complicates the use to which Foucault has been put in studies of Victorian literature. My point here is not to elaborate a revised Foucauldian reading of Victorian criminality, but to show how the older conception of the Foucauldian criminal subject has contributed to a critical neglect of the New Woman Criminal.

By focusing on female criminals, this book identifies a hitherto unnoticed feature of turn-of-the-century crime narrative: fictional female criminals tend to be more successful, more admirable, and altogether less prone to containment and arrest than male criminals. Instead of using female criminals to narrate the dangers of legal disobedience or the shame of feminine debasement, new genres of crime narrative employ these characters to model effective, autonomous agency within dauntingly complex modern social conditions. Much has been written, for example, about criminal anthropology and criminal science's influence on late-Victorian fiction. When we come to female criminals, however, this critical model simply doesn't work. In fin de siècle crime narrative, systematic or scientific efforts to explain, predict, or categorize female offenders typically fail, and the female criminal represents that which cannot be accounted for within modern systems of social control.

When we consider crime narrative's characterization of the female criminal, these genres suddenly appear to be posing entirely different questions than we have previously supposed. With the female criminal, some crime stories do tell cautionary tales about the dangers of transgressing social norms, but they also celebrate the *pleasure* of such transgression. Detective series, crime films, and dynamite narratives invite readers to admire female criminals because of their ability to evade punishment, often by manipulating beauty, glamour, disguise, cross-dressing, or other visible, imagistic means. These female criminals are remarkably protean characters, employing bodily transformation to resist social controls. Insofar as we can read such characters as supporting a dominant cultural ideology, they promote a *consumerist* rather than a *disciplinary* theory of individual identity.[6]

Careful maintenance of bodily visibility, or managing one's "public image," is a vital means of autonomous agency in turn-of-the-century crime genres. By making this point through the female criminal, these texts imagine the activity of consumption as an avenue for women's personal freedom amid a seemingly centralized and regulated modern society. Clearly, such a narrative accords with central features of late capitalism, such as the promotion of individualization via consumption, and the promise of self-actualization through commodities; this narrative also reveals, however, a fundamental *amorality* or *lack of ideological fixedness* at the root of modern social change. By using the figure of the female criminal to reveal the freewheeling power of image and style in a modern, consumerist, and image-centered society, crime genres demonstrate that under such conditions, traditional ideals governing gender, morality, self, and society can no longer operate as expected.

Explicitly or implicitly, the crime genres I consider in this study present the New Woman Criminal as capable of thriving amid the confusing and unfamiliar conditions of modern society, which all three genres characterize as fast, dangerous, and image-centric. They do this in part through form. Magazine detective series feature short, autonomous stories that do not require one to wait until the next installment for narrative resolution.[7] From 1891, they were heavily illustrated, graphically violent, and, like sensation fiction, were said to be "addictive."[8] Cinema, in its early days, appeared so immediate and lifelike that many believed it would produce perceptive shifts in viewers' bodies, directly influencing opinions and behavior; critics feared that crime film, in particular, would *cause* spectators to commit crimes.[9] Dynamite narrative focuses on "terrorists," a concept that emerged in its modern sense during this period of history, and uses a disordered narrative chronology and the trope of the explosion to associate modernity with shock and disorientation.[10] Both formally and thematically, detective series, crime film, and dynamite narrative helped disperse a tacit theory of modern experience: they portray a culture more intensely visual, more dangerous, and more thoroughly commodified than that which preceded it.

Each of these genres is also formally and thematically attentive to a modern realignment of private and public domains, suited to their depiction of female criminals. Detective fiction often portrays the opening of the home to the public gaze via the procedures of investigation. Through heavy illustration, late-Victorian detective series made this gaze visual as well as figural. Film, as a narrative form, is exhibited to crowds who sit in darkness and spy through the fourth wall into a fictional home or setting; spectators are unseen by those around them and inaccessible to actors on screen. Filmic illusion thus reiterates detective fiction's voyeurism as well as dynamite narrative's ambiguous collectivism. Dynamite narrative typically hinges on the fear that a "private" citizen, in the wrong place at the wrong time, will be victimized for a "political" issue for which they feel no responsibility. A keynote of the genre is that terrorism reveals the uncomfortable inseparability of individual and collective, private and public, personal and political. The forms and themes of these three genres thus emphasize the redistricted, unfamiliar contours of public and private in the modern world.

The following chapters describe how these popular crime genres use female criminals to make sense of social and political shifts associated with modernity, including the rise of first-wave feminism, the proliferation of consumer culture, increasing legal intervention into the private sphere, democratization, and the first sustained campaigns of terrorism in Britain. Beyond producing mere "entertainment," "titillation," or "shock," these three genres delineate new, specifically "modern" relationships among individual, society, and state. They presuppose the resolution of contentious social debates, presenting readers with a modern world that has already progressed beyond such debates.

"The woman question" is one such contentious social debate. The "first wave" of the British feminist movement coalesced in the campaign for suffrage, unleashed by groups like the National Union of Women's Suffrage Societies (founded in 1897 to unify existing organizations) and the Women's Social and Political Union (founded in 1903 on militant rather than "constitutional" principles). A long history of feminist organization and agitation preceded these developments, as throughout the nineteenth century, middle- and upper-class women won new educational and occupational opportunities and new economic and social rights. Lower-class women's experience of feminism was different. For them, feminism meant the valuing and safeguarding of labor outside the home that women were already doing, rather than the expansion of women's lives outside the home. Working-class women typically had freer access to the extradomestic sphere, but this was hardly an elected condition, as they were among the most oppressed and underpaid of all Victorian workers. This was what was "new" about the New Woman, the upper- or middle-class figure who came to symbolize feminist advancement: before the 1880s and 1890s, many British women had worked or held other public roles, but now such a life was extolled as a new *choice* or *liberty* for women who might otherwise have married or stayed home.

The New Woman was thus an imaginary icon who signified real shifts in the relative freedom and occupational choice available to many young women near the end of the century.[11] She sprang from the pages of the periodical press. Sarah Grand coined the term *New Woman* in 1894, articulating a name for a figure already at the center of cultural debates, and defined the New Woman by her insistence on a role in the public sphere: she "proclaimed for herself what was wrong with Home-is-the-Woman's-Sphere" (Grand, "New Aspect" 142). A proliferation of cartoons and other visual images of the New Woman soon appeared in the popular press. As figures 3–6 exemplify, ideographic "props" in such cartoons associated the New Woman with masculine habits and pursuits, such as scholarly books and spectacles, cigarettes, neckties, and guns. These cartoons also denote the New Woman's desire to freely navigate

"I am afraid Mother doesn't much like the latter-day girl."

Fig. 3. From *Punch,* 19 May 1894, 229

"Can I go Abroad to Finish, Ma?"
"No. It's time you were Married; and Men don't care how ill-educated a Woman is."
"You shouldn't judge everybody by Pa, Ma!"

Fig. 4. From *Punch*, 19 May 1894, 231

THE NEW WOMAN.

"You're not leaving us, Jack! Tea will be here directly!"
"Oh, I'm going for a Cup of Tea in the Servants' Hall. I can't get on without Female Society, you know!"

Fig. 5. From *Punch*, 15 June 1895, 282

A "NEW WOMAN."

The Vicar's Wife. "AND HAVE YOU HAD GOOD SPORT, MISS GOLDENBERG!"
Miss G. "OH, RIPPIN'! I ONLY SHOT ONE RABBIT, BUT I MANAGED TO INJURE QUITE A DOZEN MORE!"

Fig. 6. From *Punch,* 8 September 1894, 111

masculine space: to go abroad rather than marry, to transform the atmosphere of the drawing room to that of a male club, or to hunt outdoors for a rabbit rather than a husband.

Many of the freedoms and opportunities for women that the New Woman represented arose in tandem with consumerism and an accompanying consumerist ideology of individual choice. In the second half of the nineteenth century, amid the advertising, department stores, mass-produced commodities, and other hallmarks of modern consumer culture that flooded Britain after the Great Exhibition of 1851, advertisers, marketers, and architects of consumer infrastructure increasingly targeted women as prototypical consumers. By the end of the century, this meant new roles for women in the public sphere, such as more retail positions for "shopgirls," expanding opportunities for middle-class women to shop—and hence inhabit public space—on their own, and a proliferation of tea shops, lounges, and lavatories that made consumer space more welcoming to women.[12] Such changes were coupled with a growing sense that women should be in control of their own finances, reflected in the Married Women's Property Acts of the 1870s and 1880s.[13] Many commercial outlets happily promoted women's new rights and freedoms in the public sphere: they were, after all, good for business. In the heyday of the suffrage campaign, a number of London department stores advertised clothing appropriate for suffrage demonstrations, and constructed window displays in National Union colors (Tickner 93).

Paradoxically, however, "feminist" consumer capitalism also shifted the terms of women's oppression: under the auspices of an image-centered consumer culture, women became increasingly sexually commodified as femininity became increasingly constituted by self-administered regimes of health, beauty, fashion, and appearance. Women's bodies shifted from being the property of individual men (such as fathers or husbands), to being social property, in need of constant maintenance to meet the new cultural standards of femininity. The cartoons in figures 3–6, for example, disparage the New Woman for not looking adequately feminine. Feminist film critics like Laura Mulvey and Mary Ann Doane have described how cinema transformed representations of the female body, but the growing importance of image in establishing femininity and gender difference is also apparent in historical developments that predate film: the surge in visual advertising, the increasingly visual formats of illustrated magazines, the expansion of urban consumer culture, and the emergence of new jobs for women in the public sphere. These developments intensified the significance of women's public image in the final decades of the nineteenth century.

Turn-of-the-century crime narratives register such developments by engaging female characters in new kinds of interaction with public space—from office workers to shopgirls to suffragettes—but they also chart the escalating significance of "imagistic femininity" by portraying beautiful women criminals. Criminologists in this period insisted that the female criminal fit a "masculine" physical type, and the figural New Woman was depicted as masculine, but crime narrative's New Woman Criminals instead embody a new form of feminine glamour associated with consumer fantasy and the screen culture of the cinema. They do not validate the empirical conclusions of late-Victorian criminology, that visible traits reveal "born criminals," but rather the more abstract promises of consumer discourse: that women can effect power through style and image. Beautiful, alluring, and emphatically immoral, New Woman Criminals demonstrate how consumerism redefined femininity as a set of visual signifiers rather than behaviors, a purchasable commodity rather than a moral imperative. Femininity, with the steady growth of a visually oriented consumer culture, becomes an image rather than an ethic.[14]

The New Woman Criminal represents women's increasingly public lives not only in light of feminism and consumerism, but also in terms of a trend toward legal interventionism. The public visibility of the home and women is very much at issue in narratives of crime and detection, as Sherlock Holmes explains to Watson in the second story of Arthur Conan Doyle's series:

> If we could fly out of that window hand in hand, hover over this great city, gently remove the roofs, and peep in at the queer things which are going on, the strange coincidences, the plannings, the cross-purposes, the wonderful chains of events, working through generations, and leading to the most *outré* results, it would make all fiction with its conventionalities and foreseen conclusions most stale and unprofitable. ("A Case of Identity" 30)

Holmes goes on to uncover just such an *outré* state of affairs in the seemingly mundane, middle-class family of the New Woman typist Mary Sutherland.[15] This case is typical of turn-of-the-century detective fiction in that it features Holmes penetrating a private home and family in order to make public—via the medium of the story—an instance of crime or scandal. Although Holmes is a "private detective," public forms of legal interventionism accompanied the historical development of such a formula.

Amid the broader late-century trend toward a more interventionist state, legal interventionism meant that the domestic sphere was increasingly public, in a literal and metaphorical sense.[16] Stricter state control over the domestic arena was a progressively popular legal philosophy through the last twenty years of the nineteenth century, as Martin Weiner has established, and there was growing support for laws regulating sexuality, domestic abuse, child welfare, and other domestic concerns. Legislation against child beating and neglect, wife beating, and animal abuse required a shift in the legal understanding of the home. That the state should have jurisdiction over the home, and the expression of power within, opposed an idea of the home as inviolable, private, and patriarchal. As Frances Power Cobbe wrote in her 1878 essay "Wife-torture in England": "We are accustomed to accept it as a principle . . . that the first lesson of orderly citizenship is that no man shall be judge, jury, and executioner in his own cause. But when a wife's offences are in question this salutary rule is overlooked" (139).

By the end of the century, the "sanctity" of the father's role in the home had sufficiently dissipated for the passage of the 1878 Matrimonial Causes Act, which allowed abused women to separate from their husbands more easily.[17] Similary, legislation against child abuse and neglect came with the Prevention of Cruelty to Children Acts in 1889 and 1893. Feminists had been calling for such developments for decades, and many authors of nineteenth-century fiction made the need for such interventions a central point of their fiction. Emily and Anne Brontë, for example, in *Wuthering Heights* (1847) and *The Tenant of Wildfell Hall* (1848), illustrate the extent to which the autonomy and impermeability of the home can shelter alcoholism, abuse, and corrosive male violence. That it took so long for interventionism to take hold is a testament not only to British laissez-faire liberalism, but to the powerful ideology of patriarchal domesticity.[18] In this sense, the expansion of legal interventionism and first-wave feminism at the end of the century are not unrelated phenomena.

Critics of Victorian crime fiction have read the police infiltration of fictional homes as an ideological maneuver of a broader disciplinary apparatus, but as the following chapters show, narratives about female criminals often present interventionism as emblematic of women's increasing public significance. Michael Warner has written that twentieth-century feminism "encouraged an activist state to assert the public relevance of private life" (35); this is also true of nineteenth-century feminism. A problem with such legal developments, of course, was that they could easily be corrupted in the service of repressive aims. Judith Walkowitz has described how the final version of the infamous 1885 Criminal Amendment Act, originally intended to raise the age of consent and protect young girls from sexual abuse and exploitation, included a clause that made male homosexuality illegal, for which the act is now better known (*Prostitution*).

Legal interventionism, however, was only one part of a broader transformation in law and policing that occurred within a climate of criminological discovery. The New Woman Criminal represents consumerist rather than criminological ideals, in contrast to fictional male criminals, but the rise of criminology in the 1880s and 1890s is nonetheless a crucial context for my study. Crime narrative's emphasis on the visual manifestation of femininity echoes a wider fixation on body, image, and identity in the wake of criminological theory. Criminologists such as Cesare Lombroso and Alphonse Bertillon on the continent and Havelock Ellis, Francis Galton, and William Douglas Morrison in Britain advocated empirical strategies for visually identifying criminals, and early scientific criminology was based on the premise that one might apprehend "criminal identity" via sight.[19] The criminal's image is thus of utmost importance in turn-of-the-century crime narrative, but stories featuring female criminals emphasize the ways that criminological identification doesn't work, or the ways that it can be eluded. Female criminals use disguise, passing, cross-dressing, or cosmetics to manipulate their image; while such devices have a long literary history, here they become tactics specifically for resisting the criminological gaze, and image and bodily modification become forms of leverage for women entering the public sphere.

Critics have traced out many parallels between late-Victorian crime genres and criminological science, arguing that they constitute two new languages used to talk about crime at a time when older discourses of criminality were becoming obsolete.[20] Secularism and the emergence of social science are important contexts here: conceptions of "sin" could not adequately explain social transgression at a time when scientific conceptions of the individual—as a calculable, measurable, and predictable agent—were replacing theological notions of human behavior. In outlining this reorganization of thinking about criminality, however, no critic has accounted for the female criminal, who was pathological in criminological discourse, but glamorous and appealing in crime narrative. This radical disjunction between the female criminal as scientific subject and the New Woman Criminal in the narrative imaginary suggests that these discourses are not nearly as coterminous as critics have supposed.

Rather than reflecting contemporaneous criminological ideas, the New Woman Criminal emerges from—and diverges from—earlier fictional traditions of representing criminal women. In her peculiarly attractive badness, she is a more intensely visual or imagistic version of the prostitutes, bigamists, child murderers, and other "fallen women" of Victorian genres such as social realism or sensation fiction—*Mary Barton*'s Esther (1848), *Adam Bede*'s Hetty Sorrel (1859), or the eponymous Lady Audley (1862). She even resembles, in this respect, Daniel Defoe's Moll Flanders (1722). The New Woman Criminal tends, however, to threaten public rather than domestic institutions, and is typically motivated by economic or political desires rather than familial or sexual concerns. This marks a turn away from Victorian literary convention, in which female characters—bad or good—convey the national value of home and family.

Female criminals in other late-century genres beyond crime narrative likewise intersect with but depart from the New Woman Criminal: Oscar Wilde's *Salomé* (1896) and Thomas Hardy's *Tess of the d'Urbervilles* (1891), for example, depict the female criminal as an emblem—or victim—of decadent modernity, but not in terms of women's new public role in the modern world. Like female criminals in crime genres, Salomé uses image as a form of power, purposefully drawing or manipulating others' gaze, but Tess Durbeyfield is punished precisely for drawing others' gaze, even though the appeal is unconscious on her part. Alec d'Urberville blames her for catching his eye: "I was on the way to . . . social salvation till I saw you again!" Contrary to the New Woman Criminal, Tess feels no agency in determining whether and how she is subject to another's gaze: "I couldn't help your seeing me again!" (349).

In focusing on public and visible femininity, the new crime genres of the fin de siècle pick up on a narrative motif that long predates them: the literary fixation on the figure of the prostitute. So many critics have discussed the Victorian prostitute that she has become almost emblematic of the period: to Nancy Armstrong, she is "the figure underlying all the monstrous women" in Victorian fiction (*Desire* 182); to Walkowitz, she is a "conduit" of intercourse among disparate groups in a highly stratified society (*Prostitution* 4); to Anne McClintock, she is the "primitive" within "civilized" society, "the metropolitan analogue of African promiscuity" (56). All of these accounts position the "public woman" as a figure of orientation, a marker of boundaries and binaries. The New

Woman Criminal who emerges in the final decades of the nineteenth century represents a new cultural use for public femininity. Like the prostitute, she appeals to a range of cultural fantasies about the pleasures and horrors of feminine corruption, but she also corresponds with new conditions of gender and authority that emerge at the end of the century. In the crime genres of the fin de siècle, the female criminal is a thief, murderer, fraud, blackmailer, terrorist, or spy, but never a prostitute. In Victorian literature, the prostitute was defined by her access to public space, and was infinitely useful in locating the boundaries of "unacceptable" femininity. By the end of the century, the ideology of separate spheres had eroded to such a degree that her transgression of public space no longer carried the same symbolic weight. She did not disappear as a fictional persona, but neither does she serve the same representative functions.

A crucial absence of sentimentality distinguishes turn-of-the-century accounts of prostitutes. They are no longer wretched and pitiable, like Esther in *Mary Barton,* nor angelic and self-sacrificing, like Anne in Thomas De Quincey's *Confessions of an English Opium Eater* (1822). In some late-century writing, prostitutes are vaguely demonic incarnations of *fin de globe* decadence, as in Wilde's poem "The Harlot House" (1885). Other representations focus on economics rather than sex, reflecting women's new status in the commercial sector: Bernard Shaw's *Mrs. Warren's Profession* (1898), for example, depicts the prostitute as greedy capitalist rather than preyed-upon sufferer. Late-Victorian criminologists similarly came to view prostitutes as economic opportunists rather than victims: William Douglas Morrison wrote in 1891 that prostitution "exists among communities where destitution is an almost unmeaning word; it exists in lands where no women need be idle, and where she is highly paid for her services. In the face of such facts it is impossible to believe that destitution is the only motive which impels a certain class of women to wander the streets" (113). This contrasts with earlier accounts such as *London Labour and London Poor* (1861), where Henry Mayhew and Bracebridge Hemyng depict prostitutes as victims of male vice. Feminist advancement and the New Woman clearly inflect such depictions, wherein prostitutes become active entrepreneurs rather than passive victims of circumstance.[21]

Beyond literary depictions of prostitution, the new genres of crime narrative that emerge at the fin de siècle also draw on the transgressive women of sensation fiction, a popular genre that arose following Wilkie Collins's *The Woman in White* (1860). Indeed, as will often be apparent in this study, a web of continuities connects sensation fiction and fin de siècle crime narrative: Ann Cvetkovich groups both sensation and detective fiction, for example, with other somatic genres defined by their affective power (15). A key difference, however, is that sensation fiction is largely a domestic genre, focusing on bigamy, cross-class marriage, illegitimacy, inheritance, and family secrets, while the new crime genres of the 1880s and 1890s typically feature public and political dramas, often involving governments or terrorism. Sensation fiction undermines the notion that domesticity is the sacred seat of wholesome value in Victorian society, but never fully extricates women from that sphere. Mary Elizabeth Braddon's *Lady Audley's Secret* and Wilkie Collins's *Armadale* (1866) feature two monumental female villains of sensation fiction, for example, but the women's crimes appear to stem from the corrupting influence of violent husbands and ruinous marriages. Like sensation fiction, turn-of-the-century crime genres demythologize domesticity, but also reconfigure women's place in government, the professions, and public culture.

While the connections between late-century crime genres and earlier fictional representations of female criminality are crucial to my understanding and formulation of the New Woman Criminal, this study offers a highly contextualized view of three emergent fin de siècle genres via extensive reference to primary materials, the early film archive, periodicals, illustrations, and newspapers; for the New Woman Criminal emerged in the context of new narrative genres and media, amid various kinds of literary and filmic experimentation. This formal and thematic novelty is a crucial part of these genres' cultural role: detective series, crime films, and dynamite narrative all rely on similarly innovative aesthetic, thematic, and formal effects, just as they all insist on the "modernity" of the New Woman Criminal. The book is organized, accordingly, in three sections, each of which focuses on one of the genres.

PART ONE: DETECTIVE SERIES

The first chapter, "Private and Public Eyes: Sherlock Holmes and the Invisible Woman," considers Arthur Conan Doyle's wildly popular series of short stories about detective Sherlock Holmes, published in the *Strand Magazine* beginning in 1891. Holmes embodies the visual acumen and scientific aptitude associated with the new science of criminology in the late-Victorian period; in this chapter, however, I show how his expert eye is continually thwarted by the female body's resistance to interpretation. Conan Doyle presents a fantasy of omnipresent surveillance and omnipotent authority under modern forms of social control, but female criminals continually undermine Holmes's system of detection. Whereas with male criminals, Holmes locates "scientific" identity in the body, the identity of female criminals is consistently detached from visual and bodily moorings. Published in heavily illustrated periodical formats, Conan Doyle's detective series makes this point via uniquely visual means. I thus begin the chapter by discussing visuality and illustration in late-Victorian magazine narrative, and then move to a discussion of visibility and identification in the series, focusing on law, policing, and legal interventionism. On the surface, the stories privilege and celebrate the eye and the image, but in representing female criminals, they express profound doubt about how meaning is gleaned from the visible. This underlying ambivalence clusters around a series of problems related to femininity, publicity, and domesticity. To insist on the primacy of the visual in the making of meaning challenges the privacy of patriarchal families and the domestic sphere. In order to investigate families and homes, these spaces must be visually accessible to Holmes, yet Conan Doyle is also invested in domestic intactness, which hinges on concealment and inaccessibility. Holmes's theory of crime and criminality as visually ascertainable categories thus conflicts with the imperative to "veil" women and the home. This collision of values is most apparent when Holmes investigates female criminals and domestic crime, engaging key contemporary debates about legal interventionism and feminist challenges to patriarchal social organization.

Chapter 2, "Beautiful For Ever! Cosmetics, Consumerism, L. T. Meade, and Madame Rachel," discusses the correlation of imperialism, consumerism, and feminism in accounts of the real-life 1860s criminal cosmetologist Madame Rachel, who was convicted of fraud in 1868. Her case was extensively covered in the Victorian press and later fictionalized in L. T. Meade's 1902–3 detective series *The Sorceress of the Strand*. A "professional beautifier" who ran a London cosmetics shop and wrote a beauty manual called *Beautiful For Ever!,* Madame Rachel was the object of widespread scorn among her contemporaries. I read Meade's series, which details the exploits of a criminal cosmetologist, as a feminist intervention into the textual legacy that trailed Madame Rachel—a legacy that fueled cultural apprehension about female consumer power. In an era when advertisers and marketers were increasingly targeting women, and when detectives like Holmes dreamed of enhanced power through *looking,* consumerist rhetoric told women that *to be looked at* can be a form of power, if one has the right commodities. This chapter examines a variety of narrative and journalistic sources— from courtroom testimony to Wilkie Collins's novel *Armadale* to Max Beerbohm's essay "A Defence of Cosmetics"—to present cultural responses to Madame Rachel as an anxious foil to a popular, consumerist, pseudofeminist discourse about women's power of influence through image. Meade intervenes in this legacy by transporting Madame Rachel into 1899 London, where women's social and economic position is considerably altered, and by reimagining Rachel as a beautiful genius of science and commerce, continually able to subvert the detectives on her trail. The series fails, however, to account for the limitations of a feminism grounded in imperialist capitalism. Seeking to redefine British feminine identity in the wake of women's expanding economic role, Meade uses the rhetoric of popular imperialism to sanction female consumption. The real Madame Rachel was Jewish, and coverage of her crimes was often anti-Semitic, but Meade's version of Rachel is instead half-Indian. She provides colonial-derived cosmetics to her clients, and through these products, her English customers assert independent sexuality. Meade's stories thus "package" Anglo-feminism as an expression of imperial domination.

PART TWO: CRIME FILM

Chapter 3, "The Limits of the Gaze: Class, Gender, and Authority in Early British Cinema," extends my analysis of criminality, gender, visibility, and authority to early British crime films featuring female criminals. My endeavor is in part archaeological, as little attention has been paid to early British crime film, and no critic has yet established its relation to contemporary crime fiction. I consider crime films produced from 1896 to 1913, examining their roots in magazine detective fiction, but also how early cinema's form and context altered representations of the female criminal. Female criminals had been depicted as glamorous, rapacious consumers before the advent of motion pictures, but this portrayal is intensified in film, and takes on an overtly democratic sensibility. Because film is a distinctly visual medium, female criminals' beauty, body, and allure become even more important, completing a shift toward image-centered ideologies of femininity that is only just apparent in fiction like Meade's. Moreover, in film's earliest years, British audiences were overwhelmingly working class, fostering a populist and anti-authoritarian filmic sensibility that broke from the detective-centered structure of late-Victorian crime fiction. Rather than producing heroic "master detectives" like Holmes, early film highlights the class politics at work in crime and policing. Female thieves in early crime films steal luxury goods from wealthy aristocrats, and the women's desire to consume such commodities is presented as no less valid than a rich person's. On the other hand, many early British films focus on militant suffragettes and suffragette political crime, and these take a far more repressive approach to female deviance. Female criminals in early British film are mostly alluring thieves, whose acquisitiveness essentially accords with the individualist and consumerist values of modern, capitalist society. Militant suffragettes, in contrast, attempt to achieve social change through violent collective action, which at root was far less tolerable than individual criminal deviance. Early crime film's suffragettes are thus far less appealing than its glamorous thieves. My analysis of filmic accounts of suffragette political crime—including arson, window smashing, bombings, and sabotage—sets the stage for an in-depth consideration of female political criminals in the next section of the book.

PART THREE: DYNAMITE NARRATIVE

The final two chapters explore depictions of the New Woman Criminal as an overt political force, filling out a characterization implicitly embedded in detective series and crime film. These chapters illustrate how narratives about female crimality often correlate democracy, feminism, and consumerism as though they are necessarily allied, either to critique or promote such values. Chapter 4, "Dynamite, Interrupted: Gender in James's and Conrad's Novels of Failed Terror," treats Henry James's 1886 novel *The Princess Casamassima* and Joseph Conrad's 1907 novel *The Secret Agent*. While it is the only chapter focused on conventionally "high" culture, I contextualize both novels within a popular subgenre of "dynamite narrative" that emerged in 1880s Britain. Dynamite stories delve into the characteristically modern topic of political terror. They don't always include literal dynamite, but whether depicting an explosion, assassination, or another threat to the social order, they invariably focus on politically motivated criminal plots. Most dynamite narratives exploit fear of terrorist attacks for sensational effect, emphasizing the fragility of the social order, but James and Conrad strike a dissonant note in the mostly harmonious popular genre. Their novels contrast ineffectual and pathetic male "terrorists" with female criminals who are violent and successful, and explore the significance of contemporary controversies about feminism and gender roles. They present the feminization of public culture via consumerism—rather than radical militancy—as a threat to civilization. James locates civilization in art, while Conrad locates it in masculine endeavor, but both see feminized consumer culture as its anarchic antithesis, and use female criminals to represent consumerism's anarchic force. Indeed, the novels not only reject a feminized culture of consumption, but present it as a threat to masculine identity, linking their female criminals with the meretricious deceits of modern consumer capitalism. James and Conrad suggest that in such a society, the traditionally feminine subject position of the prostitute becomes the ineluctable position of all citizens. By interlacing topics central to late-Victorian gender debates with narratives of failed terror, they pinpoint gender ideology's use value in the political imaginary. In both novels, gender roles function as metaphorical placeholders for an emerging conception of the individual body in the modern nation-state. The novels thus characterize the prototypically "modern" subject as feminine and as inhabiting a feminized role of pliant consumption.

Chapter 5, "'An Invitation to Dynamite': Female Revolutionaries in Late-Victorian Dynamite Narrative," discusses three dynamite narratives that focus on revolutionary female protagonists: Oscar Wilde's first play *Vera; Or, the Nihilists* (1883), Olivia and Helen Rossetti's semiautobiographical novel *A Girl among the Anarchists* (1902), and *The Dynamiter* (1885), a novel by Robert Louis Stevenson and his wife Fanny Van de Grift Stevenson. Nineteenth-century iconography commonly represented "the spirit of revolution" with a beautiful woman, but only with the rise of dynamite narrative in the 1880s did female revolutionaries emerge as complex *characters* rather than abstract figures. Wilde, the Rossettis, and the Stevensons use the figure of the female revolutionary to show how modern "terrorism" and "political crime" complicate traditional notions of criminality and political representation. The unfamiliar threat posed by modern terrorist campaigns was at variance with British crime fiction's tendency to locate criminal agency in the lone individual. Not only did organized political insurgency threaten to deindividualize criminal guilt, it was often aimed at collective rather than individual targets, randomizing victimization and raising unnerving questions about the complicity of private lives in crimes of the state. Dynamite narrative, as a genre, works to convey this broadening out of criminal guilt and victimization, and women's tenuous relation to political agency made them apt subjects for the task. Wilde, the Rossettis, and the Stevensons use the female political criminal to express the new, uncomfortable sense of public/private interconnectedness embedded in modern terrorism; their female revolutionaries convey a newly modern, newly deindividualized, and newly "public" narrative of crime. By correlating their revolutionaries with New Women, however, the authors also illustrate feminism's relevance to debates about the democratization of the political sphere and the status of political "crimes" as political "acts." They position their revolutionary heroines in the context of first-wave feminism and women's swelling political voice, attaching a powerful symbolic value to the figure of the female political criminal, and linking together democracy, first-wave feminism, and political terror as modern challenges to traditional configurations of political representation.

Female criminals were widespread in late-Victorian literature, engaging popular writers as well as canonical authors. Indeed, the New Woman Criminal intersects with many levels of discourse, compelling us to see intricate interrelations between dimensions of culture that have often been viewed as discrete: between literature and cinema, between journalistic and fictional writing, and between the "low" culture of magazine detective fiction and the high literary discourse of writers like James and Conrad. Fredric Jameson has described "culture" as a "space of mediation between society or everyday life and art as such" (177). In this sense, the New Woman Criminal is a cultural figure who reveals a great deal about late-Victorian narrative, society, and the reciprocity between these two domains. Detective series, crime film, and dynamite narrative—three emergent genres of the era—use the figure of the female criminal to define a particular vision of modern life wherein feminism, democracy, and an image-centered consumer culture are mutually constitutive and mutually reinforcing rather than merely historically coincident. In making this claim, the following chapters recover the often surprising forms that feminism took at this crucial moment in women's history; they trace out a complicated and uneven relationship between feminism and consumerism, and show how an opportunistic symbiosis between the two transformed both of them in unpredictable ways. More broadly, they show that popular crime genres played a crucial role in defining major cultural and political debates.

PART ONE

DETECTIVE SERIES

"GOOD NIGHT, MR. SHERLOCK HOLMES."

Fig. 7. From "Scandal in Bohemia"

ONE

PRIVATE AND PUBLIC EYES
Sherlock Holmes and the Invisible Woman

Consider figure 7, an illustration from Arthur Conan Doyle's "A Scandal in Bohemia," the first installment in what would become a long-running, endlessly influential series of short detective stories featuring Sherlock Holmes. Outside the context of the narrative, the image seems to represent an exchange of glances between a young man passing through a nighttime street and two gentlemen on the threshold of a residence. The interplay of their gazes is complex: the walker meets one of the gentlemen's eyes, while the second gentleman looks at his companion and digs in his pocket for a key. The picture provides a full, frontal view of the itinerant young man, but an indirect view of the men on the stoop. If the image existed apart from the story, one might interpret the scene as dangerous, shady, or queer: the young man's hat is pulled low over his eyes and his posture is hunched over, while the men on the stoop appear startled and anxious to enter the house. Perhaps the walker is considering robbing the older men, or perhaps his glance is one of sexual invitation. Perhaps the gentlemen fear him as a threat, or perhaps they are disarmed at finding themselves cruised.

In the context of the story, however, the image calls for a very different set of interpretations: we learn that the young man in the picture is actually Irene Adler, Holmes's female adversary. She has cross-dressed and trailed Holmes and Watson, circumventing the trap Holmes has laid so that he will fail to close the case. Holmes's inability to find his key in this image thus reveals his larger failure as a detective: in the moment depicted here, he neglects to identify the cross-dressed Irene Adler, remarking to Watson, "Now, I wonder who the deuce that could have been" (26). As readers and viewers, we might sympathize with Holmes's failure; there seems to be no "clue" in the picture to indicate that Adler is not a man. W. J. T. Mitchell has used the Wittgensteinian concept of the "duck-rabbit picture" to describe "dialectical" or "multistable" images that seem to perfectly accommodate two or more mutually exclusive interpretations (45). Following this notion, we might "read" the picture as an allegory of imagistic ambiguity. It suggests the difficulty of interpreting the world through visual apprehension, or the fundamental inconsistency between imagistic and linguistic modes of representation, or the inevitable change of meaning that occurs when the visual is mediated through language. Without the words of the story, one would never know the walker is a woman. Without the picture, one would never grasp the disarming menace of Irene Adler's transsexual performance. Indeed, as an image and as a literary figure, Adler's identity is radically double. In the "linguistic" version of this scene, she passes by before Holmes can figure out who she is: she is Baudelaire's *passante,* the desirable but fleeting woman of the modern city who disappears before one can grasp her. Meanwhile, in the "imagistic" version of the scene, she is a criminal or cruising young man whom the other men appear to flee. Like the duck-rabbit, she is predator or prey, depending on how you look at her.

The imagistic and linguistic duality of Irene Adler previews what I will identify as a broader problem with detection and the criminal female body in the Sherlock Holmes stories. Holmes, the expert eye, finds his visual acumen continually thwarted by the female body's resistance to interpretation. Critical work on the series has focused on the stories' innovative faith in the power of vision and detection, their empiricism, their panopticism, their modern certainty about identity's location in the body, and their revolutionary merging of the science of crime and the science of physiology.[1] By focusing on Conan Doyle's female criminals, however, this chapter uncovers a crisis of image and sex that undercuts Holmes's system of visual detection. In the course of the stories, the body is extolled as the location of a new, "scientific" form of identity, as Ronald Thomas has recently argued; Holmes, however, finds that female identity is easily detached from visually comprehensible bodily moorings.[2] Published in heavily illustrated periodical formats, the detective series was generically and formally suited to make this point; thus I begin my argument by discussing the visual culture of the detective series, especially in terms of late-Victorian criminology, racial anthropology, and theories of visual epistemology. The series's treatment of race and criminality usefully reveals how Holmes prioritizes visually mediated knowledge. Such knowledge continually fails in his interactions with female criminals, however—a disparity that emerges, I argue, from a fundamental opposition: the revelatory mandates of law, policing, and legal interventionism conflict with the stories' impulse to veil the private, feminized sphere. Thus the first half of the chapter shows the female criminal as a representational problem in the series, while the second half shows the political and social ramifications of this figural crisis.

THE PICTORIAL PAST OF DETECTIVE SERIES

Victorian narrative often seems to parallel or even predict developments in visual technology, as recent critics have explored with regard to photography and realism.[3] My chapter takes up this line of inquiry in another cultural field: the visual composition of gender and criminality in Conan Doyle's detective series, 1891–1904.[4] In the years surrounding the emergence of cinema in 1896, detective series expressed with particular force a burgeoning shift toward a visually oriented culture of knowledge, and their magazine format was part of this expression. In 1891, Conan Doyle began publishing short detective stories about Sherlock Holmes in the *Strand Magazine,* a new and innovative periodical that established a distinctly visual narrative medium. Conan Doyle had already published two novels about Holmes, but the franchise only took off when packaged as a short fiction series in a thickly illustrated monthly magazine.[5] The stories and the *Strand* were immediately and enormously popular, and a host of publications with similar content and format soon cropped up. In Britain, detective series thus emerged simultaneously with the mass-market illustrated monthly magazine, and the impact of the two cultural forms is virtually inseparable.

The visual narrative form of Conan Doyle's stories was a crucial factor in the way contemporary readers perceived them. In "The Work of Art in the Age of Mechanical Reproduction," Walter Benjamin claims that vision is historically constructed, that "human sense perception changes with humanity's entire mode of existence" and that the "manner in which human sense perception is organized, the medium in which it is accomplished, is determined not only by nature but by historical circumstances as well" (222). With a "historicized" notion of sight, Conan Doyle's treatment of imagistic codes of gender, criminality, and femininity appears interwoven with concurrent developments in visual technology. Beginning in the 1890s, image-rich periodicals like the *Strand* made a tremendous cultural impact. According to Graham Law, the 1890s saw "an entirely new generation of illustrated monthly miscellanies, the first and most successful of which was George Newnes's *Strand Magazine* (1891–1950)" (32).[6] The circulation of the *Strand* was huge—around 350,000 copies a month—and its format was widely imitated (Weedon 173). This new brand of periodical was made possible by rapid shifts in publishing, which was becoming a modern, mass-market industry. Universal education and higher literacy rates had expanded the market of readers, just as the development of more efficient means of production and distribution lowered the costs of reading materials. The combined effect of these shifts was the explosion of inexpensive mass-market periodicals.[7]

Advances in printing technique had simultaneously made the reproduction of illustrations and photographs a cheaper and easier process, and as Andrew King and John Plunkett note, prominent illustration was a distinctive feature of the "New Journalism" of the 1890s and its characteristic "human interest" style (377). Illustrated periodicals had existed since the advent of lithography in the early nineteenth century, and photographs had been included in magazines and newspapers from mid-century, but the illustrated monthlies of the 1890s relied upon an intensely visual narrative format. Throughout the Victorian era, crime stories were more thoroughly "pictorialized" than other genres; George Cruikshank's famous illustrations for W. Harrison Ainsworth's *Jack Sheppard* (1839) and Charles Dickens's *Oliver Twist* (1838) helped establish a pictorial legacy within crime fiction, as Martin Meisel has explored. For most of the century, however, illustrated magazine fiction featured very few images for many pages of text; in contrast, George Newnes, the originator of the *Strand,* envisioned a magazine with "a picture on every page" (Pound 30).[8] The 1880s saw a "photomechanical revolution" in printing, according to Geoffrey Wakeman, which made a more imagistic narrative landscape possible.[9] Early editions of Newnes's *Strand* include a drawing, photograph, illustration, or cartoon on nearly every page, and many pages have multiple images. Recurring features like the "Portraits of Celebrities" series consist almost entirely of pictures, reminding us how modern forms of celebrity depend on image-rich media. Mass-market illustrated monthlies like the *Strand* thus put a great deal of weight on illustration and stimulate multiple intersections or tensions between picture and text, such as I describe at the beginning of this chapter.

The inexpensive, image-rich format of the *Strand* was instantly appealing to the British reading public. Critics have linked the publication's popularity to many different factors. Some have argued that Sherlock Holmes was responsible for its spiraling circulation; Conan Doyle's protagonist captured the imagination of his public to an unprecedented degree, and the *Strand*'s sales peaked when a Holmes story ran.[10] It is impossible to isolate how much Holmes's new context was responsible for this appeal, however; the earlier Holmes novels had not sold as well. Critics such as Ed Wiltse have argued that Conan Doyle's unique brand of serialization incited public demand for periodicals publishing such stories, and mass-market illustrated magazines of the 1890s, following Conan Doyle's success, changed their formats to emphasize narrative series over serial narratives (Law 33). Audiences found the uniquely autonomous continuity provided by this format addictive: like television sitcoms today, the series allowed readers to move effortlessly in and out of readership without the commitment necessary for reading an entire serialized novel. It didn't matter if one missed an episode or even a few. Once a reader grasped the underlying formula and the central characters, the stories could be read in almost any order.

Holmes's deepest cultural impact, however, was in many ways a specifically visual one. Conan Doyle provided his audience with an unusually visible fictional world. Many critics have discussed the "iconic" status of Holmes, the crystallization of his image in early theatrical and filmic productions, the accumulated visual detail in Conan Doyle's brand of realism, the stories' emphasis on observation and surveillance, Holmes's particularly visual mode of detection, and the author's own special interest in visual perception. Trained as a physician, Conan Doyle had received advanced preparation in ophthalmology, and as an eye specialist he was highly attuned to the human capacity for visual perception and misperception. It is hardly surprising, then, that the stories challenge the foundations of vision and knowledge amid a newly imagistic and consumerist cultural terrain; nor is it surprising that the stories exhibit, as I argue, a profound ambivalence about the image-centric culture that they seemingly showcase.

Indeed, while many critics have argued that the Victorians inveterately privileged the visual, Kate Flint has identified a counterdiscourse that challenged "the sufficiency of the visible," arguing that the visual was "of paramount importance to the Victorians," yet also "a heavily problematised category" (25). Focusing on the late-Victorian period, Jonathan Crary has argued that the 1880s and 1890s saw a "generalized crisis in perception" amid "new technological forms of spectacle, display, [and] projection" (*Suspensions* 2). The quick succession of visual innovations toward the end of the century—including cinema, x-rays, and other new technologies—demanded new kinds of attention and sight.[11] Such perceptive instability created a kind of "visual vertigo" in writers like Conan Doyle: he is powerfully attracted to the idea of visual semiotics, and palpably optimistic about the brave new world of visual technology, but often contradictory about how images make meaning. Fecund with images and marked by an accelerating rate of change in audiences' visual acumen, this era saw the rise of the image-saturated consumerist environment that we still live in today. It is no wonder that the visual innovations of the period could be confusedly deployed: not only did they transform audience's ways of seeing and knowing the world, but they dismantled cherished definitional categories such as "art" and "authenticity." Benjamin's now-familiar discussion of how the ideology of artistic "aura" was flattened by the proliferation of mechanical reproducibility suggests how visual innovations have called into question Western epistemological categories that had seemed both ageless and historically impermeable ("Work of Art"). Excavating the perceptive and cultural shifts that occurred in the context of such visual developments has long interested historians of cinema, but magazine crime series of this period likewise demanded new kinds of visual attentiveness and understanding from readers.

The Holmes stories participate in such large-scale shifts by emphasizing how identity categories such as "criminality" and "femininity" function—or don't function—as imagistic systems of signs. On the surface, the stories privilege and celebrate the eye and the image to an unprecedented degree, but on another level, they manifest deep doubt about this theory of visibility. The stories' underlying ambivalence regarding visual epistemologies and imagistic meaning clusters around a series of problems related to the female criminal. In their depiction of women, the stories acknowledge that changing visual sensibilities are entangled with shifts in ideologies of gender, privacy, and publicity. To insist on the primacy of the visual in the making of meaning challenges the imperative to "veil" the private patriarchal family or private feminized space. In order to render these social spheres meaningful, in the logic of the stories, they must be visually and publicly accessible. Thus Holmes's theory that crime and criminality are visually ascertainable categories, when subject to an expert gaze, comes into conflict with ideologies of domestic intactness and feminine concealment. This collision of values is most apparent in stories about female criminals; that such narratives are at odds with the visible criminological semiotics at work in most of the series reveals the influential resonance of contemporary debates about criminality, interventionism, and feminist challenges to patriarchal social organization.

RACE, VISUAL EPISTEMOLOGY, AND THE
CRIMINOLOGICAL GAZE

We will see how women in the Holmes series disrupt the imagistic codes of meaning that govern Conan Doyle's treatment of criminality, but let me first establish how the stories construct criminality as a set of specifically visual codes, and hence assert the primacy of visually mediated knowledge. Conan Doyle's model of visible criminality was borrowed from contemporary criminal science, which emerged as a discipline in late-nineteenth-century Europe. Early criminologists operated from the premise that European criminals were throwbacks to an earlier, more "primitive" form of humanity. Like the term *homosexual,* which also emerged in this period, *criminal* came to signify a new form of identity. Criminal experts claimed this identity could be recognized via trained observation: criminals supposedly had an atavistic physiology, a distinct physical "type," and the visual traits of inborn pathology. Early criminology echoed the logic and assumptions of physiognomy and phrenology, which came to prominence in the 1820s–1840s, but was a more empirical, visual discipline. Criminologists viewed these earlier practices as inadequately "scientific" in concept and method.

In theory as well as practice, early criminology was a correlate of late-nineteenth-century visual innovation. These decades saw visual technology exploding in manifold directions, auguring limitless new possibilities for image and sight. In the field of criminology, the disciplinary uses of vision were enthusiastically investigated, and criminologists mined visual technology to find ever-more effective means of identifying criminals. Francis Galton experimented with composite photography, amalgamating shots of various felons to generate a supposedly universal criminal image, and he developed "fingerprinting," the very name of which reveals its debt to imagistic reproducibility. Alphonse Bertillon invented what came to be called "the mug shot," and promoted anthropometric measurement to classify criminals' faces. Most prominent of all the early criminologists, Cesare Lombroso assembled galleries of criminal photographs in an effort to prove the existence of a racialized criminal type. Without resorting to technological determinism, we can see that such ideas could not have been elaborated or spread in the same way fifty years earlier: they emerged as the circulation of images in texts became a cheaper and easier process.[12]

Following the 1890 release of Havelock Ellis's *The Criminal*, which was essentially an English version of Lombroso's *Criminal Man*, such ideas were not obscure in Britain but circulated widely in texts read by the general public. Ellis's study went through four popular British editions, proffering the latest in criminological vision to a lay British audience (Radzinowicz and Hood 12). Nonfiction articles about the new science of criminology were also familiar magazine content. A piece in the *Strand* by Alger Anderson, "Detectives at School: Bertillon's New Method of Descriptive Portraits," summarized Bertillon's theories and included multiple photographs of criminals and of detectives learning to identify them; another *Strand* article by FitzRoy Gardner, "Some Sidelights on Crime," put forth a hereditary theory of criminality; an 1894 series called "Crime and Criminals" offered *Strand* readers a heavily illustrated guide to detectives' investigative methods. Published in the same volumes as the Holmes stories, such features taught readers how to perceive Conan Doyle's fictional criminals.

Conan Doyle employs contemporary conceptions of crime and image in the Holmes stories, and the relentlessly visual logic of Holmes's procedures echoes timely scientific principles and practices. Of particular relevance here is the insistence on Holmes's professional objectivity, paralleling contemporary efforts to define science in these terms. Karl Pearson, a prominent eugenicist, wrote in the *Fortnightly Review* in 1894: "Men of science are accustomed to do their own work in their own way without paying much attention to the movement of political or social thought outside the limits of their own little corner of the field of knowledge" ("Politics and Science" 140). Taking such a compartmentalization of knowledge for granted was part of the burgeoning professionalism of late-Victorian science, which Holmes epitomizes. Upon first making his acquaintance, Dr. Watson, the series' narrator, is fascinated as much by Holmes's obliviousness as by his expertise: "His ignorance was as remarkable as his knowledge. Of contemporary literature, philosophy and politics he appeared to know next to nothing" (*Scarlet* 11). Quite obviously, this characterization of "the scientist" supports an ideology of professional objectivity by depicting scientific practice as detached from political or social motivation. Significantly, Holmes's objectivity was meant to be not only logical, but visual. In the first paragraph of the first Holmes story in the *Strand,* Conan Doyle calls Holmes a "perfect . . . observing machine," and a "sensitive instrument" with "high-power lenses" ("Scandal" 5). This depiction of Holmes as a microscope or telescope is furthered in other parts of the series: in "The Crooked Man," he is said to resemble "a machine rather than a man" (157), and in "The Greek Interpreter" he is described as "inhuman" (193). As Watson tells Holmes in *A Study in Scarlet:* "you have brought detection as near an exact science as it ever will be brought in this world" (29).

Holmes's objective gaze enables his authority, and throughout the series, Watson and other characters continue to be amazed by his feats of sight. At some point in each story, Holmes puts a person or thing "under the microscope" and explains how visual phenomena reveal far more of "the truth" than most people recognize. In "The 'Gloria Scott,'" for example, merely by looking at Mr. Trevor, Holmes divines that he has feared "a personal attack" in the last year, knows how to box, has done a lot of digging, has been in New Zealand and Japan, and so on (94–95). Trevor responds: "What an eye you have!" (96). Holmes becomes less a microscope than an infrared device in "Charles Augustus Milverton": according to Watson, "Holmes had remarkable powers, carefully cultivated, of seeing in the dark" (166–67). In "The Golden Pince-Nez," not only darkness but history itself succumbs to Holmes's penetrating gaze. As the story begins, he is "engaged with a powerful lens deciphering the remains of the original inscription upon a palimpsest" (218).[13]

Although the stories celebrate Holmes's purportedly objective visual stance, his visual practice relies on assumptions grounded in late-Victorian criminology and anthropology, and his debt to pernicious racial theories is now only too apparent.[14] Flint has argued that Victorian critics tended to "see" in visual art what they already "knew," revealing how the visual is mediated through "hidden forces of ideology" (166), and the same could be said for Holmes's tendency to see what he believes to be true about race. A key principle of early criminology, for example, was the nineteenth-century anthropological tenet that "ontogeny recapitulates phylogeny"—that the evolution and development of a species follows the same trajectory as the development of an individual organism within that species. By extension, this idea became foundational to theories of atavism and racial degeneration in scientific conceptions of criminality. Utilizing the metaphor of the human life-span—childhood, adulthood, and decline—to describe the evolution attained by various cultures and races, criminologists concluded that criminals who do not adhere to the behavioral norms of their society must be atavistic throwbacks to an earlier evolutionary stage. As Ellis wrote in *The Criminal,* "our own criminals frequently resemble in physical and psychical characters the normal individuals of a lower race. This is that 'atavism' which has been so frequently observed in criminals and so much discussed" (206–7). For his part, Holmes not only believes that ontogeny recapitulates phylogeny, he advocates the theory as his own invention: "I have a theory that the individual represents in his development the whole procession of his ancestors" ("Empty House" 23).

Revealing his consistency with the foundational principles of criminology, Holmes peppers his conversation with references to contemporary theorists and corroborates their faith in the power of the gaze to reveal social aberration. In "The Naval Treaty," for example, Watson depicts Holmes as a devotee of Bertillon: "His conversation, I remember, was about the Bertillon system of measurements, and he expressed his enthusiastic admiration of the French savant" (235). As Ronald Thomas has discussed, Bertillon was most famous for developing a system to organize photographs of criminals and measurements of criminals' bodies as a means of easing police identification. Holmes's reliance on the accumulation of visual data bears a salient resemblance to Bertillon, and Holmes likewise depends on myths about the human body and visual difference perpetuated by criminologists like Lombroso and Ellis.

The debt that Holmes owes to anthropological theories of racialized criminality is apparent throughout the series. Metaphorical descriptions of "the dark jungle of criminal London" ("Empty House" 13) set up an elaborate parallel between criminals and "savages" and between the role of the detective and that of the anthropologist, as Joseph McLaughlin has explored in the Holmes novels. Holmes's visual capacity as an observer, cataloger, and classifier of human and criminal "types" echoes the imperialist, "master-of-all-I-survey" gaze that Mary Louise Pratt describes in *Imperial Eyes.* In "The Six Napoleons," for example, Holmes describes a photograph of Beppo—an Italian workman who turns out to be the story's felon—in terms that associate its subject with the criminal type: "It represented an alert, sharp-featured simian man with thick eyebrows, and a very peculiar projection of the lower part of the face like the muzzle of a baboon" (182). Beppo's photograph evokes the galleries of criminal photographs in Lombroso's and Ellis's criminological tomes—a link supported by the story's visual depiction of Beppo's capture (see figure 8)—and references to Beppo's "simian" characteristics reveal criminal typology's debt to theories of racial degeneration.[15] We learn later in the story that Beppo lives in an area of London "where the tenement houses swelter and reek with the outcasts of Europe" (186).[16] In Conan Doyle's depiction, the "Italian colony" (193) evokes a bacterial colony, a festering breeding-ground for criminals, but Holmes's initial "diagnosis" of Beppo is through a photograph, which displays only his visual features and not his social context. Holmes gleans that the photograph "was evidently taken by a snap-shot from a small camera" (182), but otherwise it presents no information beyond Beppo's visual appearance. Here, photographic evidence—in the new form of the "snap-shot"—renders the world of the visual in isolation from context. Beppo's "primitive" body becomes the determining aspect of his identity, the apparent cause of his "criminal" instincts. This accords with what critics such as Stephen Arata and Simon Joyce have seen as a general tendency within crime fiction to cite individual rather than social or systematic explanations for criminal deviance.[17]

Conan Doyle's stories often depict male criminals as perfect specimens of the criminal type, as with Colonel Sebastian Moran in "The Empty House:" "one could not look upon his cruel blue eyes, with their drooping, cynical lids, or upon the fierce, aggressive nose and the threatening, deep-lined brow, without reading Nature's plainest danger-signals" (19). Describing Moran's features as "Nature's plainest danger-signals," Conan Doyle suggests not only that the expert eye can discern traces of pathology in criminal faces, but that such visible signals have evolved in nature as a means of imagistic semiotics.[18] Visible phenomena thus constitute a more "natural," less mediated means of signification than language or speech. The imagistic language of criminality is also apparent with Professor Moriarty in "The Final Problem." Moriarty appears not only underevolved but positively primordial: "his forehead domes out in a white curve, and his two eyes are deeply sunken in his head. . . . his face protrudes forward, and is for ever slowly oscillating from side to side in a curiously reptilian fashion" (254). The side-to-side turning of Moriarty's head silently echoes the aesthetic of the mug shot, and illustrations accompanying the story allow readers to see Moriarty's criminal visage for themselves (see figure 9). Holmes explicitly links Moriarty's criminal physiology with an innate condition:

"WITH THE BOUND OF A TIGER HOLMES WAS ON HIS BACK."

Fig. 8. From "The Six Napoleons"

"PROFESSOR MORIARTY STOOD BEFORE ME."

Fig. 9. From "The Final Problem"

"the man had hereditary tendencies of the most diabolical kind. A criminal strain ran in his blood" (252). Moriarty's "bad blood" visually manifests in an antediluvian, "reptilian" appearance. Near the end of the story, Holmes tells Watson that in hunting down Moriarty, he is confronting a problem "furnished by Nature rather than those more superficial ones for which our artificial state of society is responsible" (263).[19] As with Beppo, this corroborates the idea that criminality is an inborn rather than situational characteristic, and that criminal features are a "natural" rather than constructed visual code.

Some of the Holmes stories suggest, with particular ferocity, how such theories of visual, racial, and bodily signification offered ideological justification for cruelty toward masses of individual human bodies. The description of an Andaman Islander named Tonga in *The Sign of Four,* for example, reminds us that such ideas contributed to genocidal atrocities such as the European colonization of Africa and the Holocaust:[20]

> a dark mass, which looked like a Newfoundland dog . . . straightened itself into a little black man . . . with a great, misshapen head and a shock of tangled, dishevelled hair. Holmes had already drawn his revolver, and I whipped out mine at the sight of this savage, distorted creature. . . . that face was enough to give a man a sleepless night. Never have I seen features so deeply marked with all bestiality and cruelty. His small eyes glowed and burned with a sombre light, and his thick lips were writhed back from his teeth, which grinned and chattered at us with half animal fury. (85–86)

Conan Doyle's reliance on scientific notions of primitivism is quite apparent here, but the passage depends on a particularly *visual* form of racist apprehension. Tonga begins "looking like" mere "mass," then a dog, and finally "a little black man": his climb up the great chain of being—in Watson's assessment—is imagistic. Watson describes Tonga's head as "misshapen," his hair as "dishevelled," and his body as "distorted": the sequence of negative-prefixed words indicates that he apprehends Tonga's figure in relation to a normative visual code. Watson remarks that he draws his revolver, like Holmes, "at the sight of" Tonga. Tonga's appearance—not behavior—elicits their repulsion. Watson describes this archetypal confrontation with the Other in almost exclusively visual terms, although "race" was not an exclusively visual category in nineteenth-century conceptions. The Holmes series, as a whole, makes a case for the immediacy and authority of visual epistemology in terms of race and criminality.

THE FEMALE BODY AND THE FAILURE OF
IMAGISTIC SEMIOTICS

If the stories imagine race as a straightforwardly visible ontological category, gender proves to be far more protean. Indeed, while establishing the immediacy and authority of visual epistemology in terms of race and criminality, Conan Doyle's stories are uncertain when it comes to visualizing gender, sexuality, and femininity, and women often represent barricades to Holmes's visual methodology. In "The Greek Interpreter," as in other stories, Watson says that Holmes has an "aversion to women" (193), but in most of his interactions with them, he appears merely inattentive. In *The Sign of Four,* for example, upon meeting Mary Morstan, Watson exclaims, "What a very attractive woman!" Turning to Holmes, Watson is met with indifference: "He had lit his pipe again and was leaning back with drooping eyelids. 'Is she?' he said languidly; 'I did not observe'" (17). That Holmes, an expert in seeing, did not "observe" Morstan seems remarkable, but Holmes's visual capacities are often not as effective with women as with men.[21] Throughout the series, Holmes complains to Watson that women's inner lives are impossible to determine by their outward appearance: "the motives of women are so inscrutable. . . . Their most trivial action may mean volumes, or their most extraordinary conduct may depend upon a hair-pin or a curling-tongs" ("The Second Stain" 912). References to a "hair-pin" and "curling-tongs" indicate that part of women's inscrutability for Holmes has to do with their employment of imagistic transformation via beautification ritual.

Women are not only more difficult for Holmes to read, but they often block his detection in active and passive, conscious and unconscious ways. Especially in stories that feature a wife or fiancée of a murdered man, women tend to hurt rather than help Holmes's investigations, regardless of innocence or guilt. In "The Crooked Man" and "The Dancing Men," the wives of murdered men have nervous breakdowns and remain silent and inaccessible to Holmes throughout the stories. Although the two women are the only witnesses to the murders, and are also suspects, neither can shed any light on the investigation. In "The Crooked Man," Mrs. Barclay is struck "insensible" (160) by her husband's death, and remains closed to Holmes's criminological gaze throughout the course of the story: "No information could be got from the lady herself, who was temporarily insane from an acute attack of brain fever" (162). Holmes must solve the case without "reading" the text that she represents. Similarly, in "The Dancing Men," Mrs. Hilton Cubitt is the main witness and suspect in her husband's murder, but a bullet has "passed through the front of her brain," and she remains unconscious for the rest of the story (85). In both cases, the women's bodies provide no useful information for Holmes: their enigmatic physicality hinders his investigations.

Sometimes, women's bodily inscrutability is intentional rather than unconscious. In "The Abbey Grange," a wife again proves useless as a witness or source of information concerning her husband's murder, but in this case she is lying rather than cataleptic. Despite Lady Brackenstall's beautiful appearance, Holmes is wary of her from the beginning: "The lady's charming personality must not be permitted to warp our judgement" (277), he tells Watson. Her lovely physical appearance and aristocratic manner hide unsavory secrets: she has been physically abused by her husband, who was consequently killed by the man she loves. When Holmes tries to question her, Lady Brackenstall's beautiful face sets "like a mask" (282), failing to reveal any information. Both she and her maid "deliberately" lie to Holmes, and he determines "we must construct our case . . . without any help from them" (279).

That the women prove indecipherable in this story is especially remarkable since Lady Brackenstall's body bears the physical evidence of her husband's abuse.[22] At the onset of the story, Sir Eustace Brackenstall is dead, but his wife retains the marks of his violence: she has a black eye from when he "welted her across the face with [a] stick" (288), and her arms are spotted with stabs from hatpins. She covers such signs of abuse, claiming in one instance that the "hideous, plum-coloured swelling" over her eye was given to her by a burglar (268, 270). Holmes does eventually solve the case, but not through the evidence on Lady Brackenstall's body. Instead, the murder is solved through the frank and honest admission of Captain Crocker, who killed Eustace Brackenstall under circumstances that, in Holmes's opinion, justify his act. The openness and candor of Crocker, whom Watson considers "as fine a specimen of manhood as ever passed through" Holmes's door (285), contrast sharply with the masked, inexpressive body of Lady Brackenstall.

Similarly, in "The Musgrave Ritual," a woman whose former fiancé has been killed presents an inscrutable obstacle to Holmes's investigation. In contrast to the other three stories, where the female suspects are eventually cleared, this woman does prove to be responsible for the man's death. Although Holmes deduces Rachel Howells's guilt, however, he is never able to establish crucial details about the crime, her motive, nor even her present whereabouts. Holmes cannot determine whether Howells actively murdered Brunton, the victim, or passively allowed his death to occur: "Was it a chance that the wood had slipped and that the stone had shut Brunton into what had become his sepulchre? Had she only been guilty of silence as to his fate? Or had some sudden blow from her hand dashed the support away . . . ?" (131). At the end of the story, these questions remain unanswered. Holmes finds some explanation for the crime in Howells's "Celtic" heritage (131), believing her Welsh ancestry makes her prone to impulsive violence.[23] He cannot, however, apprehend her racialized body, as the final lines of the story emphasize: "Of the woman nothing was ever heard, and the probability is that she got away out of England, and carried herself, and the memory of her crime, to some land beyond the seas" (133). Howells disappears without a trace; her secrets remain a mystery. Holmes raises the possibility that Howells was pregnant with Brunton's child when she murdered him, making her womanly body an explicit source of mystery in the story: "What smouldering fire of vengeance had suddenly sprung into flame in this passionate Celtic woman's soul when she saw the man who had wronged her—wronged her, perhaps, far more than we suspected . . . ?" (131). The final line of the passage suggests that Howells was pregnant when her fiancé abandoned her, and references to her recent illness support this idea (122), but the story leaves the question of her motive open. Conan Doyle's female characters continually represent enigmatic texts; their uncooperative bodies counteract and challenge the idea that visual vestiges of crime and criminality are immediate, patent, and obvious.

Immediate, unmediated knowledge that derives from careful visual apprehension seemingly abounds at the beginning of the series' first story, "A Scandal in Bohemia," but in the course of the narrative, Irene Adler interrupts and challenges Holmes's visual methodology. Many critics have discussed how Adler defeats the great detective; Frances Gray, for example, claims she "offers an endless destabilization and disruption of what seems fixed" (13). I want to focus specifically on Adler's employment of feminized visual spectacle to elude Holmes's eye. At the beginning of the story, Holmes's visual authority is established not only in that he is compared to a microscope, but through his expert apprehension of other people. Though his client chooses to hide his identity behind a mask and use a false name, Holmes sees through his disguise.

After Holmes calls him "your Majesty," the King of Bohemia "with a gesture of desperation . . . [tears] the mask from his face" (12). Images of the king both masked and unmasked appear alongside the text in the *Strand* (figures 10 and 11), establishing Holmes's flair for unmasking.

The central predicament of the case also emphasizes the primacy of visual knowledge: the king's former lover, Adler, possesses a photograph of the two together, and he fears she will blackmail him on the eve of his impending marriage. Holmes treats photography in this case as a fetishized or idealized form of reality and an utterly transparent window into history. His conversation with the king presumes the superiority of imagistic signification over writing: "If this young person should produce her letters for blackmailing or other purposes, how is she to prove their authenticity?" The king responds,

> "There is the writing."
> "Pooh, pooh! Forgery."
> "My private note-paper."
> "Stolen."
> "My own seal."
> "Imitated."
> "My photograph."
> "Bought."
> "We were both in the photograph."
> "Oh, dear! That is very bad! Your Majesty has indeed committed an
> indiscretion." (13)

If the past was once a forgeable document, this passage suggests that in the age of photography, it is an inexorable force.

André Bazin, an early theorist of film, argued in his influential 1945 essay "The Ontology of the Photographic Image" that photographs make the object they depict *more real*. He claimed that "The photographic image is the object itself, the object freed from the conditions of space and time that govern it" (14), and that "Only the impassive lens . . . is able to present [its object] in all its virginal purity to my attention and consequently to my love" (15). Holmes's treatment of photography in this story anticipates a Bazinian philosophy of images: photography "purifies" reality by emptying it of contextual material. It is an incorruptible entity because it is a pristinely visual one. At the end of the story, Holmes requests a photograph of Adler—alone in an evening dress—as his reward from the king. Watson treats this image as a surrogate for

"A MAN ENTERED."

Fig. 10. From "Scandal in Bohemia"

"HE TORE THE MASK FROM HIS FACE."

Fig. 11. From "Scandal in Bohemia"

Adler herself: "when [Holmes] speaks of Irene Adler, or when he refers to her photograph, it is always under the honourable title of *the* woman" (29). There is no separation between Adler the woman and Adler the image here, as though by acquiring her photograph Holmes somehow acquires her. Since Adler outwits and eludes Holmes in this case, his possession of her image can be viewed as a surrogate means of "apprehending" her.

Still, the idea that images purvey identity comes under question in the opening pages of the story, when Holmes establishes his visual acumen by putting Watson under the microscope. After looking over his friend's body, Holmes declares that Watson has gained seven and a half pounds, returned to practicing medicine, recently been caught in the rain, and that he has a "clumsy and careless servant girl" (6–7). Watson, as usual, is mystified by Holmes's logic ("You would certainly have been burned had you lived a few centuries ago"), but here, perhaps unwittingly, the text's illustration challenges the idea that the story seems to be expressing: that visual images are reliably transparent. Holmes tells Watson, to explain his deductions, "my eyes tell me that on the inside of your left shoe, just where the firelight strikes it, the leather is scored by six almost parallel cuts. Obviously they have been caused by someone who has very carelessly scraped round the edges of the sole" (7). In the story's original magazine publication, an illustration of this passage accompanies the text, inviting readers to "see" like Holmes and seemingly reinforcing the passage's endorsement of visually ascertained knowledge (figure 12). Ironically, however, the story's words do not provide anchorage or relay—the two conventional text-image relationships that Roland Barthes has described (38)—for this image, but instead conflict with it: the instep of Watson's right foot, not his left, faces the fire, and given the position of his foot in the illustration, it would be impossible for Holmes to view the firelight on Watson's left instep. What is more, the illustrator, Sydney Paget, has framed the image so that the reader cannot see the effect of the firelight on Watson's right instep either.[24] What is visually available to Holmes in the story is not available in the illustration, both because of the "error" in the picture and because of its perspective.

It is easy to view the discrepancy between image and text as a mere mistake or miscommunication between author and illustrator, and Victorian readers who noticed the lapse might well have seen it as evidence of illustration's inauthenticity in contrast to photographic verisimilitude. The inaccuracy highlights, however, an underlying counterpoint to the story's narrative thrust: vision is not a transparent, unmediated, or direct

"THEN HE STOOD BEFORE THE FIRE."

Fig. 12. From "Scandal in Bohemia"

process, but is "framed" by conditions both internal and external to the viewer. Even photographs are subject to such framing: in any medium of perception, the orchestration of space, image, concealment, and revelation function to shape visibility and discernment. In the world of the stories, everything from houses to clothes to furniture serves as an elaborate control on what others perceive. Such a philosophy of imagery, which sometimes emerges in the stories, is closer to the ideas of Sergei Eisenstein than André Bazin. Eisenstein was interested in montage and visual dialectics; his works show that the placement of an image within a carefully orchestrated sequence and arrangement would imbue the image with meaning. In "Through Theater to Cinema," for example, he wrote: "Everyone who has had in his hands a piece of film to be edited knows by experience how neutral it remains, even though a part of a planned sequence, until it is joined with another piece, when it suddenly acquires and conveys a sharper and quite different meaning than that planned for it at the time of filming" (*Film Form* 10). In this idea of visuality, meaning does not *exist* in the image, as criminological theory would have it, but emerges through context. In representing female criminals, the Holmes stories begin to develop such a notion of visual meaning; vision then becomes a far different procedure than in the series's representations of male criminals.

Language's inadequacies as a means of signification are obvious in the Holmes series: personal testimony is dubious since characters are continually lying, repressed, or blackmailed; letters and government documents are often stolen; notes and handwriting are forged; newspapers and reporters are depicted as unreliable and easily manipulated in stories such as "The Six Napoleons" and "The Final Problem." Even the stories themselves, we are to understand, are not "faithful" reproductions of Holmes's detective work. As the narrator, Watson is the linguistic mediator between the reader and Holmes's cases, and Holmes continually gripes that Watson's sentimentality and sensationalism corrupt the raw material: "You have degraded what should have been a course of lectures into a series of tales" ("Copper Beeches" 271). Audiences may be grateful not to read the "severe reasoning from cause to effect" (270) that Holmes would prefer, but such metafictional commentary nonetheless reminds us that textual conventions and narrative point of view shape the reality of realism.

While the stories seem to propose that visual, imagistic signification is thus more authentic or truthful than the spoken or written word, when depicting women, they suggest that vision has its own failures as a means of knowing the world. Adler is perhaps the most obvious example of Holmes's visual limitations. She is beautiful and in no way adheres to the "criminal type," despite being an "adventuress" who threatens to blackmail the King of Bohemia. Indeed, her appearance does not match her behavior in any of the ways others expect. From the king's first description of Adler, the story emphasizes that her outward display of femininity conceals an inward rejection of the norms of feminine behavior: "She has the face of the most beautiful of women and the mind of the most resolute of men" (14). The disjunction between Adler's "face" and "mind"—between her performance and internalization of gender—is what allows her to outwit Holmes.

Watson's conclusion to the story reveals that Adler remains a fixture in Holmes's imagination, as the adversary who "beat" him, long after the case is closed: "And that was how a great scandal threatened to affect the kingdom of Bohemia, and how the best plans of Mr Sherlock Holmes were beaten by a woman's wit. He used to make merry over the cleverness of women, but I have not heard him do it of late" (29). Adler "beats" Holmes, as we have seen, by manipulating outward visual codes of gender. When Holmes meets the cross-dressed Adler on the street, her voice is familiar but he fails to recognize her image:

> We had reached Baker Street, and had stopped at the door. He was searching his pockets for the key, when some one passing said:
>
> "Good night, Mister Sherlock Holmes."
>
> There were several people on the pavement at the time, but the greeting appeared to come from a slim youth in an ulster who had hurried by.
>
> "I've heard that voice before," said Holmes, staring down the dimly lit street. "Now, I wonder who the deuce that could have been." (26)

In this scene, we witness the failure of Holmes's reliance on visual means of knowledge. He recognizes Adler's voice, but cannot see through her disguise. Adler is identified as "some one passing," but she is passing in more ways than he is aware. As I discuss at the beginning of the chapter, the illustration that depicts this scene provides no visible hint that the "slim youth" is Adler or even that "he" is a woman (figure 7).

Adler's disguise suggests, quite obviously, the extent to which outward displays of gender can be manipulated and faked: public, visual markers of gender are not a "natural" expression of innate subjectivity.

Cross-dressing may have a long literary history, but here it points to a broader problem with women and femininity in the Holmes stories. Throughout the series, Conan Doyle suggests that women present a challenge to conventional Western conceptions of truth as associated with public space, visibility, and transparency. Jürgen Habermas's theory of the public sphere, for example, details how publicity, openness, visibility, and the pursuit of truth have been coterminous in Western discourse, following the Greek notion of the *agora* or public market as the place of communicative rationality. Adler's means of inhabiting open space, however, involves an elaborate masking rather than a revelation. Habermas argues that the foundation of the rational public sphere, since the Enlightenment, depended upon a separation between the visible public and the invisible intimate or domestic sphere. But here, not only is the boundary between these gendered spheres disrupted, their associations with revelation versus concealment are also disarranged.

Superficially, Conan Doyle's stories seem to support the conventional idea that "public" and "visible" are coterminous with authentic truth. Holmes's metaphors to describe the solving of cases, for example, reveal the extent to which visibility and truth have been coupled in the English language. In "The Final Problem," as in other stories, Holmes uses "exposing" and "clearing up" as visual metaphors to represent the apprehension of truth (253). Similarly, Conan Doyle often evokes publicity to signify discovery. A character in "The Naval Treaty," for example, says: "If we keep our courage and our patience, the truth must *come out*" (235; emphasis added). In "The Norwood Builder," Mrs. McFarlane, whose son has been wrongfully accused of murder, connects manifest truth with a specifically Christian visual epistemology: "There is a God in heaven, Mr Holmes, and that same God who has punished that wicked man will show, in His own good time that my son's hands are guiltless" (38). Her use of a visual metaphor to describe what she sees as absolute truth indicates an underlying presumption of visibility in the Christian notion of "revelation." Despite such conventional usage, however, throughout the series, images and visibility again and again prove unreliable as means of knowledge, particularly problematic with regard to gender identity.

To Holmes, Adler is not only memorable because she outwits him, but because she embodies something distinctively womanly. Referring to her, he subsumes her whole identity into womanliness, as though "woman" signifies that which he can't account for:

To Sherlock Holmes she is always *the* woman. I have seldom heard him mention her under any other name. In his eyes she eclipses and predominates the whole of her sex. It was not that he felt any emotion akin to love for Irene Adler. All emotions, and that one particularly, were abhorrent to his cold, precise, but admirably balanced mind. . . . And yet there was but one woman to him, and that woman was the late Irene Adler, of dubious and questionable memory. (5)

Watson continues to refer to Adler in such terms, but in this initial description he also offers assurance that she is no longer a social threat: reference to her death dulls the menace that she poses from the opening lines of the story.

Similarly, at the end of the story, Conan Doyle reprivatizes Adler's public body, nestling her in conventional domesticity via marriage. When she marries Godfrey Norton, a lawyer "of the Inner Temple," she enters the impermeable domestic sanctum where femininity is contained and concealed (17). Adler's ability to burrow into such a position, despite her "dubious" public reputation, suggests that the coverage of domesticity not only "protects" women from public danger, it also imparts to them the means of secreting and manipulating public perception. This has a broader sociopolitical relevance: as women gain more public access on the crest of first-wave feminism, the story suggests, they bring to public culture a proclivity for privateness, veiling, and secreting, dismantling the association between "publicity" and "openness."

As a character, Adler suggests that the visual, bodily language of gender and femininity paradoxically becomes *more* important as feminism provides women greater public access. By means of cross-dressing, Adler eludes Holmes's visual system of detection, but throughout the story her behavior enacts a complicated semiotics of visibility and invisibility, highlighting her mastery of public displays and concealments of self. She has learned this skill, perhaps, through her career as an actress: she is a public celebrity who has learned to exist under cover from the public eye.[25] The king calls her "the well-known adventuress," and assumes her "name is no doubt familiar." Adler is a woman in public circulation, existing, promiscuously, at a level beyond intimate acquaintance. Indeed, Holmes is familiar with more than her name: his files record her birthdate, birthplace, and other facts concerning her identity (12). Despite the fact that her life is in public circulation, Adler masterfully retains control of her physical image. At the end of the story, she leaves a note for Holmes explaining how she outwitted him: "Male costume is nothing new to me. I often take advantage of the freedom which it gives. I sent John, the coachman, to watch you, ran upstairs, got into my walking clothes, as I call them, and came down just as you departed. . . . I followed you to your door. . . . Then I, rather imprudently, wished you good-night" (28). Adler calls her drag outfit "walking clothes," which, as Joseph Kestner notes, suggests that a male identity allows Adler a public, peripatetic freedom otherwise unavailable to her (77). Even on the metalevel of the story's publication, she retains control over her image: though the story has several pictures of Adler, none show her in a putatively "true" state. We see her crossed-dressed and veiled, but never in a "natural" condition. The story makes no mention of a veil in Adler's wedding (19), for example, but in the illustration of the ceremony, her face is covered by a semitransparent veil (figure 13). We have no undisguised, unmediated picture of the "real" Adler, casting doubt on the idea that such pictures exist at all.

LEGAL INTERVENTIONISM AND THE POLITICS OF VISIBILITY

Women's appearance and concealment in public and private spheres is at issue throughout the Holmes series, and Conan Doyle often employs the backdrop of legal interventionism to convey the broader political relevance of this theme. The visibility of women is not only an imagistic and narrative difficulty in the stories, but also a social one. As I discuss in the introduction, the late-Victorian legal landscape was marked by a series of developments that expanded the jurisdiction of governmental influence over private life, opening the home to greater governance. Often, such legal developments occurred at the behest of women's political groups, which marshaled opposition against wife beating, child abuse and neglect, and violence against animals. Prominent feminist Frances Power Cobbe, for example, appealed to state protectionism in advocating for women's suffrage, against wife abuse, and against vivisection; in her 1877 pamphlet "Why Women Desire the Franchise," she wrote: "the natural and artificial disabilities of women demand in their behalf the special aid and protection of the State" (220). Victorian legal interventionism, as a social movement, challenged patriarchal social organization; many interventionist developments depended on women's political organization, and on a more symbolic level, they suggested that the father or man of the house was no longer the ultimate

"I FOUND MYSELF MUMBLING RESPONSES."

Fig. 13. From "Scandal in Bohemia"

arbiter of authority over the home and family. By opening domestic space to the scope of public concern, interventionism correlates with women's increasing public significance amid feminist reform. As a component of momentous social changes in modern conceptions of state, power, gender, and subjectivity, legal interventionism is a key context for late-Victorian fiction, and nowhere is its importance better articulated and explored than in detection and sensation genres. Typically, in such stories, the home is exposed to the public gaze, not only on the level of plot—in which investigators may commandeer the domestic arena—but on the metafictional level of publication and readership. In the forum of illustrated mass-market magazines, 1890s detective series propped open figurative windows to show intimate images of domestic crime and scandal to an ever-wider reading public.

As in "Scandal in Bohemia," the Holmes series often depicts intimate crimes that bear directly on state or governmental interests. Public and private are virtually indistinguishable in this scenario, just as Holmes himself is not an *official* police agent. A private detective, he is nonetheless aligned with what Louis Althusser would call the repressive state apparatus. Not only does Holmes frequently work with the police and Scotland Yard, he often lets them take credit for cases he solves.[26] Even when Holmes helps to conceal a crime rather than expose it— significantly, all such cases involve a woman criminal or victim—the stories emphasize Holmes's commitment to the spirit of the law if not its bureaucratic realities.[27] Indeed, Conan Doyle depicts Holmes as an ardent nationalist, hand in glove with state power and authority: in "The Musgrave Ritual," Holmes honors Queen Victoria by decorating his wall with bullet holes in the shape of "a patriotic V. R." (113). He often safeguards royal or governmental power, covering up not only the private scandals of the ruling class but also their violations of public trust, as in "The Beryl Coronet." In his quasi-official capacity, Holmes thus enacts an authorized intervention into the homes and families of Britain. Several of the stories use visual or spatial metaphors to illustrate this role. Recall the moment in "A Case of Identity," discussed in the introduction, when Holmes fantasizes about having more domestic access than he already does: "If we could fly out of that window hand in hand, hover over this great city, gently remove the roofs, and peep in at the queer things which are going on . . . it would make all fiction . . . most stale and unprofitable" (30). Similarly, while riding a train in "The Naval Treaty," Holmes enjoys a privileged view into suburban residences: "It's a very cheering thing to come into London by any of these lines which run high and allow you to look down upon the houses like this" (228). The pleasure that Holmes takes in such domestic voyeurism is the pleasure of uncovering hidden vileness, like finding a nasty slug beneath a rock; all too often, when Holmes pokes his nose into someone's home, he finds something slithery and loathsome.

Critics have viewed this interventionist strain in the Sherlock Holmes stories as a symptom of increasing surveillance and discipline of individual bodies by state and society, as theorized most thoroughly by Michel Foucault. Lydia Alix Fillingham, for example, argues that Holmes—as an extragovernmental agent—functions to reconcile British liberalism with a newly interventionist police force. Conan Doyle's detective series, however, crucially represents state interventionism as a specifically *feminist* strike against a distinctively *patriarchal* authority. Many of Holmes's cases suggest that the foundations of the "respectable" British home are rotten or crumbling; the source of such decay is nearly always male violence, which serves in the series to justify an interventionist legal philosophy. In "The Boscombe Valley Mystery," Holmes discovers that the estate of a wealthy northern family was built on the spoils of colonial highway robbery. John Turner, who turns out to be a murderer in the case, admits to Holmes that he made his wealth in Australia as "what you would call over here a highway robber." After amassing a fortune, he returned to England, "determined to settle down to a quiet and respectable life. I bought this estate . . . I married, too" (98). Despite its accoutrements of respectability, Turner's home has brutal origins, exemplifying the violent past of colonial booty. In "The Copper Beeches," Holmes again associates private domesticity with violent abuse; he tells Watson that the image of a country farmhouse, rather than evoking wholesome English homeliness, makes him think of "the impunity with which crime may be committed there." Watson is bemused—"Good heavens! . . . Who would associate crime with these dear old homesteads?"—but Holmes replies, "They always fill me with a certain horror. . . . the lowest and vilest alleys in London do not present a more dreadful record of sin than does the smiling and beautiful countryside" (280).

To Holmes, rural areas are more dangerous because they are detached from the social and legal pressures pervasive in populous areas:

The pressure of public opinion can do in the town what the law cannot accomplish. There is no lane so vile that the scream of a tortured child, or the thud of a drunkard's blow, does not beget sympathy and indignation among the neighbours, and then the whole machinery of justice is ever so close that a word of complaint can set it going, and there is but a step between the crime and the dock. But look at these lonely houses, each in its own fields, filled for the most part with poor ignorant folk who know little of the law. Think of the deeds of hellish cruelty, the hidden wickedness which may go on, year in, year out, in such places. . . . (280)

Passages like this have led many critics to view the stories as apologies for panoptical surveillance, but note Holmes's emphasis on the abuse of wives and children: "the scream of a tortured child, or the thud of a drunkard's blow." Feminists in this period were calling for women and children to have equal protection under the law, and this passage presents a genuine need for such protection. The passage reverses conventional notions of domesticity and rural life as idyllic, safe, and peaceful: taking a page from sensation novels such as *Woman in White,* Conan Doyle depicts the isolated family home as a seat of "hellish cruelty" rather than a heavenly sanctum presided over by an "angel in the house." Disciplinary and feminist objectives are not mutually exclusive, nor are they necessarily related, but Conan Doyle's emphasis on paternal violence throughout the series does appeal to a decidedly feminist sensibility of the period. His stories articulate a feminist moral imperative for broader state control over the private sphere. As I discuss in chapter 5, contemporaries such as Oscar Wilde and Olivia and Helen Rossetti make feminist arguments *against* interventionism, but in the logic of Conan Doyle's stories, interventionist legal developments do not represent a new kind of infringement on individual liberty so much as a means of protecting the liberty of the disempowered.

The ideology behind paternalistic, private familial structures depended on the belief that women and children were *better off* when taken care of under the auspices of patriarchy. Such a notion is utterly exploded in the Holmes stories, which present a battery of fathers, stepfathers, and husbands who are not only poor caretakers of their dependents, but actively injurious and destructive. In what was perhaps a nod to women's temperance organizations, much of this abuse is alcohol-related. Several of the stories depict wives and children trapped under the dominance of drunken men. In "Abbey Grange," discussed earlier in this chapter, Eustace Brackenstall's wife attributes his abusive behavior to drink: "Sir Eustace was a confirmed drunkard. To be with such a man for an hour is unpleasant. Can you imagine what it means for a sensitive and high-spirited woman to be tied to him for day and night? It is a sacrilege, a crime, a villainy to hold that such a marriage is binding" (269). Conan Doyle takes the opportunity not only to highlight the ravages of alcohol abuse and the failures of patriarchal social organization, but to impress upon readers that marriage should not be treated as an indissoluble institution.[28] In "Black Peter," Black Peter similarly abuses his wife and daughter under the influence of drink: "The man was an intermittent drunkard, and when he had the fit on him he was a perfect fiend. He has been known to drive his wife and his daughter out of doors in the middle of the night, and flog them through the park until the whole village outside the gates was aroused by their screams" (137). Chasing his family outdoors at night and waking the neighbors, Black Peter's abuse reveals the interconnectedness of the domestic and the public, a central contention of first-wave feminism.

As illustrations of negligent patriarchy, Eustace Brackenstall and Black Peter strike notes in a cultural crescendo: a resounding call for a legal response to abuse in the family sphere.[29] In the world of the series, legal interventionism appears as a salutary corrective to domestic injustice, and a legitimately necessary social change. Rather than alcohol, other stories focus on money, inherited wealth, and capital as sources of paternal cruelty. Many of Holmes's cases pry open the home to reveal greedy, grasping fathers rather than drunkenly abusive ones, and yet the two groups can be equally merciless and violent. "A Case of Identity," for example, depicts a stepfather who disguises himself as a suitor, engages himself to his stepdaughter, Mary Sutherland, and then summarily abandons her after swearing eternal devotion. He does all of this to retain control over her small fortune. "The Speckled Band," published a few months later, features an even more vicious stepfather, who murders one stepdaughter and attempts to murder another by means of a poisonous snake. His motivation is their fortune. A few months later, "Copper Beeches" depicted a father, not a stepfather, who imprisons his daughter and attempts to trick her fiancé into abandoning her, all for her wealth. Conan Doyle published these three stories within nine months, and all feature a father or stepfather stooping to unimaginable cruelty to prevent a daughter's marriage and retain her independent fortune.[30] The prevalence of this plot echoes a contemporaneous debate about women's increasing property rights and the extent to which such changes would affect conventional, familial relationships between men and women.[31]

Via new occupations and new laws such as the Married Women's Property Acts, women were beginning to assert more independence in the economic realm, which indicates how the trend of legal interventionism was intertwined with women's increasing power and voice in the public sphere. The Holmes stories tacitly support an ideology of interventionism, effectively erasing the legal boundary between public and private, which functioned in part to cordon women off from political and social power. They call into question women's traditional social position of domestic obscurity, by extension recognizing women as public figures. In this way, Conan Doyle becomes the unlikely ally of Sarah Grand, who wants to erode distinctions between "woman's sphere" and the public sphere. Yet his series remains ambivalent and even suspicious of women's public power. Conan Doyle himself, according to Derek Longhurst, was a "well-known opponent" of the women's suffrage campaign, and "berated the movement for its criminal acts against property and offered the opinion that in this exceptional case he was in favour of lynching" (65). In response to such denunciations, militant suffragettes chucked sulphuric acid into his letterbox (Stashower 295). Daniel Stashower cautions that is "unfair to dismiss [Conan Doyle] as an opponent of women's rights" on the basis of his antagonism toward the suffragettes (130), but regardless of his personal feelings, the stories' aversion toward women's new public roles does conflict with their interventionist message.

The stories' ambivalence about women in public is obvious from a particularly fragile visual metaphor that appears throughout the series. A recurring motif depicts a woman standing in a doorway, at the threshold of light/dark, public/private, visible/invisible. Emphasizing this irresolute image, Conan Doyle invokes and reassesses a familiar symbolic function for women in Victorian fiction: to demarcate the line between public danger and domestic safety. In *The Sign of Four,* for example, Watson describes his future wife, Mary Morstan, standing beside Mrs. Forrester at the doorway of their home: "As we drove away I stole a glance back, and I still seem to see that little group on the step—the two graceful, clinging figures, the half-opened door, the hall-light shining through stained glass. . . . It was soothing to catch even that passing glimpse of a tranquil English home in the midst of the wild, dark business which had absorbed us" (51). Watson contrasts the "tranquil" home with the "wild, dark business" of crime, using the language of sentimental domesticity, but also emphasizes the fluidity between the two realms: the "half-opened door" and "hall-light shining through stained glass" suggest porosity and permeability.

Conan Doyle uses an identical visual trope in "The Man with the

Twisted Lip." Here, Watson depicts his first encounter with the wife of Neville St. Clair—a man who has disappeared—at her London suburban home:

> I followed Holmes up the small, winding gravel drive which led to the house. As we approached, the door flew open, and a little blonde woman stood in the opening, clad in some sort of light *mousseline-de-soie*, with a touch of fluffy pink chiffon at her neck and wrists. She stood with her figure outlined against the flood of light, one hand upon the door, one half raised in eagerness, her body slightly bent, her head and face protruded, with eager eyes and parted lips, a standing question. (136)

This threshold tableau, like the last, occurs in a doorway and is equally diaphanous: the woman is associated with lightness and luminosity ("blonde," "light," "fluffy pink chiffon"), but her body connotes irresolution rather than enlightenment: her hands, posture, head, face, and lips are all dualistic rather than unified. The ambiguity of the moment foreshadows the story's ending. While this image taps into a sentimental iconography of home, with Mrs. St. Clair awaiting her lost husband like a suburban Penelope, the conclusion projects a retrospective irony onto the scene: St. Clair, as it turns out, has financed his home, wife, and comfortable private existence by pretending to be a beggar on the London streets.

In "The Engineer's Thumb," Conan Doyle twice makes use of this recurrent visual tableau to depict Elise, the female accomplice of a counterfeit gang. The engineer describes how Elise, despite her criminal ties, risked her life to save him: "Suddenly a door opened at the other end of the passage, and a long, golden bar of light shot out in our direction. It grew broader, and a woman appeared with a lamp in her hand, which she held above her head, pushing her face forward and peering at us" (208). Elise, like the other women, is a figure of protrusion at the boundary of light and dark. On the next page, she appears in a nearly identical image: "Suddenly, without any preliminary sound in the midst of the utter stillness, the door of my room swung slowly open. The woman was standing in the aperture, the darkness of the hall behind her, the yellow light from my lamp beating upon her eager and beautiful face" (209). In both passages, Elise appears "suddenly," emphasizing that she marks a rupture in the textual landscape, a figurative manifestation of the stories' conflicting beliefs about female visibility.

Conan Doyle's continual use of the ambiguous threshold image connotes a crisis in the Victorian sentimental idiom of "women" and "home." Opening up the home to the detective's gaze, the image suggests, entails a changed conception of women's social role. This is particularly apparent in stories that depict female criminality. In "The Beryl Coronet," for example, Conan Doyle links a misapprehension of women's changed role with a failure to recognize female criminality. In this story, Alexander Holder is responsible for a priceless coronet, entrusted to his bank as collateral by an anonymous member of the royal family. The case is sensitive because an artifact of national heritage has become security for a private loan: "as it was a national possession, a horrible scandal would ensue if any misfortune should occur to it" (248). In an astounding example of his faith in the safety and impermeability of his domicile, Holder decides to take the coronet home rather than leave it in the bank safe: "I felt that it would be an imprudence to leave so precious a thing in the office behind me." The coronet is stolen that night.

Analogous with the coronet is Holder's niece, Mary, whom he adopted as a daughter after the death of his brother. Just as Holder believes the coronet to be safe in his home, so he believes Mary to be a sheltered girl. When Holmes asks Holder if the family participates "in society," Holder responds, "Mary and I stay at home. We neither of us care for it. . . . She is of a quiet nature" (254–55). In the course of the story, however, Holder loses not only the coronet, but also his adopted daughter. Mary, it seems, is not as secluded and sequestered as Holder believes, and both she and the coronet exit the house through the sponsorship of the same man, Sir George Burnwell. Mary has stolen the coronet from Holder's bureau and ferried it out of the house into Burnwell's waiting hands. When Holmes reveals these facts to Holder, he depicts Burnwell as a penetrator of a closed domestic ring: "Neither you nor your son knew the true character of this man when you admitted him into your family circle. He is one of the most dangerous men in England" (264). By paralleling Mary with the beryl coronet, the story follows the conventional literary trope of associating women with precious jewels, the same correlation Wilkie Collins uses in *The Moonstone*.[32] Unlike Collins, however, Conan Doyle articulates the breakdown of a gendered code wherein the visibility and invisibility of daughters can be managed like precious jewels, secured in the confines of the home and publicly displayed on special occasions as exemplars of a family's prestige. After a range of social shifts, women are less subject to patriarchal management, and Mary, the seemingly docile female criminal, remains virtually invisible throughout the story: her skin is continually described as exceptionally pale and white, a blank page.

"The Second Stain" has several significant parallels to "The Beryl Coronet": a man again entrusts an object of national significance to the security of his home, again the object is stolen, and again a woman in his immediate family proves to be the thief. In this case, the stolen object is a letter, which Mr. Trelawney Hope, Secretary for European Affairs, has taken home for safekeeping. The peril in this case is not due to the letter's value as an artifact of national heritage, but to the possibility that it will be published. The letter, from "a certain foreign potentate," has such incendiary rhetoric that according to Trelawney Hope, "within a week of [its] publication . . . this country would be involved in a great war" (295). Trelawney Hope explains to Holmes that the letter "was of such importance that I have never left it in my safe, but I have taken it across each evening to my house . . . and kept it in my bedroom in a locked dispatch-box" (293).

Trelawney Hope's faith that the letter would be safe in his bedroom rests on his belief that he has tightly sealed off political matters from the intimate sphere of his home. Even his wife, he assures Holmes, knew nothing of the letter's existence, and the premier himself praises Trelawney Hope for his ability to hold a national secret "superior to the most intimate domestic ties" (293). The assumption of women's irrelevance to the public realm proves mistaken yet again, however, and Holmes quickly realizes that the theft must have been an inside job. The story features a nestlike narrative structure: within the outer frame of the political drama are twin domestic dramas concerning the Trelawney Hope marriage and the murder of Monsieur Fournaye at the hands of his wife. Fournaye, a secret agent, led a double life and believed, like Trelawney Hope, that "he kept his life in water-tight compartments" (307). His lives prove more permeable, however, and his wife ends up murdering him in a jealous rage, confusing his secret political life with a secret sexual affair. The story accounts for Madame Fournaye's murderousness via race—she is "of Creole origin" and is prone to "attacks of jealousy which have amounted to frenzy" (305)—but the stereotype of the "mad Creole wife," familiar from *Jane Eyre,* does not preclude its broader point regarding the impossibility of divorcing the political from the feminine.[33]

Paralleling Mme. Fournaye's crime is the theft performed by Lady Hilda Trelawney Hope: she was blackmailed into furnishing her husband's letter to M. Fournaye, fearful that he would expose an "indiscreet" letter from her youth. Her husband, she believes, "would have thought [the letter] criminal" (314), yet she maintains that even so, she would not have stolen his letter if she'd had any sense of its significance. Her husband's insistence on concealing all political matters from her notice, according to Lady Hilda, is to blame for the theft: "There is complete confidence between my husband and me on all matters save one. That one is politics. On this his lips are sealed. He tells me nothing" (301). It was this ignorance about her husband's political affairs, she says, that made her prey to Fournaye: "terrible as it seemed to take my husband's papers, still in a matter of politics I could not understand the consequences, while in a matter of love and trust they were only too clear to me" (315).

In attempting to repair the situation, Lady Hilda proves to be a skillful cross-dresser and an adept manipulator of feminine embodiment, like Irene Adler and other New Woman Criminals whom I consider in this study. After learning of M. Fournaye's murder, she goes to his house to salvage her husband's letter, and manages to coax the policeman guarding the house into letting her inside. To accomplish this, she uses disguise and flirtation: dressed as a young working woman, claiming to be looking for a position as a typist, Lady Hilda projects and embodies a type of femininity very different from that of a married aristocratic woman. Under questioning by Holmes, the policeman admits, "she was a well-grown young woman. I suppose you might say she was handsome. Perhaps some would say she was very handsome. 'Oh, officer, do let me have a peep!' says she. She had pretty, coaxing ways, as you might say, and I thought there was no harm in letting her just put her head through the door" (310). Lady Hilda dexterously manipulates her sexuality and her image, but her success in conning the policeman has as much to do with her ability to rein in her body as to reveal it. Holmes asks the officer: "How was she dressed?" He responds: "Quiet, sir—a long mantle down to her feet" (310). Dressed extremely modestly, Lady Hilda convincingly plays the part of a respectable young girl. The officer sees no threat in letting her into the house precisely because he imagines that no one could be less connected to the crime than a woman so covered up. Again, while male criminals in the series prove unable to hide manifestly pathologized bodies, female criminals masterfully transform their image and orchestrate visibility.

The subtlety with which Lady Hilda enacts various feminine roles suggests the plasticity of her image: at various moments in the story, she is the noble wife of a prominent aristocrat, a stealthy thief, an innocent but flirtatious girl, and, at the end, a supplicating woman penitent. All trace of audacity disappears in the final scene amid her Magdalenesque theatrics:

> The butler had hardly closed the door behind him when Lady Hilda was down on her knees at Holmes's feet, her hands outstretched, her beautiful face upturned and wet with her tears.
>
> "Oh, spare me, Mr Holmes! Spare me!" she pleaded, in a frenzy of supplication. "For God's sake don't tell him! I love him so! I would not bring one shadow on his life, and this I know would break his noble heart. . . . Oh, Mr Holmes, I would cut off my right hand before I gave him a moment of sorrow! There is no woman in all London who loves her husband as I do, and yet if he knew how I have acted—how I have been compelled to act—he would never forgive me." (313–14)

Naturally, Holmes agrees to screen her. Lady Hilda's "frenzy of supplication" parallels Mme. Fournaye's "frenzy" earlier in the story (305), again linking the two women's crimes. After admitting her agency in the theft, Lady Hilda carefully corrects herself ("how I have acted—how I have been compelled to act"), but the story indicates that both women are indeed unacknowledged actors in the political careers of their husbands.

THE PERILS OF PUBLIC VISIBILITY

Conan Doyle's resistance to visually identifying the female criminal sometimes appears, nonetheless, as a denial of women's public subjectivity, a refusal to grant women full citizenry by refusing to grant them full criminality. The anonymous female avenger in "Charles Augustus Milverton" perfectly exemplifies this tendency in the series. Despite the violence of the murder she enacts, Holmes keeps her publicly invisible by chivalrously covering up her deed; her name remains a secret even to readers of the story. This is not the only case where Holmes opts not to pursue legal redress after discovering a crime, but it is the most obviously illegal instance, since he actually witnesses the murder. On the night in question, Holmes and Watson break into the home of Milverton, a blackmailer, to secure some letters written by Holmes's client, Lady Eva. While searching his study, they inadvertently witness Milverton's meeting with a lady's maid who has offered to sell him her mistress's letters.

"YOU COULDN'T COME ANY OTHER TIME—EH?"

Fig. 14. From "Charles Augustus Milverton"

The maid turns out to be a former victim in disguise. Milverton previously exposed her secret letters to her husband, who died from the shock, and she has returned to enact revenge.

In describing the interplay between Holmes, Milverton, and the avenger, Conan Doyle orchestrates a complicated interplay of the visible and the invisible. An illustration of the avenger shows her thickly veiled—utterly obscured by the accoutrement of feminine propriety (figure 14). Secreted behind a curtain, Holmes and Watson witness her visual revelation: "The woman without a word had raised her veil and dropped the mantle from her chin. It was a dark, handsome, clear-cut face which confronted Milverton, a face with a curved nose, strong, dark eyebrows, shading hard, glittering eyes, and a straight, thin-lipped mouth set in a dangerous smile" (171). While suggesting formidability, this description counters the visual criminal theory of criminologists like Lombroso, who claimed female criminals have racialized or masculine features such as a heavy jaw (102). The avenger speaks:

> "It is I . . . the woman whose life you have ruined. . . . you sent the letters to my husband, and he—the noblest gentleman that ever lived, a man whose boots I was never worthy to lace—he broke his gallant heart and died. . . . You will ruin no more lives as you ruined mine. You will wring no more hearts as you wrung mine. I will free the world of a poisonous thing. Take that, you hound, and that!—and that!—and that!"
>
> She had drawn a little gleaming revolver, and emptied barrel after barrel into Milverton's body, the muzzle within two feet of his shirt front. . . . Then he staggered to his feet, received another shot, and rolled upon the floor. "You've done me," he cried, and lay still. The woman looked at him intently and ground her heel into his upturned face. She looked again, but there was no sound or movement. I heard a sharp rustle, the night air blew into the heated room, and the avenger was gone. (171–72)

This passage depicts one of the most violent murders committed by a woman in turn-of-the-century fiction, and its graphic illustration brought that violence home to readers (figure 15). Despite the woman's ferocity, however, Conan Doyle takes pains to rationalize—even defend—her act. Her invocation of her husband and her insistence on her own humility position her squarely in the tradition of self-renunciatory Victorian wifeliness. The scandalous letters do not challenge this charac-

"THEN HE STAGGERED TO HIS FEET AND RECEIVED ANOTHER SHOT."

Fig. 15. From "Charles Augustus Milverton"

terization: we know from Lady Eva's case that most of the letters in which Milverton traffics were written when the women were young and unmarried, and Holmes describes Lady Eva's letters as "imprudent, Watson, nothing worse" (159). Watson's reference to Milverton's killer as an "avenger" also serves to justify her act, as does her seemingly selfless invocation of Milverton's future victims.

Holmes and Watson choose not to expose the avenger. When Inspector Lestrade of Scotland Yard tries to enlist Holmes's help in solving the case, obviously unaware that he witnessed the murder, Holmes replies, "there are certain crimes which the law cannot touch, and which therefore, to some extent, justify private revenge. . . . My sympathies are with the criminals rather than with the victim, and I will not handle this case" (174). Even in the moment of watching the woman unload her pistol into Milverton's breast, while Watson reacts, Holmes holds him back:

> No interference upon our part could have saved the man from his fate; but as the woman poured bullet after bullet into Milverton's shrinking body, I was about to spring out, when I felt Holmes's cold, strong grasp upon my wrist. I understood the whole argument of that firm, restraining grip—that it was no affair of ours; that justice had overtaken a villain. . . . But hardly had the woman rushed from the room when Holmes, with swift, silent steps, was over at the other door. He turned the key in the lock. At the same instant we heard voices in the house and the sound of hurrying feet. The revolver shots had roused the household. With perfect coolness Holmes slipped across to the safe, filled his two arms with bundles of letters, and poured them all into the fire. Again and again he did it, until the safe was empty. Someone turned the handle and beat upon the outside of the door. . . . "This way, Watson," said he; "we can scale the garden wall in this direction."
> (172–73)

Holmes not only keeps quiet about the murder, but seizes the opportunity to actively cover it up and destroy all of the compromising letters in Milverton's safe. Committed in cold blood, with premeditation, this crime would presumably be quite disturbing to contemporary readers: a woman shooting a man with a phallic gun in his own study is a perfect example of the kind of invading and destructive threat that characterized many representations of first-wave feminism.[34] In covering the woman's act, however, Holmes ensures that the avenger will remain outside of the public forums of the newspaper, courts, and legal system. Indeed, the female avenger remains anonymous even on a metafictional level, for Watson refuses to reveal her name even to the "public" readership of the story.

Conan Doyle's discomfort with women in public cannot alone account for his shocking and remarkable female avenger, however; it does not explain why he makes her at once so appalling *and* so appealing. He takes a potentially threatening woman and normalizes her by providing justification for her act and presenting her as a loyal and loving wife; but he goes on to present her, like Irene Adler, as an object of public desire, idolization, and glamorization. At the end of the story, gazing into "a shop window filled with photographs of the celebrities and beauties of the day," Holmes recognizes what we might call the "mug shot" for the anonymous avenger:

> Holmes's eyes fixed themselves upon one of [the photographs], and following his gaze I saw the picture of a regal and stately lady in Court dress, with a high diamond tiara upon her noble head. I looked at that delicately curved nose, at the marked eyebrows, at the straight mouth, and the strong little chin beneath it. Then I caught my breath as I read the time-honoured title of the great nobleman and statesman whose wife she had been. My eyes met those of Holmes, and he put his finger to his lips as we turned away from the window. (174–75)

Shop window photography promoting "celebrities and beauties of the day" was part of the new visual landscape of Victorian consumerism. Just as magazine illustrations and newly visual textual formats transformed the medium in which readers encountered crime fiction and other narratives, the display of famous women's photographs as a means of selling products helped shift public culture toward the visual, consumerist, and feminine. Here, Conan Doyle portrays one such woman—displayed in all her aristocratic splendor to encourage others' consumption—as a murderer, a sharp distinction from what she appears to signify on a visual, imagistic level. The Holmes series on the whole presents criminality and truth as visually ascertainable categories, but when depicting female criminality, it suggests that the orchestration and framing of an image determines its meaning. Here, the murderer's photograph is a marketing tool, not a revelation of essential identity. Rather than a low brow, sensuous lips, or a misshapen ear, she has a tiara.

The photograph represents the avenger's invulnerability: she gets away with murder in part because of her social standing, but more obvi-

"FOLLOWING HIS GAZE I SAW THE PICTURE OF A REGAL AND STATELY LADY IN COURT DRESS."

Fig. 16. From "Charles Augustus Milverton"

ously because of her image. Conan Doyle's depiction of the avenger encapsulates the entire series' ambivalence about the female criminal, who represents a newly roused feminist power, the failures of patriarchy, and the consumerist appeal of feminine disobedience. The anonymous avenger is not a figure of criminal degeneracy, but of glamour and beauty; she is appealing rather than repulsive to readers. As the illustration accompanying this scene shows, she is literally a representation for the public to admire (figure 16). Thus, while Conan Doyle's stories do commodify feminine victimization, their commodification of feminine violence and criminality is even more significant. At a historical moment when a faction of the suffrage campaign was becoming ever more violent in its acts of civil disobedience, Conan Doyle's 1904 story banks on the allure of feminine disobedience for readers. The avenger puts the anger of first-wave feminism into an exquisite, consumable package. Like other female offenders in the series, her image and body project fantasy and glamour rather than criminological stigmata; she suits a consumerist model of vision rather than an anthropological or criminological one. In consumerist discourse, as I discuss in the introduction, to be visible and noticeable is a form of power rather than submission. Late-nineteenth-century advertisers and marketers preached, unlike Holmes, that it was better to be looked at than to look. They also defined, however, what kind of feminine embodiment was worthy of the gaze. Consumerism redefined femininity as public and visible, but only when it conformed to the logic of consumerism.

Given the series's apparent investment in a criminological theory of vision, one would expect its female criminals to be easily identifiable, but envisioning women is an activity fraught with problems for Holmes, the otherwise expert eye. Women criminals prove capable of resisting the detective's gaze, and Conan Doyle makes a sustained case for legal interventionism, which he associates (not unproblematically) with state feminism rather than state paternalism. Thus, at the turn of the twentieth century, Conan Doyle's stories put forth a far more compound and ambivalent theory of gender, vision, and the public than has been previously acknowledged; they support the authority of the gaze and locate ontology in image, *except* when depicting women criminals. In these instances, Conan Doyle's detective fiction prefigures filmic genres like film noir, in which *femmes fatales* reveal a great "truth" about the visual landscape of modern urban culture: that the unknowable is not signified by the invisible, but by a peculiarly modern disjunction between the visible and the real.

BEAUTIFUL FOR EVER!

TWO

*Cosmetics, Consumerism, L. T. Meade,
and Madame Rachel*

At the end of the last chapter, I turned from the criminological gaze to the consumerist image: let me briefly recapitulate why this move is central to my project. As an image and representation, the female criminal unites two distinct and conflicting conceptions of visibility in late-Victorian crime fiction. In criminological discourse, as we saw in the last chapter, imagistic semiotics was understood as a powerful new domain of knowledge for positivist social science and the empirical science of social control. Consumerism, in contrast, was an "image centered" rather than "gaze centered" discourse. Women were increasingly targeted by marketing and advertising in the final decades of the nineteenth century, and the message embedded in these media was, as in criminology, a message about vision and power. While criminologists envisioned enhanced power through observation and the gaze, however, consumerist rhetoric fed women an essentially opposite theory of the image: to be looked at can be a position of power, if one vigorously consumes in order to construct the image that affords the most power and control.[1]

Thus late-Victorian women were increasingly encouraged to exercise power via image and consumption; at the same time, fictional female criminals in detective series emerge as an anxious foil to a popular, consumerist, pseudofeminist discourse about the power of feminine influence through image. The last chapter, for example, concluded with a discussion of shop-window photography and the anonymous avenger of "Charles Augustus Milverton." At the end of the story, the detective "identifies" the criminal, as is typical of detective fiction, but identification in this case does not correspond with the disappearance or containment of the criminal. Rather than repressively pinning down her identity, the reproduced image of the female criminal instead serves as an object of display to encourage other women's purchases.

This chapter treats another fictional female criminal who promotes women's consumption and whose power emerges from image manipulation; L. T. Meade's detective series *The Sorceress of the Strand* depicts cosmetics, beauty, and feminine consumption as powerful deflectors of the criminological gaze. Meade's series is in many ways very much like Arthur Conan Doyle's: it was published in the *Strand Magazine* with numerous illustrations, it follows Conan Doyle's successful format of autonomous serialization, and it theorizes the relationship among femininity, visibility, and criminality. Both series explore what I argue is a central paradox of late-Victorian crime fiction: they depict women's suddenly expanded visibility in the public sphere, via consumerism and first-wave feminism, but simultaneously emphasize the opaqueness and indecipherability of female criminality. The central difference between the two series is in Meade's feminist perspective: she addresses pertinent feminist questions about gender, body, image, and visibility far more explicitly than Conan Doyle.

An extremely prolific author, L. T. Meade is chiefly remembered as a writer of fiction for girls, but she also made extensive contributions to the literature of crime.[2] She was an advocate of feminist causes, and critics such as Sally Mitchell and Mavis Reimer have argued that her writings facilitated mainstream Victorian feminism by depicting strong female heroines and by establishing a separate subculture for girls.[3] While her stories were printed in the same organ as Conan Doyle's, in a similar form and with a similar visual context, they would not necessarily have been viewed as having the same audiences or goals. In Reginald Pound's history of the *Strand,* he describes Meade's work for the magazine as part of an effort to meet "women's fiction needs" in a publication that sometimes "went to press with no story or article of compelling interest to women" (70). Meade's stories are an important feminist intervention into the gender narrative that the Holmes series puts forth, yet as the latter section of this chapter explores, they fail to account for the limitations of a liberal feminism grounded in economic empowerment and imperialist consumption.

To assess Meade's depiction of vision and image in these stories, my analysis goes back to a hitherto unnoted source for her series: *The Sorceress* is an overt rewriting of the strange case of Madame Rachel, a notorious female criminal of the 1860s. *The Sorceress* features a master criminal named Madame Sara, a thinly disguised—but far more lethal—impersonation of Madame Rachel. The connection between Meade's stories and her source would have been quite obvious to contemporary readers: the villain of her series is named Madame Sara, and Madame Rachel's full name was Sarah Rachel Leverson.[4] More strikingly, the two women share an unusual vocation: like Madame Rachel, Meade's Madame Sara is a "professional beautifier" who operates a perfumery and cosmetics shop in London's West End ("Madame Sara" 388). Both Rachel and Sara purport to make women look younger and more beautiful through cosmetic products and procedures, but this promise is primarily a lure that allows them to inveigle wealth and riches from unwitting clients. Madame Sara's name, shop, and business clearly identify her with Madame Rachel, and Meade even uses real incidents from Rachel's life to form some of the plots in *The Sorceress*.[5]

Meade evidently found a wealth of inspiration in Rachel's well-documented criminal saga, which she employs less prominently in another crime series called *The Brotherhood of the Seven Kings* (1898). Her recycling of Madame Rachel's case was unusual, however, in the length of time that elapsed between Rachel's mid-Victorian crimes and Meade's fictionalization of them. Crimes with a lot of coverage in the press guaranteed audience interest for Victorian writers, and Richard Altick notes that many authors "thrived on the public's consuming appetite" for coverage of contemporary crimes (531). If Meade was seeking to feed a "consuming appetite" for stories about Madame Rachel, however, her audience's gratification was quite delayed: *The Sorceress* was published twenty-two years after Rachel's death.[6]

The gap between Rachel's 1868 trials and Meade's 1902 series provides a fascinating case study of how turn-of-the-century feminist writing transformed the terms of cultural debate about women's visibility in Victorian society. As handed down in newspapers and other popular sources, the story of Madame Rachel had been used to legitimate broad cultural apprehension about women's foray into the expanding urban commercial marketplace in the second half of the nineteenth century, but Meade alters her source material in significant and fascinating ways. She transports Rachel into the fictional setting of 1899 London, where women's social and economic position was considerably different from the 1860s, and thus traces the shifting character of consumer capitalism and "the woman question" in the late-Victorian period. Her stories connect earlier discussions about women in the commercial sphere with turn-of-the-century debates about women's entry into new bastions of male economic privilege, such as science and the professions. At the same time, the series seeks to redefine what constitutes British female identity in the wake of women's expanding social and economic roles. Exploiting the exotic and foreign elements of Madame Rachel's commerce, Meade imagines a new kind of feminine identity defined not by exclusion from the economic sphere, but by a global marketplace for women's consumption. The rapidly escalating demands of feminine image, fashion, and appearance are framed, in this series, as manifestations of women's new economic agency *and* exemplars of England's imperial dominance.

"SHREWD WOMEN OF BUSINESS": THE CASE OF MADAME RACHEL

Critical work on *The Sorceress* has not yet acknowledged Madame Sara's real-life prototype, but historians and critics have documented the strong cultural resonance of Madame Rachel in the Victorian period.[7] Madame Rachel, or Sarah Rachel Leverson, was indicted for fraud three times: in 1865, 1868, and 1878. The 1868 case was particularly momentous, protracting for nearly a year and occasioning a media frenzy.[8] In this case, Rachel was charged and imprisoned for swindling money, jewelry, and goods from a wealthy lady customer of her Bond Street shop. Her five-year prison sentence was unusually harsh for the crime of fraud, suggesting how much the case unsettled her contemporaries. Over the course of two trials, the first of which closed without a verdict, the press struggled to understand what "Madame Rachel" signified about her society. The London *Times* alone ran no fewer than fifty articles, reports, letters, and editorials about the 1868 trial, from June 1868 to June 1869. Rachel also spawned cartoons and lampoons in *Punch,* parodic vaudeville renditions, a popular street ballad, and literary allusions that persisted for more than a century.[9] In September 1868, Madame Tussaud's wax museum prominently promoted Rachel's induction into their collection, and the next month, the Stereoscopic Company advertised portraits of Madame Rachel and her accuser, made "from sketches in Court," in the *Times*. The slogan for Rachel's shop engendered the widespread Victorian catch-phrase "beautiful for ever," signifying puffery (Altick 542), and Rachel even became the namesake for a New Zealand spring called Madame Rachel's Bath (Boase 323). The cultural impact of the trial was enormous and far-reaching. In court, the prosecutor himself admitted the case had not "involved a great catastrophe or a grave crime," but still called it "one of the most extraordinary which had ever been brought into a court of justice" because "it was one of such a remarkable nature" (4).[10]

What was so "remarkable" and "extraordinary" about the case? In the years leading up to the proceedings, Madame Rachel had become famous by marketing and vending her own line of beauty products. Though illiterate, she had even authored via dictation an 1863 "how to" manual entitled *Beautiful For Ever!*[11] George Boase, writing in *Notes & Queries* in 1894, asserts that Rachel originally set up shop around 1860, but that "on August 13, 1861, she was insolvent on her own petition . . . [and] remanded to Whitecross State Prison" (322–23). Upon her release from debtor's prison, Rachel reopened her business, and this time was far more successful because of the hyperbole and omnipresence of her advertisements. A 1908 memoir called *London in the Sixties* recalls her shop as phenomenally popular: "Everybody consulted Madame Rachel" (280).

It was not simply her fame that made Rachel's case "remarkable," however, but what she herself represented. In journalistic and popular sources, the discourse surrounding Madame Rachel is predicated upon a vexed entanglement of gender, ethnic, and economic anxieties: Rachel's villainous persona came to symbolize threats to traditional English national identity posed by feminism, immigration and cosmopolitanism, and consumerism. To position Meade's series in the context of such representations is to locate both *The Sorceress* and the Madame Rachel case within a network of late-Victorian cultural debate, largely conducted in the periodical press, about femininity, nationalism, and consumerism. Meade's particular redaction of Rachel's story exemplifies not only the dissemination of feminism in popular discourse, but also feminists' intervention into cultural narratives that cordoned women off from various forms of public and economic engagement.

When considering Victorian writing about Madame Rachel, the boundaries between accuracy, embroidery, and hysteria aren't always easy to determine. Contemporary sources suggest Rachel's "beauty shop" provided more services than the merely cosmetic, but Victorian authors are not forthcoming about what precisely these entailed. Boase wrote in 1894, "it would not do to enter into the particulars of the various services which Rachel rendered to some of her clients, in addition to selling them enamels and perfumes" (323). Some accounts indicate Rachel was a "madam" in more ways than one: William Roughead claims she "dealt in other wares than those exposed to public wonder in her windows," and that her shop's "primary purpose" was "procuration and blackmail" (96). If this is true, it lends a particularly ironic tone to the slogan posted over her shop door: "Purveyor to the Queen."

Wilkie Collins's 1866 novel *Armadale* suggests another source for the iniquitous legacy that surrounded Madame Rachel: through Mother Oldershaw, a character modeled on Rachel, Collins implies that backroom abortions were provided in her shop. *Armadale* predates the media frenzy surrounding Rachel's 1868 trial, suggesting that unsavory rumors had developed prior to her indictment. Mother Oldershaw's shop is in Pimlico rather than on Bond Street, and thus is of a lower social status than Rachel's shop, but Oldershaw sounds very much like Rachel when discussing her vocation. She tells Lydia Gwilt, the villainess of the novel: "I have had twenty years' experience among our charming sex in making up battered old faces and worn-out old figures to look like new. . . . If you will follow my advice about dressing, and use one or two of my applications privately, I guarantee to put you back three years. . . . when I have ground you young again in my wonderful mill, you [won't] look more than seven-and-twenty in any man's eyes living" (160). With the image of her "wonderful mill," Oldershaw becomes an industrial capitalist, a woman of industry, which corresponds with Collins's depiction of her abortion racket.

Oldershaw does not perform abortions herself, but her shop adjoins the office of Doctor Downward, "one of those carefully-constructed physicians in whom the public—especially the female public—implicitly trust" (341). The novel refers to "the risks the doctor runs in his particular form of practice" (499), and a lawyer in the novel, who "has had a large legal experience of the shady side of [women]" (358), whispers to protagonist Allan Armadale some awful secret about Oldershaw's business. Collins thus indicates that Downward provides abortions under the sponsorship of Oldershaw's shop. Oldershaw tells Lydia, "One of the many delicate little difficulties which beset so essentially confidential a business as mine, occurred . . . this afternoon" (209), and Lydia later refers to this incident as "some woman's business of course" (214). Both Oldershaw and Downward are "filled with wicked secrets, and . . . perpetually in danger of feeling the grasp of the law" (345–46). Toward the end of the novel, the shop closes down because of an apparent problem with the medical side of its commerce: Downward refers to a "business difficulty connected with our late partnership in Pimlico" (586). In its correlation of makeup, commerce, and female criminality, *Armadale* anticipates depictions of the New Woman Criminal in the new crime genres of the fin de siècle.

We cannot know how much Collins borrows from the Madame Rachel story, how much he invents, and how much he paraphrases from rumors circulating about her shop. Altick maintains, when discussing *Armadale,* that "Madame Rachel may not, in fact, have been involved in an abortionist racket" (543), but it is also true that she may well have been. In 1928, crime chronicler Horace Wyndham made the same insinuation as Collins, writing that Rachel supplied clients with "'medical treatment' of a description upon which the Law frowns" (242). Some of the rhetoric in Madame Rachel's *Beautiful For Ever!* does echo advertising copy for late-Victorian abortion-inducing patent medicines: her method of "cleansing the system from many of its impurities, which may arise from different causes" (20) is perhaps an oblique reference to abortifacients, which were discreetly advertised in the Victorian periodical press in such terms. The title *Madame,* by the same token, was common among providers of abortions or abortifacients in nineteenth-century culture.[12]

Despite speculations about a greater extent to her illegal activities, Rachel's actual indictment concerned only the relatively minor crime of fraud. Her seemingly petty crimes nonetheless occasioned an astounding degree of vitriol among her contemporaries. Tammy Whitlock notes that Rachel's trial performed cultural work well beyond its alleged purpose of determining Rachel's "guilt" or "innocence" of defrauding customer Mary Tucker Borradaile of fourteen hundred pounds: "there were actually a series of 'trials' within the larger frame of the criminal trial. Rachel was on trial as a perpetrator of fraud, but she was also on 'trial' for her participation in retail trade" ("A 'Taint'" 30); consequently, she was judged "guilty not only of her crime, but of lacking the respectability, class, ethnic origins, and morality of a Victorian lady" (36). Rachel was illiterate, thrice-married, separated from her husband, and Jewish, yet she had managed to amass a degree of social capital unusual to her situation. Over the course of her trials, newspaper readers learned that she held a box at the opera and owned a home in the suburbs, that her children had traveled and been educated in Paris, and that Lord Ranelagh frequently visited her shop. She represented an affront to Victorian class and gender strictures, and such effrontery gave contours to the presumption of guilt that hung over the trial. Newspaper coverage, for example, marshaled public opinion against Rachel's character. The *Express* argued: "Criminals do not acquire the deep cunning and terrible proficiency in evil displayed by Rachel without having served a long and painstaking apprenticeship . . . how many other victims are there who have sunk quietly and unresistingly out of sight!" (117). Even the *Times,* which doubted there was enough evidence to justly convict Rachel, reasoned: "whatever may be the difference of opinion about the prisoner's legal guilt, about her moral guilt we take it that there can be no doubt whatever" (107).

Popular depictions of Rachel as a procuress, a prostitute, and an abortionist hovered over the press coverage, suggesting that her villainous appeal was due to widespread apprehension about women's participation in public, capitalist enterprise. Reports from Rachel's various trials suggest that she was perfectly cognizant of such apprehension, and was willing to manipulate it to her own ends when it suited her. During her 1865 trial, when Rachel was sued for fraud by Aurora Knight, the defense attempted to discredit Knight by depicting her as a woman overly engaged in the public sphere and thus "not a lady, as she represents herself." Not only had Knight "lately come from America," which linked her with travel, traffic, foreignness, and domestic unrootedness, but she was also "known at the Café de Lyons by various names." Most telling of all is Rachel's argument as to why her course of beauty treatments didn't work for Knight: Knight "had suffered from an attack of smallpox and wished to have the marks removed. Madame Rachel . . . recommended her to take baths. Of course Madame Rachel would not admit a woman who had just recovered from smallpox into her private baths, and she sent her to some baths in Argyll-place. But the complainant went to the Endell-street public baths" ("Marlborough-Street"). Rachel's testimony suggests that her beautifying treatments aren't effective in "public" baths, because such places are impure. By telling this story in court, Rachel associates her accuser with public, transnational contagion. The irony, of course, is that she relies here upon the same conventional associations— between privacy and purity, publicity and contamination—that corrupted her own character in the minds of her contemporaries. Rachel's expansive, ubiquitous advertising campaign and her engagement in public commercial exchange had exposed her to exactly the same kind of censure.

Rachel was not only a woman, however, but a "Jewess," so her public image was tainted by ethnic as well as gender and class stereotypes. Newspaper reports of her trials often reminded readers of Rachel's Jewishness, evoking not only anti-Semitic fears of racial difference and cultural otherness, but also fears associated with immigration, job competition, cosmopolitanism, and the dilution of English national identity. Rachel's first appearance in court, for example, was in 1858, when she sued her landlord for assault after he allegedly locked her up and attempted to push her down a flight of stairs. In its coverage of the case, the *Times* describes Rachel as "an English Jewess," and at the trial itself, the defense attempted to gain sympathy for the landlord by appealing to ethnic stereotypes. As evidence against Rachel, though it had nothing to do with the alleged assault, the defense produced one of her advertising circulars, where she refers to herself as "Madame Rachel, of London, and also of New York" ("Court of Queen's Bench"). At another point, a witness testified that Rachel often spoke German with her mother. Rachel denied to the court that she had ever been in New York and denied that she spoke German, but such allegations were clearly intended to cast doubt on her "Englishness," to present her as foreign and cosmopolitan, transnational and untrustworthy. The United States and Germany were Britain's primary economic competitors, so Rachel's commercial endeavors are figured as threats to English capitalist enterprise rather than manifestations of it. Similarly, when Rachel was convicted of debt in 1862, the *Times*'s account began: "The insolvent, a young Jewess . . ." ("Insolvent"). Representing the bankrupt Rachel as an economic drain on her society, the report takes pains to emphasize her Jewishness. Coverage of her 1868 trial performed similar discursive maneuvers. The *Saturday Review* called her a "Jewish purveyor of feminine charms" (119), associating Rachel's business with exotic Eastern mysticism, which, in this account, is racially and commercially antagonistic to Englishness.

If Rachel's gender and ethnicity were on trial, the 1868 case also served as a trial of the victim, the widow Mrs. Borradaile, whose own failure to adhere to Victorian standards of respectable feminine behavior nearly lost her the case. According to Borradaile, Rachel had swindled her by leading her to believe Lord Ranelagh wanted to marry her, provided she underwent a series of expensive beautification treatments and lent him a good deal of money through Rachel's intercession. Borradaile was around fifty years old, which made this story seem ludicrous enough to Victorian readers, but rumors surrounding the trial painted a much more sordid picture: that Ranelagh had watched Borradaile bathing in Rachel's back room, with her consent, and that Rachel's baths were specially designed to allow such voyeurism. Other rumors indicated that Borradaile had had an affair with Ranelagh years earlier, while she was still married, and that he had fathered one of her children. Most damaging to Borradaile was the argument used by the defense: that the Lord Ranelagh story was completely false, and that Borradaile was using it to shield her real "paramour," William.

The prosecutors denied all of these allegations, but Borradaile's image and appearance didn't attest to her respectability. Her lawyer later described her as "a spare, thin, scraggy-looking woman . . . her hair was dyed a bright yellow; her face was ruddled with paint; and the darkness of her eyebrows was strongly suggestive of meretricious art. She had a silly, giggling, half-hysterical way of talking" (qtd. in Roughead 109). To be visibly made-up was still considered indecent in the 1860s, according to Neville Williams's history of cosmetics in England, and the falseness of Borradaile's appearance perhaps led jurists to doubt her testimony: in the first attempt to try the case, the jury failed to reach consensus because of disagreement about her reliability as a witness. Commentators on the case, too, were critical of her. The *Saturday Review* said her letters, brought as evidence in the trial, were a "very ugly romance of a vulgar and disgusting chapter of sin and shame." They were skeptical of her claim that she wrote them while bewitched by Rachel (121). Even the prosecution, aware of their star witness's limitations, called her "weak, credulous, foolish, and vain" in closing statements (94).

The trial came down to the question of which of these two repugnant women the jury would believe: Madame Rachel or Mrs. Borradaile. Accordingly, both lawyers were at pains to prove their clients' allegiance to an ethos of proper Victorian femininity, and emphasized their devotion to their families while playing down their savviness in the consumer sphere. Transcripts from the trial suggest the extent to which, in the late 1860s, proper feminine character was established not only by proof of domestic ties, but by opposition to all forms of financial intercourse. The prosecutor repeatedly referenced Borradaile's familial and social status, calling her a "gentlewoman . . . for she was gentle in birth, manners and demeanour" (100), and noting that her husband had been a respected army officer. According to the *Times,* he "asked [the jury] to believe Mrs. Borradaile upon the ground that she had been a virtuous wife, and since her husband's death a virtuous widow, and that the slightest stain or slur could not be cast upon her. It was true that charges against her had been whispered, but he challenged [them]" (6). He also portrayed her as the innocent dupe of Rachel's business acumen, emphasizing that she was "a lady fresh from the country" (96) and that "Rachel, being a woman of great craft and very considerable mind, brought that craft and mind to bear upon her victim" (95).

The defense, on the other hand, implied that Borradaile was "a woman of loose habits" (9) and questioned her commitment to the feminine sphere of home and family: "That there was something strange on the part of Mrs. Borradaile was clear, else why was she living in London, moving about from coffeehouse to coffeehouse, while her daughter and other relations were all living in Wales?" ("Central Criminal Court, Sept. 24"). Emphasizing Borradaile's nomadic life and supposed domestic negligence, they presented her as more comfortable in the public consumer sphere than she let on: the defense brought in a jeweler whose shop Borradaile had visited, and he testified that "she took a look round as ladies will do. She appeared to understand what she was about, and to be a shrewd woman of business" (66). They also put a linen draper on the stand, who said that Borradaile had spent 150 pounds in his store and had "appeared to be a woman of business" during the transaction (66). In his closing statement, Rachel's lawyer revisited this line of argument, insisting that "so far from being a fool, [Borradaile] appears to have been a shrewd woman of business, and quite capable of knowing what she was doing" (78). Given her profession, it was not possible for the defense to deny Rachel's involvement in the consumer sphere, so her lawyer portrayed her efforts at commercial success as prompted by devotion to her children, an appropriately feminine motivation, rather than the mere desire for financial gain. Emphasizing that Rachel's seven children were enormously well educated, considering their mother's social standing, the lawyer reasoned, "whatever might be said against the prisoner, this must be admitted that she had given her children a good education" (77).

CONSPICUOUS CONSUMPTION: FEMINISM,
VISIBILITY, AND CONSUMERISM

As these "trials within trials" suggest, Rachel's case resonated with Victorian cultural debates about the status of gender and social identity in the expanding commercial marketplace and economy. As the ideology of consumerism spread and the accumulation of wealth became enough to ensure one's social capital, fears about the denigration of established social hierarchies came to the surface of popular discourse. That

Rachel was a vendor of cosmetics heightened her symbolic relevance to such debates: her very trade entailed making people appear more attractive than they "really" were. Paula Black notes that the beauty industry and the beauty salon as an institution emerged in tandem with the mid-nineteenth-century rise of advertising aimed directly at women (20); thus Rachel's shop represented not only consumer culture's penchant for obliterating supposedly "natural" divisions among gradations of humanity, but also its feminization of public culture and the visual landscape of public life. Rachel's case represented a trial of Victorian femininity and English national identity in the face of rampant commercialism, and an attempt to determine what would happen to respectable, domestic women as the city and the marketplace expanded to include them. As women became established as the preeminent consumers in the new commercial economy, Rachel's trial posed profound questions, questions that Meade would take up in her fictionalization of Rachel's story: What kinds of financial intercourse were socially permissible for women in the modern marketplace? What social changes were entailed in Victorian ladies becoming "shrewd women of business"? And what did all of these changes mean for the status of English national identity?

By the time Meade was writing in 1902, the presence of "respectable" women in the city marketplace was a reality experienced by millions of British urbanites. The expanding consumer economy had created a whole new class of young, single, working women, often from the country, who came to London to work and support themselves. Such women found jobs in a service economy that included shopgirls, office workers, typists, and other occupations that had not existed for women of Rachel's generation. At the same time that such working-class "girls" were negotiating a legitimate presence in the city, leisured middle-class women had established their own urban status as shoppers, charity workers, and political agitators. The New Woman had become a staple of popular discourse, articulating real shifts in the relative freedom and occupational choice available to women.[13] In *The Sorceress,* Meade creates Madame Sara as a New Woman by emphasizing not only her commercial success, but also her scientific and medical prowess; in this way, her stories translate the gender anxieties aroused by Madame Rachel into the era of the New Woman.

Feminist critics who have discussed women's role in the nineteenth-century consumer sphere have tended to take either a Marxian or historicist position. Marxian critics have read the expanding consumer marketplace as merely another arena for sexist oppression, in many ways worse than the domestic sphere. When women become enmeshed in modern consumer capitalism, the argument goes, they are subjected to an illusory false consciousness of the world in which their very perceptions and desires are afflicted by commodity ideology. Because of their lack of power in relation to men, women have a heightened vulnerability to the dehumanizing, objectifying prerogatives of consumer capitalism. Susan Buck-Morss claims that "Sexual liberation for women under capitalism has had the nightmare effect of 'freeing' all women to be sexual objects (not subjects)" (124). Rachel Bowlby has similarly argued that consumer capitalism in the nineteenth century developed according to preexisting models of domination supplied by the example of patriarchy: "the making of willing consumers readily fit into the available ideological paradigm of a seduction of women by men, in which women would be addressed as yielding objects to the powerful male subject forming, and informing them of, their desires" (20). Consumer capitalism, according to Bowlby, instills the illusion that customers, in buying, exercise a mode of power that echoes male sexual domination: "the very image used of the relation between commodities and buyers is one of seduction and rape: commodities cannot ultimately 'resist' the force of him who would 'take possession of them'" (27). According to this model, the attraction of the consumer marketplace for Victorian women was the allure of a masculine, rapine form of power available in the sphere of the shop, if not anywhere else. Needless to say, in shopping, women were actually not powerful at all, but were recapitulating and reinforcing an oppressive gendered division of labor and an oppressive patriarchal-capitalist system.

In contrast to these readings of the nineteenth-century consumer marketplace, some recent feminist critics have taken a more broadly historicist approach, rather than one based on critiques of ideology, and concentrated on the impact consumer culture had on the daily lives of Victorian women. Doing so, they have viewed the expansion of consumer culture quite differently. Sally Ledger, for example, reflects that "the department stores, like the arcades, boulevards, and cafés, constituted a half-public, half-private social space which women were able to inhabit comfortably, so that the rise of consumerism was not *all* bad as far as women were concerned. The metropolitan department store enabled leisured women in particular to look, socialise, and simply to stroll" (*New* 155). Judith Walkowitz, discussing women in 1880s London, suggests that the road to women's public and political engagement was in many ways smoothed by the growth of consumer society. Female shoppers, enticed by new metropolitan retail development, carved out a space for middle- and upper-class women in the public spaces of the city. Along with lower-class shopgirls and "girls in business," such a presence made the urban landscape a "contested terrain" rather than the sole bastion of men and prostitutes (*City* 11). This was a necessary prerequisite for women being "drawn into the vortex of political and religious activity" in 1880s London (73).

The conflict between these two critical perspectives revisits many of the same questions at issue in Madame Rachel's trial. As Rachel's success suggests, there *was* a connection between the growth of the consumer economy and women's emancipation in late-Victorian culture, which is one reason that entrepreneurs like Rachel elicited such anxiety from their contemporaries. To view patriarchy and consumer capitalism as utterly analogous is to ignore how the commercialization of culture broadened the lives of many women in the last decades of the nineteenth century, and how consumer culture participated in the weakening of strict social hierarchies such as Victorian gender roles. The memoir *London in the Sixties* by "One of the Old Brigade," for example, offers a glimpse into upper-class male resentment at the gender-leveling consumerism occasioned. The text is a nostalgic account of clubs, drinking, gambling, and after-dark carousing in the 1860s, but it was written in 1908, six years after Meade's stories:

> London in the sixties was so different from the London of to-day. . . .
> Streets have been annihilated and transformed into Boulevards . . .
> night-houses and comfortable taverns demolished and transformed into plate-glass abominations run by foreigners and Jews, whilst hulking louts in uniform, electro-plate and the shabby-genteel masher have taken the place of solid silver spoons and a higher type of humanity.
> . . . [I]f any night-bird of those naughty days were suddenly exhumed, and let loose in Soho, he would assuredly wander into a church . . . and so unwittingly fall into the goody-goody ways that make up our present monotonous existence. (1)

The author goes on to bemoan the loss of "recreations which, if indulged in now, would be tantamount to social ostracism, or imperilling the 'succession'" (1–2), and the existence of "vigilance societies . . . and fifty institutions with their secretaries and staff . . . supported by seekers after morality" (43). Many of the changes that the author decries were occasioned by a consumerist-feminist effort to "clean up" the city, easing urban access for women. The widening of the streets, the installation of large windows, and the presence of vigilance societies made the urban center a more attractive place for "respectable" women, working girls, and bourgeois female shoppers. To court women customers, businesses were perfectly happy to contribute to this effort, facilitating greater public freedom for women by making the city marketplace a safer and more respectable place to be.

Nevertheless, it would be a mistake to theorize late-Victorian consumerism as a straightforwardly progressive step toward female emancipation. The relationship between consumerism and sexist oppression, I would argue, was not one of opposition or partnership, but of multiple contingent and variable effects. Women's new urban "freedom," for example, offered little benefit for poor, disenfranchised women who could profit neither from new jobs in the consumer sphere nor from new opportunities for female consumption. Likewise, prostitutes were adversely affected by urban commercial development at the end of the nineteenth century, as Buck-Morss and Walkowitz (*Prostitution*) both describe. Less obviously, the extent to which even bourgeois women "paid a price" for new freedoms at the end of the century is a significant question for critics of culture, and one that is particularly crucial in discussions of image, body, and appearance.

Meade's stories highlight the crux of this issue by associating the rise of feminism and the rise of cosmetics in the second half of the nineteenth century. The proliferation of cosmetics and other feminine beauty products signifies how the feminization of consumer capitalism shifted the terms of women's oppression, so that women became increasingly sexually commodified under the auspices of an image-centered consumer culture. As recent feminist critics have argued, since the Victorian period, the category of "femininity" has been constituted more and more by self-administered regimens of health, beauty, fashion, and appearance.[14] Women's bodies have shifted from being the property of individual men (such as fathers or husbands) to being social property, in need of constant maintenance to meet the new cultural standards of femininity. Such a condition is oppressive for women, but not in conventionally "patriarchal" terms, wherein power is held or exercised by men. Consumerism afforded women greater access to and engagement with the public sphere, but did it also distort their desires so that they "advanced" merely to become their own oppressors—or the oppressors of others?

Meade's stories and the case of Madame Rachel suggest that neither a Marxian nor a historicist approach can fully account for the complex relationship between feminism and consumerism at the end of the nineteenth century. While many feminist objectives were aided by the expansion of consumerism, some may have become unrecognizably altered in the process. Rachel's story is a case in point: she was a lower-class and illiterate woman who became a successful business-owner, but she attained success by exploiting economically autonomous women and by insisting that women conform to commercialized "norms" of feminine image and appearance. Indeed, Rachel's sales tactics, as exemplified in *Beautiful For Ever!,* could be Machiavellian. In one section, she claims: "How frequently we find that a slight blemish on the face, otherwise divinely beautiful, has occasioned a sad and solitary life of celibacy— unloved, unblessed, and ultimately unwept and unremembered" (18). Yet "if ladies bestow an extra hour at the toilette, it is to delight and please the sterner sex. It is therefore our endeavor to prove that a lady cannot be too careful in the arrangement of her toilette, as the future happiness of her life may depend upon her first appearance in society" (18). Black notes that in the late nineteenth century, the "beauty business provided one of the few sources of employment open to women where their expertise propelled them to the highest levels of authority and entrepreneurship" (28). Yet clearly, Rachel's success also depended on her capacity to bolster oppressive ideology as a means of selling her products. Rachel owed her business success to women's increasing consumer independence in the 1860s, but by insisting such women have an obligation to "buy" physical femininity, her advertising prose forges them a new set of manacles.

L. T. Meade revises Rachel's story, in part, by complicating the degree to which her cosmetic business corresponds with patriarchal interests. Meade's Madame Sara gains her influence over women with quite a different tactic than those employed in Madame Rachel's *Beautiful For Ever!* Instead of encouraging her female clients to beautify themselves to please men, Sara encourages them to disobey men by taking advantage of her services. For Sara's female clients, physical transformation and bodily modification become acts of ownership, independence, and rebellion rather than capitulation or compliance. The male relations of her female victims are continually complaining to Eric Vandaleur and Dixon Druce, the detectives on the hunt for Madame Sara, about their wives' and relations' use of Sara's services. In the first story of the series, for example, Jack Selby describes his wife's attraction to Sara as though it's a disease: "my wife is also infected. I suppose it is that dodge of the woman's for patching people up and making them beautiful. Doubtless the temptation is overpowering in the case of a plain woman, but Beatrice is beautiful herself and young. What can she have to do with cosmetics and complexion pills?" ("Madame Sara" 394). In another story, "The Bloodstone," Vandaleur worries that one of his patients is seeing Sara. A police surgeon, doctor, and forensic detective, Vandaleur is a powerful representative of masculine authority, but he worries that Sara's appeal overwhelms his influence: "I warned Lady Bouverie on no account to consult [Sara] medically, and she promised. But, there, how far is a woman's word, under given circumstances, to be depended upon? . . . She is losing her looks; she gets thinner and older-looking day by day. Under such circumstances any woman who holds the secrets Madame Sara does would compel another to be guided by her advice" (199). Here, far from being a means of covering up a blemish that could occasion "a sad and solitary life" without men, the use of Sara's services constitutes a rebellion *against* authoritative men.

Indeed, part of Sara's genius lies in how she manages to criminalize or corrupt her female clients at the same time that she victimizes them, by encouraging them to disobey their husbands and doctors. In order for the victims to expose the crime, they must also expose themselves, and thus Sara achieves the perfect crime: one in which no one is innocent. The prosecutor in Rachel's case, as Whitlock also discusses, likewise emphasized her sullying influence. According to the *Times* he "wished all the ladies who had heard or read this case would learn that if once they crossed the threshold of such places [as Rachel's shop] they would come out with a taint upon them" (*Extraordinary* 96). Meade literalizes this concept of the "taint" in "The Blood-Red Cross." Here, a young woman named Antonia Ripley asks Sara to remove a disfiguring mole from her neck. She has been warned not to consult Sara, but wants to get rid of the mole before her wedding, where she must wear a low-cut dress to show off an heirloom pearl necklace. Sara has uncovered a secret from Antonia's past, and after giving her chloroform, she tattoos the secret onto her body: "The words were very small and neatly done—they formed a cross on the young lady's neck . . . : 'I AM THE DAUGHTER OF PAOLO GIOLETTI, WHO WAS EXECUTED FOR THE MURDER OF MY MOTHER.'" Sara writes the words with nitrate of silver, so they will be invisible until exposed to light; once exposed, they will be permanently indelible (513–14). An illustration in the text realized this chilling scene for readers (figure 17).

Sara's plan is to blackmail Antonia with a cross-shaped necklace that will prevent the tattoo from being exposed to light, in return for the

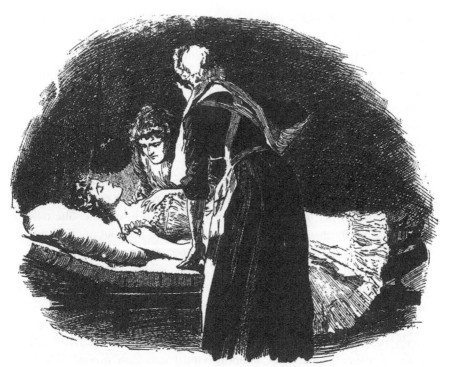

" MADAME WROTE SOMETHING ON HER NECK."

Fig. 17. From "The Blood-Red Cross"

heirloom pearls. Antonia has literally left Sara's shop with "a taint upon her": hereditary theories of crime were prevalent at the turn of the century; thus her body will be visibly criminalized if she refuses to abet Sara's theft.[15] Vandaleur uncovers the plot, however, and treats her neck with "cyanide of potassium," an antidote that obliterates nitrate of silver: "You have nothing to fear," he says, "your secret lies buried beneath your white skin" (517). Meade had a source for this story in Rachel's real-life interactions with Mrs. Pearce (see note 5), but the tattoo is wholly her invention. With the trope of the tattoo, her version forcefully asserts the significance of *writing* in determining how women's bodies are interpreted, viewed, or "read." Whether fiction, journalism, or advertising, the written word has the power to direct the way women's bodies are seen. Vision and perception in this story are not transparent, immediate, or unmediated processes, as in criminological discourse, but are structured by language and words. Meade's task as a feminist writer thus emerges clearly: she exposes how women's bodies are "written on" and protests women's bodily subjection to the perilous semiotics of image and respectability.

That the perception of female respectability is a particularly malleable sensation would be no surprise to Madame Sara. Her penchant for ruining her victims' reputations, as a means of preventing the exposure of her crimes, is most patently illustrated in "The Bloodstone." Here, Sara first casts doubt on the good name of her victim, Violet Bouverie, by involving her in a series of clandestine monetary transactions. Violet had been under the guardianship of Druce while still unmarried and named Violet Sale. Now, she enlists his help in accessing her fortune without her husband's knowledge; she won't tell why, but later it comes out that Sara had duped her into believing her brother was in trouble. She tells Druce: "I am in great trouble just now . . . I have not told my husband anything about it, nor do I wish him to know. It is not my duty to tell him, for the affair is my own, not his." Druce replies, "I cannot understand any circumstances in which a wife could rightly have a trouble apart from her husband" (201).

Violet's mother left her in "complete control of quite a large property" (198), but she cannot access it independently. She tells Druce, "I want to realize [some rupee coupon bonds] into cash immediately. I could not do so personally without my husband's knowledge" (201). Though unable to retrieve her own inheritance, Violet is clearly capable of being a "shrewd woman of business," as her maiden name (Sale) implies. Her married name (Bouverie) evokes Madame Bovary, of Gustave Flaubert's 1856 novel, whose surreptitious economic transactions ruined her husband and signified her deep moral corruption. Unlike Madame Bovary, however, Meade's Mrs. Bouverie resorts to secrecy to access her *own* property, not her husband's, and she herself has a detailed understanding of the financial markets: "I want you to sell them for me at the best price. I know the price is low owing to the fall in silver, but as they are bearer bonds there will be no transfer deeds to sign, and you can take them to your broker and get the money at once" (201). Druce reluctantly agrees to help, but is obviously uneasy about facilitating Violet's private financial dealings.

Having first cast doubt on her victim's reputation, Sara next impersonates her while stealing the "bloodstone," a Persian treasure owned by a guest of the Bouveries, ensuring that there is a witness to the crime. Seemingly in possession of eyewitness testimony, even Violet's husband believes her guilty, and calls the police to arrest her. Violet's recent ploys to obtain money have considerably damaged her credibility. Vandaleur eventually clears her, however, through scientific analysis of a handker-chief left on the scene; he determines that the chemical composition of the residual bodily fluids does not match Violet's. Nevertheless, like "The Blood-Red Cross," this story highlights how all women who get involved with Sara become "tainted"; the rouge, eyepencils, and other "paint" she vends symbolize how women's reputations are convention-ally sullied—unjustly, in Meade's stories—by engagement in commercial intercourse.

Cosmetics are an apt symbol for Meade to employ in this way be-cause they provided a very visible sign of the changes that, by 1902, had altered women's position in British society so drastically from Rachel's day. In the 1860s makeup was still considered disreputable, but by the end of the century it was widely used. In his history of cosmetics in En-gland, Williams claims the 1890s "saw a great advance in the popularity of cosmetics among women of all ages . . . the visible signs of woman's emancipation were painted faces and rational clothes. Make-up was, in-deed, one of the most striking expressions of *Fin de Siècle*. The new woman had arrived" (114). More recent scholars would dispute Williams's association of cosmetics with the New Woman, who tended to espouse a more androgynous style, but makeup did rise in correlation with women's social and sexual freedom. Hygienic dress reformer and aesthetic tastemaker Mary Haweis, wife of a prominent minister, wrote in 1878 that "because paint is considered to be a characteristic of a cer-tain showy vulgarity which we cannot wish to imitate, an unnecessary amount of contempt and contumely has been cast on cosmetics," but that she saw no "harm or degradation in avowedly hiding defects of complexions, or touching the face with pink or white" (196). A decade and a half later, an 1894 cartoon from *Punch* depicts common use of cos-metics among "respectable" women (figure 18).

As is evident in Meade's stories, the cosmetic boom near the end of the century hinged upon women having enough social and financial freedom to buy such products. What is more, use of makeup denotes a pronouncement of one's self as a sexual being, a departure from the per-formance of sexual disinterest compulsory in earlier Victorian formula-tions of respectable femininity. For Meade's readers, Sara's business was thus a reminder of the changing social role of women. That cosmetics are a troubled signifier of women's emancipation, however, is clear from Max Beerbohm's essay "A Defence of Cosmetics," published in *The Yel-low Book* in 1894. While proclaiming it "useless" for men to protest women's growing attachment to cosmetics, Beerbohm suggests, with

"A PAINTED LADY."

"O, Mummy dear, why did Papa say he was thinking of having you painted by Sir John Millais? I'm sure he wouldn't do it better than you do it Yourself!"

"Ethel, dear, I think you had better go and play in the Nursery with your little Brother!"

Fig. 18. From *Punch*, 27 January 1894, 45

tongue firmly in cheek, that men should instead embrace the development. Makeup, he claims, will stem the tide of women engaging in archery, tennis, golf, bicycling, typing, and other New Womanly "horrors" (69), and will force them to go back to their appropriate position of "repose" (70): "When the toilet is laden once more with the fulness [sic] of its elaboration, we shall hear no more of the proper occupation for women" (74).

Meade's stories express a conflicted response to the more general use of cosmetics at the end of the century. A visual signifier of women's shifting sexual and social roles, potentially connoting ownership of body and self, makeup also denoted artificiality and duplicity, and was incompatible with traditional Victorian values of feminine artlessness and naturalness. This explains Beerbohm's enthusiasm for it: claiming that "within the last five years the trade of the makers of cosmetics has increased immoderately—twentyfold, so one of these makers has said to me," he calls makeup a "great sign of a more complicated life" (67). *The Yellow Book* was the principal aesthetic literary journal, and Beerbohm one of the movement's key figures. His essay uses cosmetics to extol aestheticism's antinaturalist values: "of all the good things that will happen with the full renascence of cosmetics, one of the best is that surface will finally be severed from soul. . . . Too long has the face been degraded from its rank as a thing of beauty to a mere vulgar index of character or emotion" (71).

Outside of aesthetic circles, however, the prospect of the masked, made-up women Beerbohm describes—whose faces reveal nothing of their inner lives—was to be feared rather than welcomed. *Degeneration,* Max Nordau's best-selling 1895 diatribe against the excesses of modernity, calls women's hair dye a "symptom" of cultural degeneration (8). Cesare Lombroso's criminological study *The Female Offender,* also published in England in 1895, claims that "the art of making up . . . disguises or hides many characteristic features which criminals exhibit" (101). Havelock Ellis, in 1894, similarly proposes that the "artifices of the toilet" are proof of women's natural, "almost physiological" tendency to deceive, a trait leftover from the pressure of sexual selection: "a woman instinctively hides her defects, her disorders, if necessary her age—anything which may injure her in the eyes of men" (*Man* 175).[16] Like Sherlock Holmes, Nordau, Lombroso, and Ellis are deeply unnerved by the prospect of feminine opacity, but even feminists who share few of these social scientists' assumptions might dread the kind of developments Beerbohm predicts. In enabling performativity, makeup enhances women's power of parody, mimicry, or masking, but also constrains them to the burden of playing "beautiful."

Meade captures this difficulty in her depiction of Madame Sara, who uses makeup to present a guileless and innocent face to the world. Novels such as *The Picture of Dorian Gray* (1891) and *The Strange Case of Dr. Jekyll and Mr. Hyde* (1886) suggest broad fin de siècle interest in the disjunction between innocence and its outward appearance, but here Meade overtly connects this theme to the expanding feminine context of cosmetics and consumer fantasy. Sources indicate that Madame Rachel had not personally benefited from her beautification talents, but Meade depicts Sara as a strikingly lovely woman whose appearance is undoubtedly artificial and calculated. In "The Bloodstone," Druce claims, "Sara, by her own showing, was an old woman, and yet . . . [her] face was brilliant, not a wrinkle was to be observed; her make-up was so perfect that it could not be detected even by the closest observer" (206). In Sara, the ostensible line between cosmetic artificiality and "genuine" beauty is obliterated. Druce knows she must be made-up, but cannot find evidence for it, which as a detective he finds maddening: "I hate all mysteries—both in persons and things. Mysteries are my natural enemies; I felt now that this woman was a distinct mystery" ("Madame" 390). Here, as in the Holmes series, the female criminal is an unstable element in the scientific system of criminal detection. Just as Francis Galton believed that fingerprints were but "faintly developed" in women (*Finger Prints* 59), making female criminals difficult to detect, Sara's cosmetics help her maintain a "distinct mystery" of identity that baffles her pursuers. Though it is primarily Sara's genius, rather than her appearance, that accounts for her criminal success, she repeatedly employs her image to escape punishment and avoid detection. Sara's manipulation of others' perception suggests that the cultural shift toward commercialized femininity can be advantageous for women, but Meade also depicts the desperation gripping Sara's clients, conveying the peril of inculcating a social duty of attractiveness in women.

GLOBAL CONSUMPTION AND ANGLO-FEMINISM

By presenting Sara's cosmetically enhanced appearance as a tool of sympathetic appeal, Meade highlights a connection between the perception of virtue and the visual manifestation of whiteness in English society. In the first story, Druce and Vandaleur manage to have Sara arrested (the only instance in the series where they succeed at this endeavor), but she "appeared before the magistrate, looking innocent and beautiful, and managed during her evidence completely to baffle that acute individual. . . . Thus Madame escaped conviction" ("Madame" 401). The court rules that one of Sara's dark-complexioned Brazilian assistants, now conveniently absent from the country, must be guilty of the poisoning for which she has been charged. Sara's escape from conviction underscores the powers of cosmetic adulteration in a society that ascribes visual, racial significations of value. At the same time, however, the stories depict a sharp disjunction between Sara's ethnic identity and her appearance, presenting racial and national categories as surprisingly unstable. Sara is described as "a most lovely woman herself, very fair, with blue eyes, an innocent, childlike manner, and quantities of rippling gold hair. She openly confesses that she is very much older than she appears. . . . by birth she is a mixture of Indian and Italian" ("Madame" 388). Sara's blonde and childlike appearance is doubtless a nod to Lady Audley, but it is also at odds with her Indian and Italian identity, hinting again that her appearance is unnatural. Her use of cosmetics to achieve this disjunction reinforces makeup's role in the text as a signifier of the breakdown of social hierarchies—in this case, racial hierarchies.

Note that in her portrayal of Sara, Meade alters Rachel's ethnicity from Jewish to Indian and Italian. Meade refrains from using Madame Rachel's story to evoke stereotypes about Jewish business owners, as many writers had before her; instead, she Orientalizes and exoticizes makeup by associating it, and Sara, with non-European countries. Sara reveals in the first story, for instance, that she learned her trade "partly from the Indians and partly from the natives of Brazil" (389). By associating cosmetics and beauty procedures with India and Native America, the stories connect the emergence of Western women as sexual subjects with the objectification of colonial subjects. Because the English women whom Sara beautifies are initiated into sexual and bodily power via colonial-derived cosmetics, their sexual empowerment depends upon the disempowerment of non-Europeans, inherent in the extraction of such products under colonial regimes; cosmetics in these stories thus generate and convey the sexual power dynamics couched in colonial conquest and domination. Krista Lysack notes in a reading of Christina Rossetti's 1862 poem "Goblin Market" that the Victorian imperial marketplace "created the conditions for specifically gendered desires" (161), as "capital sought to incite women's participation in Empire . . . to inscribe women within its imperial project through the construction of women as consumers of oriental goods" (143). Meade's series not only interpellates women into imperial capitalism, however: it renders women's participation in the imperial market as coterminous with feminism. Women's economic liberty to buy colonial products conveys, in this series, their emancipation in late-Victorian society; this emancipation, in turn, becomes "proof" of national superiority, justifying the colonial project.[17]

The rise of the "New Imperialism" in 1890s Britain, characterized by a more virulent insistence on racial and national superiority as a justification for imperial expansion, provides a context for Meade's mode of depicting women, cosmetics, and colonialism. Madame Sara is nearly always attended by subservient colonial men, reinforcing the stories' association of Western female independence and Western imperial hegemony. Though Indian and Italian, she represents female economic autonomy in English society, and her "dazzlingly fair" complexion ("Madame" 389) is a visual focus of the narrative. Her mastery over dark, Eastern, male servants thus reinforces the stories' message that women's social and sexual emancipation in Britain is evidence of national superiority. At the beginning of the series, for example, Sara appears with two Brazilian attendants and "an Arab, a handsome, picturesque sort of fellow, who gives her the most absolute devotion" (388). Her Arabian servant surfaces throughout the series, always characterized by his dark skin and slavish demeanor toward Sara. In "The Blood-Red Cross," she brings him to a country house party, much to her hostess's bewilderment: "she has also brought her black servant, an Arabian, who goes by the name of Achmed. I must say he is a picturesque creature with his quaint Oriental dress. He was all in flaming yellow this morning, and the embroidery on his jacket was worth a small fortune" (510). Achmed is just one example of Sara's penchant for conspicuous displays of colonial finery. In one story, she dresses in "rich Oriental stuffs made of many colours, and absolutely glittering with gems" ("Madame" 393). In another, she engages in a series of machinations to obtain "Orion, the most marvelous diamond that Africa has produced of late" ("Teeth" 285). By dominating colonial men and flaunting colonial splendor, Sara asserts her wealth and prowess as a London entrepreneur; as a woman of Indian heritage, however, she also exhibits the perceived depravity of colonial nations, conventionally associated with femininity, sexuality, bondage, and duplicity, as Edward Said has argued.

Meade's use of exotic colonial imagery to market Anglo-feminism was not without a source in the story of the real Madame Rachel. In promoting her cosmetics, Rachel touted the supposedly exotic and foreign origins of her products. Wyndham claims that "a small black boy in [a] turban" ornamented her shop (243), and Rachel even trademarked her products with the so-called Royal Arabian Signet.[18] Sexualized descriptions of non-European nations, in Rachel's advertising prose, encouraged Western women to consume such nations by means of her products. *Beautiful For Ever!* describes a plethora of Eastern and Oriental cosmetics, including products from Armenia ("Armenian Liquid for Removing Wrinkles"); North Africa ("Magnetic Rock Dew Water of Sahara for Removing Wrinkles" and "Egyptian Kohl"); China ("Pure Extracts of the China Rose"); India ("Indian Coal" [*sic*]); and, most commonly, Arabia ("Royal Arabian Cream," "Arab Bloom Powder," "Arabian Perfume Wash," "Arabian Fumigated Oils," "Disinfecting Powder of the Choicest Arabian Odours," and "The Royal Arabian Toilet of Beauty as arranged by Madame Rachel for the Sultana of Turkey").[19] All of these products, marketed and vended together, produced the illusion that the London female shopper had the entire globe at her economic disposal, all in the service of beautifying her body.[20] Particularly common in Rachel's inventory were brand names that connote Eastern patriarchal despotism: "Sultana's Beauty Wash," "Sultana's Bouquets Perfume," "Favorite of the Harem's Pearl White Powder for the Complexion," or "Favourite of the Harem's Bouquet Perfume." References to sultans, sultanas, and harems were perhaps intended to bottle the pleasures of sexual dominance and submission. Rachel's product names fetishize her cosmetic commodities, associating them with imaginary constructions of Eastern gender, power, submission, and sexuality. By referencing harems, for example, Rachel organizes her clients' fantasies around conventionally Orientalist images of colonial sexual excess and debauchery. Eastern "enslavement" thus authenticates Western women's "freedom" to buy and use Rachel's products and to consume the exotic treasures of the East.[21]

In *The Sorceress,* Meade uses colonial imagery in much the same way that Madame Rachel did: to magnify Western women's sexual and economic agency. This strategy was particularly salient in Meade's time, however, not only in light of New Imperialism, but also due to the suffrage movement and the general progress of feminism. If British national identity had long depended on an ideology of female domesticity, wherein the feminized space of home and hearth constituted the "heart" of what made the nation great, turn-of-the-century feminists like Meade had the task of rewriting nationhood so that women were no longer excluded from the realm of economic, political, and public exchange. Interested in establishing women's rights and freedoms outside the domestic sphere, Meade employs empire—rather than home—as the organizing principle of British nationalism. Her series could be said to marry feminist and imperialist ideologies: women still play a key role in the construction of nationhood, but the role is independent and commercial rather than domestic.

DANGEROUS BREW: WOMEN, POISON, SCIENCE

Madame Sara's whiteness and beauty thus play a weighty role in the series, signifying both her economic empowerment and her artificial duplicity, but Meade refrains from attributing Sara's success solely to her appearance or to other traditionally "feminine" means of influence, which is a significant intervention into Rachel's story. Madame Rachel's contemporaries, unwilling to understand her achievements outside a paradigm of female power limited to the occult, conjectured that she could "bewitch" or "mesmerize" her victims; Meade, by contrast, makes Sara a far more successful criminal than Rachel, and though she does title the series *The Sorceress of the Strand,* she resists accounting for Sara's abilities via maleficent magic. Instead, Meade locates Sara's power in her "genius" and her "marvelous scientific attainments," a model of female achievement scarcely believed to exist a decade earlier.[22] The stories thus employ an imperialist model of global consumption as a justification for feminism, but their principal feminist innovation is in the depiction of science.

Sara's scientific talent is apparent throughout the series, and though she exercises that talent in the cosmetics trade, she also directs it to other ends. In "The Talk of the Town," she outsmarts Professor Piozzi, a scientist who is purportedly "a phenomenon, a genius, probably the most brilliant of our times" (68). Sara manages to steal an abstract discovery Piozzi has made, which she quickly recognizes can be turned to "a means of manufacturing artificial foods in a manner which has long been sought by scientific men" (78). Hot on Sara's trail, Vandaleur tells Piozzi: "you did not grasp the deduction from your most interesting discovery . . . [but Sara] read your notes, and at a glance saw what you have not grasped at all, and what I have taken days to discover" (78). Here, Meade depicts Sara's scientific genius as an explicit challenge to traditional feminine roles: rather than making food in the kitchen, she makes food through mathematical and chemical formulas. Like the cosmetics that she sells, Sara's crimes artificially parody femininity. In the Piozzi case, she steals a theory that enables the engineering of artificial food, thus fulfilling a conventional feminine role as feeder in a way that is both masculine—because scientific—and criminal. Indeed, Sara not only steals Piozzi's theories, but later attempts to kill him by poisoning his milk. Piozzi is stunned when he learns the source of his near-death: "Poisoned milk! I confess I do not understand. The thing must have been accidental" (73). Milk is uniquely associated with maternal nurturance, and thus Sara uses chemistry again to parody essential femininity: she bestows milk, but the milk is poisoned.

Late-Victorian social scientists believed the instinct to mother, nurture, and feed was the primal drive of female psychology, which made the female poisoner a particularly distressing figure.[23] That a woman might commit murder via her natural role as feeder and nurturer—seemingly the very opposite of killer—was appalling and fascinating, as evidenced by an extensive fictional, scientific, and journalistic literature about female poisoners. Criminologists said that women were much more likely to commit murder by poison than men (Morrison 151), and many real-life cases of women who poisoned their husbands made sensational headlines throughout the era.[24] Many criminologists believed, moreover, that most women poisoners were never detected. In his 1912 study *Women and Crime,* Hargrave Adam wrote: "there is far more secret poisoning of husbands by their wives than is generally known. If only half what the police know in this connection were made public, there would be consternation among the married men of this nation" (331–32).

Through her depiction of Sara, Meade reclaims the popular, misogynist "poison panic" for feminist purposes: in representing Sara's expert use of chemical poisons, she invariably emphasizes Sara's "scientific genius." Ironically enough, cosmetics fit into this constellation of associations as well, for during the nineteenth century, common poisons were often used as cosmetics. Arsenic was applied to whiten the skin, and belladonna was dropped in the eyes. Wilkie Collins's 1875 novel *The Law and the Lady* depicts a woman who poisons herself with arsenic, after unsuccessfully using it to treat her complexion. Madeleine Smith was accused of poisoning her ex-fiancé with arsenic in 1857, and Florence Maybrick for poisoning her husband with arsenic in 1883. In their trials, both women used what we might call "the cosmetic defense" to explain why they possessed arsenic at the time of the men's deaths.[25] Meade's work draws upon such events. In the final story of the series, a woman named Julia Bensasan admits, "I poisoned my husband . . . I hated that feeble man. I poisoned him with arsenic" ("Teeth" 290). "The Blood-Red Cross" features a nurse named Rebecca Curt, recently escaped from prison after committing "forgery, with a strong and very daring attempt at poisoning" (512). This character reflects a contemporary fascination with the nurse poisoner: Nordau's 1895 best seller *Degeneration,* for example, recounts the 1884 case of a Swiss nurse—Marie Jeanneret—who fatally poisoned nine victims out of sadistic impulses (277–78). Unquestionably, Meade exploits sensationalist preoccupation with such cases, but her three female poisoners also function to destabilize essential femininity: Rebecca Curt is a nurse, Sara poisons Piozzi's milk, and Julia Bensasan poisons her husband presumably via food or drink. All these crimes mimic conventional feminine caregiving. Meade's depiction of female chemical villainy thus transforms age-old stereotypes of female witchery into modern New Woman Criminals, whose powers lie in scientific expertise rather than the eye of newt.

Sara's expertise is quite apparent to detective Druce when he visits her beauty shop. He finds a site resembling Frankenstein's workshop or Dr. Jekyll's laboratory rather than the collection of rouge-pots and perfumes he expects of a "professional beautifier":

> There stood a . . . table, on which lay an array of extraordinary-looking articles and implements—stoppered bottles full of strange medicaments, mirrors . . . brushes, sprays, sponges, delicate needle-pointed instruments of bright steel, tiny lancets, and forceps. Facing this table was a chair, like those used by dentists. . . . Another chair, supported on a glass pedestal, was kept there, Madame Sara informed me, for administering static electricity. There were dry-cell batteries for the continuous currents and induction coils for Faradic currents. . . . Madame took me from this room into another, where a still more formidable array of instruments were to be found. Here were a wooden operating table and chloroform and ether apparatus. ("Madame" 392)

The back room of Sara's shop, with its operating table and anesthetics, may have reminded readers of rumors that Madame Rachel was an abortionist. Indeed, the specter of this prospect hangs about the stories: "[Sara's] clients go to her there, and she does what is necessary for them. It is a fact that she occasionally performs small surgical operations" ("Madame" 388). Such insinuations represent Sara as a challenge to nineteenth-century medical professionalization, a trend that had led to the dwindling of midwives and other traditional female medical providers in the Victorian era. By the end of the century, a few women had managed to break the ranks of male professionalism to attain medical degrees, and 1902 (the year that Meade's series was published) also saw the passage of the Midwives' Act, which made midwifery an established profession with standards of training and regulation. Meade's series underscores women's ongoing incursion into male medical professionalism: whereas in *Armadale,* Collins uses the intermediary male figure of Doctor Downward to provide abortions in conjunction with Oldershaw's shop, Meade positions Sara herself at the operating table. Sara acknowledges in "The Bloodstone" that she does not have professional medical training ("I do not hold diplomas" [206]), but throughout the series, she acts in the capacity of doctor and dentist. The back room of her shop confirms that she is poised, like the New Woman, to infiltrate not only science and commerce, but also the professions.

In her 1898 crime series *The Brotherhood of the Seven Kings,* Meade provides an extended consideration of the female practitioner as a threat to medical professionalism, a theme she only sketches out in *The Sorceress.* Like Madame Sara, the villain of this series is modeled on Madame Rachel: Madame Koluchy, as she is called, is a doctor, medical consultant, and leader of a secret criminal organization, "able to restore youth and beauty by her arts" ("At the Edge" 87–88). Also like Sara, Koluchy is a scientific genius: "That woman has science at her fingers' ends" ("Winged" 146). Meade depicts Koluchy's medical success as a direct assault on male professionalism. In the first story, she heals a young boy, "succeed[ing] where the medical profession gave little hope" ("At the Edge" 87), and in the second story, "the men of the profession are mad with jealousy, and small wonder, her cures are so marvellous" ("Winged" 139). Part of their jealousy stems from the fact that she ignores professional norms of compensation, "taking, it is true, large fees from those who could afford to pay, but, on the other hand, giving her services freely to the people to whom money was scarce" ("Luck" 379). To disregard the presumption that medical services are a "labor" to be exchanged for "capital" is to deny medicine's very status as a profession. Koluchy's fellow scientists and doctors frown upon her success, and Meade pinpoints a distinctively British professionalism as the source of their resentment. The narrator of the story, an English scientist named Norman Head, declares: "I am sick of her very name. . . . She has bewitched London with her impostures and quackery" ("At the Edge" 87).

Dr. Fietta, a devious foreign physician, disagrees: "As a medical man myself, I can vouch for her capacity, and unfettered by English professional scrupulousness, I appreciate it" (90). With Madame Sara and Madame Koluchy, Meade employs the themes of science, medicine, and professionalism to adapt Madame Rachel's story to the new front lines of feminism.

Madame Rachel's trial turned on key mid-Victorian debates about women entering the commercial marketplace, but Meade provides Madame Sara with a much stronger grasp on the domain of capitalism than her predecessor, and her cosmetic powers reach a level of scientific and professional proficiency of which Rachel could not have dreamed. In this way, Meade zeroes in on emerging cultural debates about women's abilities and education, debates of less consequence in Rachel's day, when women (like Rachel herself) were routinely denied the most basic level of education and literacy.[26] Thus, while Meade uses Madame Rachel's story to signify Victorian women's expanding role in the consumer sphere in the second half of the nineteenth century, with Sara she also demarcates the boundaries of new territories that turn-of-the-century women were on the verge of penetrating. Meade presents women's expansion into these new roles as part and parcel of British imperial ascendancy; in this way, despite her focus on an evil female villain, Meade's series actually popularizes and normalizes the ideals and objectives of Anglo-feminism by packaging them in the rhetoric of New Imperialism. New Women's commercial, professional, and scientific advancement, in this series, becomes a symbol of national and racial superiority. Thus, while many British feminists of this era argued against imperial domination, racial inequality, and capitalist consumerism, Meade's series reveals that mainstream Anglo-feminism, in the heated era of suffrage agitation, also exhibited its compatibility with capitalist and colonialist ideologies as a means of ingratiating itself with mainstream audiences.

PART TWO

CRIME FILM

THE LIMITS OF THE GAZE

THREE *Class, Gender, and Authority in Early British Cinema*

Historians of film debate such basic questions as who invented cinema and what year it first appeared, but all now agree that the early film archive, once relegated to the embarrassing category of "primitive" filmmaking, is a rich trove for understanding modern developments in culture, narrative, and visuality.[1] In Britain, the Lumière brothers' films first appeared on movie screens in 1896, while Thomas Edison's "peepshow" films debuted a few years earlier, but what happened for the next fifteen or twenty years was, for a long time, of little interest to literary and cultural critics. This chapter considers early British crime films about female criminals, and its endeavor is partly archaeological, as critics have not yet established early British crime film's relation to contemporaneous crime literature, nor the broader relations between literature and film of this era.[2] I will examine early crime film in relation to the cultural practices I have identified in detective series, and my chronological scope will include cinema from 1896 to 1913; these films reproduce crime fiction's New Woman Criminal, but the unique form and context of early cinema also transform the cultural meaning of this figure. Because of early cinema's cultural status as working-class entertainment, crime films address far more directly than crime fiction the class politics of female consumption. Moreover, while we have seen that female criminals were glamorous, rapacious consumers before the advent of film, this characterization expands and evolves in motion pictures due to early cinema's promotion, as Paula Black has put it, of "femininity as a process of image selection" (33).

Before I turn to the films themselves, let me offer a few pertinent remarks on early cinema, rather than slipping seamlessly from a discussion of magazine fiction to a discussion of another medium altogether. Because filmmaking is an "industry" to a greater extent than fiction writing, many critics have assumed that it is more bound by capitalism's implicit and explicit forms of censorship, and for many years, film was hardly thought to be an "art" at all, since an enormous gap appeared to exist between the artist as Romantic individual and a crew that engages in both technical and creative labor. Film was not yet industrialized or integrated in its earliest years, however, but sat somewhere between artisanal and entrepreneurial, and one might argue that appreciation of film as an art form correlated with its adoption of bourgeois ideology.

While these early, volatile years of British film can thus offer surprisingly heterodox narratives, radical shifts in filmmaking did occur in the seventeen years that constitute the scope of my study. Tom Gunning has called films from 1896 to 1906 a "cinema of attractions," whose chief *raison d'être* was to create a spectacle, trick, or thrill rather than to compose a narrative. In contrast, he and other film historians often term 1906–13 a period of "narrative integration," which saw the solidification of the film industry, the "language" of continuity editing, and the conventions of filmic storytelling. In Britain as in other countries, economic and social pressures contributed to such formal and aesthetic developments. Britain's hodgepodge of pre–1913 filmmakers bears little resemblance to the vertically integrated studio system of Hollywood's golden age, much less the transnational, cross-marketing conglomerates that dominate the entertainment industry today, but when the British Board of Censorship was inaugurated in January 1913, it ushered the industry into a new age of relatively systematic, centralized film regulation. Though this censorship organ was not state-controlled, its introduction marks the advent of a more incorporated and less erratic age of film production.

For all these reasons, pre–1913 films invite the same terminological dilemmas one also faces in writing about crime fiction, magazines, and other "popular" or "mass" cultures. "Popular culture" suggests organic cultural forms that emerge spontaneously from authentic audience endorsement or desire; "mass culture," on the other hand, implies forms that have been imposed on audiences by a centralized capitalist culture industry with sophisticated means of manufacturing audience desire.

Early film lies somewhere between these formulations. Like detective fiction, film often regulates, normalizes, and performs other "mass cultural" disciplinary functions, but in its earliest years in Britain, it attracted an almost exclusively working-class audience, and often addressed class-specific pain and indignation. The same could not be said of early U.S. cinema, which according to Miriam Hansen had a "heterogenous" audience, "mostly the new urban middle class" (61). Audience composition is a contentious issue among scholars of early U.S. cinema, but not early British cinema. Films that cost a nickel in U.S. nickelodeons were only a penny in Britain, less than half as much in exchange rates of the day (Burrows, "Penny Pleasures" 71). Because it was "cheaper to see a film than to attend any other form of organized entertainment," as Nicholas Hiley writes, the British cinema "appealed to those people who were too poor to join other paying audiences" ("Fifteen" 106). British film's early marginality temporarily mounted a genuinely "popular" culture, which often celebrates antibourgeois and antiauthoritarian values.[3] It was not a utopian or extracapitalist space: Britain's film pioneers often made tidy profits (Barnes 2:8), and even rabidly antibourgeois films tend to endorse and naturalize a voracious urge to consume. Its audiences were clearly not stupefied into ideological submission, however, and its appeal elicited widespread fears about the rise of a working-class mass medium, not unlike earlier debates surrounding the penny press and the taxes on knowledge in the first half of the nineteenth century.

Besides having a different audience, early film was also far more international than contemporary fiction, and a film's national origin had much less to do with its presence in the British public than was the case for magazine series or novels. French and U.S. film dominated the British market from early on: in 1909 and 1910, for example, only 15 percent of the films shown in Britain were British (Low 54).[4] Film's cosmopolitanism was part of its association with the "new," but it also begs the question of why this chapter should focus exclusively on films made in Britain. British films did have unifying stylistic elements, such as an antiauthority sensibility, and British companies certainly employed the *idea* of a national style to market their films: a 1910 advertisement in the *Bioscope* reads, "BRITISH FILMS FOR BRITISH AUDIENCES. You are in business to make money—the easiest way to do so is to please your Audiences. They being English prefer ENGLISH PICTURES;" Hepworth Manufacturing Company touted in another advertisement, "ALL BRITISH PRODUCTIONS. PICTURES which your audience can APPRECIATE and UNDERSTAND."[5] Despite the simplistic nationalism underlying such claims, I limit my analysis to British films because they are enmeshed in the intricacies of historical and cultural localism, including the narrative discourse of crime, gender, and female criminality that my other chapters examine. British crime films didn't begin from scratch in 1896, but grew out of generic practices already in place, such as in detective series and dynamite narrative.[6]

If early British film picks up on the preexisting figure of the New Woman Criminal, it also offers a vital reinvention of this narrative persona. I argue in this chapter that film's visual and spectacular form, as well as its unique audience and context, occasioned pivotal shifts in the New Woman Criminal's cultural role. In a visual medium so dependent upon characters' bodies, female criminals' physical glamour becomes increasingly significant in motion pictures. Early film thus illuminates a shift toward image-centered conceptions of femininity, incrementally apparent in the fictional genres that precede cinema. Film also adapts the New Woman Criminal to the sensibilities of a proletarian audience. British cinema's working-class public fostered an antiauthoritarian political sensibility that is largely absent from contemporaneous literature; thus filmic female criminals reveal the underlying class regulation at work in narratives of theft. A sharp contrast emerges, however, when we compare such New Woman Criminals to filmic representations of suffragettes. At the end of the chapter, I turn away from conventional crime films to consider films about militant suffragette violence, and here we see the limits of film's antiauthoritarianism. En masse feminist political action aroused far more filmic hostility than female criminals' individual violations of property law, which paradoxically served to *uphold* consumerist, individualist ideologies; thus early crime films both complement and complicate crime fiction's depictions of authority, gender, and criminality.

GLAMOUR AND THE GAZE: GENDER IN EMERGING
FIELDS OF VISION

I want to begin by discussing how film's visual form intersected with a scopophilic turn in the narrative representation of female criminals. Authors of detective fiction as well as sensation fiction depict transgressive women as uniquely apt subjects for the erotic gaze, but this maneuver becomes even more significant when projected erotically on screen. Criminal women are overtly sexualized, for example, in the 1898 film

Duel to the Death.[7] Produced by British Mutoscope and Biograph Company, *Duel to the Death* features two women fighting with daggers, and could function as a primer on why criminal women tend to be filmed erotically.[8] As the film begins, the actresses strip down to their undergarments, so they wear only petticoats and bodices during the duel. Tropical flowers and palm fronds garnish the film's mise-en-scène, summoning conventional associations between the exotic and the erotic, and though the women's dress does not appear foreign, criminality marks them as alien, sexual, and titillating. They circle around one another and pounce. As they wrestle, the straps of their chemises slide down, revealing bare shoulders incrementally like a striptease. Eventually, one woman's breast is partially exposed to the camera. The seminude women stare intently into each other's eyes as they fight, and finally, one stabs and kills the other.

This film demonstrates how criminality can function to designate women as appropriate subjects of the erotic gaze. Constance Balides writes of early U.S. cinema: "pornographic and erotic films from this period justify the display of women by relying on the pretext of a theatrical performance or out of the ordinary situation" (20). Criminal behavior—definitionally eccentric to norms—is a perfect "out of the ordinary situation" to "justify" erotic display. Female criminal transgression legitimates the sexual voyeurism of the camera, while the revelation of the women's bodies transforms the duel into a sexually charged spectacle. It is not altogether clear, however, that *Duel to the Death* simulates the "male gaze" that feminist critics since Laura Mulvey have described, as its actresses enact both diagesis and spectacle. Examples of erotically depicted women are readily available in early British film, as in *Duel to the Death,* but typically do not follow a stable division between male action and female spectacle, such as Mulvey finds in classic Hollywood cinema. As Hansen writes in her analysis of U.S. silent film, "early cinema was no less patriarchal than its classical successor . . . [but] lacked the formal strategies to predetermine reception in the classical sense" (38). Recent critical work in film as well as literature has challenged an overly rigid conception of the "male gaze," as Deborah Parsons describes (4–6). I am less interested in engaging with this specific term than with identifying emerging, historically specific modes of representing sexuality, vision, and power at the turn of the century.

The formulation of modern visual/sexual sensibilities, I argue, was bound up with social shifts such as women entering the workforce and gaining more access to the public sphere, and with the rise of cinema and other visual culture. The "to-be-looked-at-ness" of the female criminal body, to use Mulvey's term, thus plays an important but uneven role in early film. I find the term *glamour* more useful than *spectacle,* in describing this to-be-looked-at-ness, because it captures the ambiguity of film's emerging sexual tone in depicting female criminals. Peter Bailey has used the term *glamour* to describe a new sexual "middle ground" at the end of the nineteenth century: sexuality that was neither domesticated nor illicit, but existed in "everyday settings" like "the expanding apparatus of the service industries, and commercialised popular culture" (148). Glamour, in this sense, is an elusive desirability primarily visual in nature: "Glamour and its stimulus to the sexual pleasure in looking . . . gave a new emphasis to the visual element in the changing sexual economy" (167–68).

Bailey does not link glamour with Charles Baudelaire's *passante,* but the two concepts might be profitably connected. Both glamour and the *passante* refer to a new kind of modern femininity defined by visibility, attraction, and remoteness. Parsons has discussed the *passante*'s "ability to evade being fixed by the male gaze," claiming she is a "metaphor" for "modern, autonomous" women (64), parallel to my formulation of glamorous female criminals. Filmic women, elusive as flickering light, are perhaps the perfection of Baudelaire's *passante,* for the rise of photography contributed to the development of this new model of femininity. Susan Sontag claims that with photography, "new conventions about what was beautiful took hold. What is beautiful becomes just what the eye can't (or doesn't) see: that fracturing, dislocating vision that only the camera supplies" (91). Glamour, in this sense, is a specifically *photographic* visual effect: it is always mediated and never perceived directly. This is why, in Bailey's analysis, the barrier provided by the bar is what makes the barmaid glamorous.

The concepts of glamour and the *passante* provide useful models for discussing the female body in early film. Glamour, like the *passante,* is characterized by distance, achieved through "the traditional device of the stage; more recently by the shop window or the distance inherent in the mechanical representations of photography, film and television" (Bailey 152). While theater also relies on the distance between actor and audience to imbue the stage with meaning, film intensifies the sense of distanced desire by exacerbating the separation between the performer and spectator, and by creating an illusion of intimacy through close-ups, lighting, and other filmic effects. The uniquely mediated intimacy of film was the perfect forum for representing glamorous female offenders:

the distance between the spectator and the image on screen is heightened by criminality, positioning such women at an even further remove. Films such as *Duel to the Death* capitalize on the female criminal's "outlaw" position to voyeuristically parade her sexuality; thus the glamorous female criminal was often much more sexualized in early film than in crime fiction.

The 1909 Cricks and Martin film *Salome Mad* comically satirizes the modern interconnectedness of cinematic glamour, transgressive women, and distanced desire.[9] At the time of the film's release, Britain was in the grip of "Salomania," as Philip Hoare describes it, and Maud Allan's erotic dance performance *Vision of Salomé* was all the rage. Like a filmic female criminal, Allan's rendition of Salomé was transgressive yet alluring, criminal yet beautiful. *Salome Mad* exacerbates the distance between the filmic Salomé and her admirer to comic effect, and links this particular form of impossible desire to the visual illusion of cinema. The film depicts a man who falls in love with Salomé, or rather with her picture on a poster in a shop. He buys the poster, but loses it in the wind, and chases it across town. So enamored is he with Salomé's image that he pursues the poster up a ladder, through a bedroom window, into a movie theater, and under the sea. On the seafloor, the poster comes alive, and Salomé performs her erotic dance for the man's visual pleasure. In his ecstasy, he attempts to embrace and kiss her, but before he can grasp her, his rescuers fish him out of the ocean. Salomé's dance, it turns out, was merely the near-death illusion of a drowning man. In depicting a love affair between a man and a poster, the film comically mocks the absurd physical and emotional connections that can obtain between humans and visual commodities under modern capitalism.

Rudyard Kipling's "Mrs Bathurst" (1904) is a less comedic, more haunting take on this idea. In the short story, a British serviceman in South Africa becomes fixated on the image of his former love, Mrs Bathurst, after watching her in an actuality film at a traveling circus. He ends the story burned to a crisp in an electrical storm. Nicholas Daly reads the cryptic narrative as a parable of cinematic technology, and views Mrs. Bathurst as a version of the cinematic "it" girl, a personification of filmic glamour: "the cinema apparatus magnifies Mrs Bathurst's 'It' to the point that her on-screen representation does not simply attract Vickery—it obsesses him" (76). Interestingly, while Daly suggests that the cinematograph "seems to exert more power over [Vickery] than the woman herself" (76), Kipling's story refers three times to Mrs. Bathurst's "blindish" way of looking. On film, for example, "she looked out straight at us with that blindish look" (287), as though she too is dazzled by the flickering light of cinema. Kipling thus presents the gaze as unidirectional and chimerical, yet treacherous to both viewer and subject.

In different ways, both *Salome Mad* and "Mrs Bathurst" indicate that glamour is a concept inextricable from Marx's notion of commodity fetishism. Glamour, like commodity fetishism, is an intangible generator of indefinite desire; unlike commodity fetishism, however, glamour adheres to a person—more precisely, the image of a person—rather than an object or commodity. Mindful of Benjamin's Marxian reading of the *passante* in *Charles Baudelaire,* we can view glamour, like the *passante,* as a phantasmagoric abstraction of consumer capitalism, part of the "consumerist" or "image-centered" models of body and visuality that I discuss in chapter 2. Consumerism's new means of manipulating desire via vision and distance—as with large plate-glass windows and prominent department store displays—anticipated the spectatorship of filmic glamour.[10]

If glamour suggests a new visual-sexual order for the modern world, we have already seen how criminal science outlined a seemingly opposite modern relation between visuality and power. As I discuss in chapter 1, the decades preceding the 1896 emergence of cinema saw widespread innovation in the field of visual technology, and the disciplinary uses of vision were eagerly investigated as criminologists mined visual technology for means of identifying criminals and tightening social controls. Criminal theorists like Galton, Bertillon, Lombroso, and Ellis imagined the gaze in terms of knowledge rather than feeling; unlike consumerist appeals to vision, they considered the eye as powerful and controlling rather than vulnerable and desiring. Benjamin's distinction between "trace" and "aura" helps explain this crucial difference between criminological and consumerist notions of visibility: "The trace is appearance of a nearness, however far removed the thing that left it behind may be. The aura is appearance of a distance, however close the thing that calls it forth. In the trace, we gain possession of the thing; in the aura, it takes possession of us" (*Arcades* 447). The criminological gaze, we might say, apprehends the visible as what Benjamin calls trace, whereas the consumerist gaze perceives aura or glamour.

Fictional detectives like Sherlock Holmes operate in tandem with new criminological theories of vision, and the Holmes series thematizes the prospect of near-perfect surveillance and authority in modern criminal science. Tom Gunning has located a similar predisposition toward the criminological gaze in early cinema.[11] He uses a 1904 U.S. film, *A*

Subject for the Rogues' Gallery, to exemplify cinema's indebtedness to visual theories of criminology. The film depicts a female criminal who resists police efforts to take her photographic "mug shot." Gunning argues that the film reveals the "ineffectiveness" of her resistance ("Tracing" 27), and thus the "process of criminal identification represents a new aspect of the disciplining of the body which typifies modernity" (20); but his analysis fails to account for the woman's manipulation of her appearance, which defies the criminological gaze of the police. A very attractive woman, she sits smilingly and complacently until the camera is trained on her face, at which point she grotesquely contorts her features and begins to bawl violently, to distort the photographer's image. The moment the camera is withdrawn, however, she shuts off her tears like a faucet and affectedly smoothes her hair. The sharp contrast between her vanity and beauty (captured by the off-screen camera) and her contorted, anguished mug shot (captured by the on-screen camera) indicates the failure of the criminological gaze: she has no singular appearance or particular bodily identity to be fixed, recorded, or caught.[12]

The crime films that I discuss in this chapter similarly interweave the criminological gaze of power and the consumerist gaze of desire and lack, but just as in crime fiction, filmic representations of female criminals do not simply map onto a visual binary between female transgressive spectacle and male authoritative gaze. The presence of female detectives and other woman "gazers" in early film strongly challenges such a division. The 1910 Cricks and Martin film *Bumpkin's Patent Spyopticon,* for example, imagines the augmentation of conventionally *feminine* authority by means of new technologies of vision. The film no longer exists, but was described at length in contemporary film magazines.[13] A wife "leaves the house on a shopping expedition" and "passes an 'Amusement Arcade.'" She is "attracted by a poster advertising a 'Spyopticon'—a wonderful instrument which reveals the action of absent persons without their knowledge," and "pays her penny to peep into the instrument." In the device, "she witnesses her hubby entering a sitting-room with an attractive young lady" and "observes the couple . . . embracing shamelessly."[14] The wife later gets revenge by enjoying a shameless embrace of her own. The film posits a relationship between the ongoing scientific "progress" of modernity, signified by the "patent spyopticon," and the feminization of the public sphere, signified by women's shopping, sexual equality, and enhanced visual surveillance. Here, women are part of modernity's incremental encroachment into patriarchal autonomy; technologies of visual authority are not aligned with the expert male eye, but with egalitarianism and the feminization of public politics and public life.

Early British films about female detectives and female figures of visual authority pose a challenge to overly rigid conceptions of male visual power at the turn of the century, but many of these films presume the *undesirability* of women exercising the gaze of social control. The 1908 film *If Women Were Policemen* capitalizes on antisuffrage sentiment by satirically depicting "militant suffragettes" who "take over [the] police force" (Gifford no. 01805). The 1910 B & C (British and Colonial Kinematograph Company) film *When Women Join the Force* illustrates, according to a contemporary film periodical, "the state of affairs which would obtain if the police force accepted female recruits, and . . . the picture is not a very reassuring, though an extremely humorous, one."[15] The film's policewomen flee burglars, dog thieves, and wife beaters, but arrest a small boy for stealing an apple. Britain had no policewomen until 1915, so such satires comically stoke anxiety about the possibility of women's advancement into positions of visual and social authority.

Like contemporaneous fiction, many early British films exhibit a preoccupation with "new" and "modern" modes of femininity and with women who work in the public sphere. Some suggest that women's emancipation will disrupt family relations, such as *The New Woman* (1905), in which a woman "makes [her] husband do housework while she goes to his office" (Gifford no. 01172). Others exploit the volatile new sexual realm opened up by women's more general public employment. For example, a 1904 film called *Once Too Often* depicts an "exciting scene between thief and shop girl" (Gifford no. 00911), while *The Mill Girl,* a 1913 Hepworth film, features a "factory girl" named Lizzie whose foreman frames her for theft after she "indignantly repulses" his "attempts to make love to her." At the end of the film, "the foreman is rushed off to the police station by an irate crowd of women," "Lizzie is immediately released," and "the foreman is arrested on the charge of conspiracy."[16] A few months before this, B & C released *A Factory Girl's Honour,* which depicted a factory girl who is fired after refusing her manager's sexual advances, but ultimately avenged when she saves the factory owner's daughter from a fire.[17] Building on the theatrical genre of the factory melodrama, these films sympathetically ponder working-class women's new economic role on the heels of industrial and consumer revolutions.

The figure of the female typist—a paradigmatic New Woman, as

Christopher Keep has argued—also commonly appears in early British film. As factory girl melodramas do for industrial space, films about typists ponder the seismic sexual shifts occasioned by women's entry into the new frontier of the white-collar workplace. A 1904 film called *The Lady Typist,* for example, shows a boss kissing his typist as his wife enters the room; the film revisits the scenario of one of the earliest and most influential of surviving British films, *The Maid in the Garden* (1897), in which a wife catches her husband kissing the maid behind a clothesline. *The Lady Typist* also portrays a working woman as disrupter of bourgeois domesticity, but transplants this landmark scene from the home to the "middle ground" of the office, where women's new public roles present a threat to domestic stability.

On the other hand, *Foiled by a Girl,* a 1912 Clarendon film, depicts a lady typist as hero: after a theft in the office, she poses as an amateur detective and uncovers the perpetrator of the crime.[18] The opening shot of the film again revisits the recurring gag from *The Lady Typist* and *The Maid in the Garden:* the typist Dora steals kisses with her officemate, Dick, but the two quickly "look busy" when another coworker enters the office.[19] Billed as a "sensational drama," *Foiled by a Girl* features a standard plot progression—crime, detection, and arrest—but is unusual in that a woman functions as detective and rescuer. Dora manages to prove that her coworker, Blunt, has stolen money from the office safe and framed her sweetheart, Dick. To catch Blunt, she trails him while cross-dressed in her brother's clothes, and ultimately threatens him with a gun. The film ends with her rescue of Dick, who has been kidnapped, bound, and gagged. As in Arthur Conan Doyle's "Scandal in Bohemia," the plot turns on Blunt's failure to "see" Dora beneath her cross-dressing, and on his broader failure to appreciate the lowly female typist in the corner of the office. Like the female detectives of contemporaneous crime fiction, Dora exploits the fact that outside the periphery of the erotic or desiring gaze, women are often not seen at all, which can be a form of power in itself.[20]

EVERYBODY AGAINST THE POLICEMAN: CRIME ON FILM

The similarity between *Foiled by a Girl* and "Scandal in Bohemia" is one of many intertextual links between late-Victorian crime fiction and early British crime film, for with the emergence of film as a new narrative form the popularity of crime and detective plots flourished. According to Rachael Low, some early proponents of cinema in Britain believed the crime story was the most inherently filmic of genres: it was "said that of all types of plot those dealing with crime and its discovery were best suited to the film medium. Undoubtedly they were in vogue throughout the period, with a popularity which was probably greatest between 1908 and 1911, but which never failed" (197). Though often dismissed as a marginal cinema, the British film industry made significant contributions to crime film as an international genre. Jonathan Auerbach argues, "As early as 1901 British filmmakers had combined crime with the chase to create an exciting kind of fast-paced drama that powerfully influenced Porter and other Americans" (810). With crime fiction's ubiquity in the literary marketplace, magazine crime series' heavily imagistic narrative format, and the interlocking histories of visual technology and policing, crime narrative transitioned easily to the visual medium of film. In Conan Doyle's stories, for example, the fictional focus on the detective's expert "eye" made crime narrative a visual genre even before it was taken up by film.

Two of the earliest narrative pictures in British film history were crime stories. Birt Acres's *The Arrest of a Pickpocket*—the "first dramatic photoplay made in England"—was a Kinetoscope film that debuted in April 1895 (Barnes 1:230). R. W. Paul's *The Arrest of a Bookmaker* was, according to Denis Gifford, projected on screen in May 1896, only a few months after the Lumière brothers' Cinématographe arrived in England. Both films climax in the "arrest" of a wrongdoer who succumbs to authority's grasp. The Sherlock Holmes tradition is apparent in this plot structure: each of Conan Doyle's stories focuses on a particular investigation, and whether or not they conclude with an arrest, Holmes usually asserts his authority by unraveling the case. It did not take long for early British filmmakers to depart from this formula, however, and even actively to satirize it. British crime film is obviously in debt to the generic conventions of crime fiction, but there are substantial differences between the two forms. As early filmmakers adopted the literary conventions of crime fiction, they also altered the formula: in film, the line between "cops" and "robbers" is more ambiguous, figures of authority are less effective, and the narrative perspective is more sympathetic toward criminals.

Prior to World War I, British cinema audiences were almost exclusively working-class, and these audiences took pleasure in a different kind of crime narrative than the "master detective" stories that dominated fiction.[21] In his history of early British film, Michael Chanan writes, "The enormous social impact of cinema reached the most remote corners of society long before the upper echelons knew what it was really all about. Previous new inventions, like the telephone and the phonograph, entered the market somewhere near the top and then filtered down. Film, after initial screenings for society audiences, went the other way" (206). Some early British crime films followed the same narrative structure as the Sherlock Holmes stories, depicting thieves being caught at the end of the story.[22] More often, however, early crime films favor neither narratives of effective social authority nor master detectives like Holmes, and filmic police and detectives are more apt to produce disorder than to contain it.

A survey of film titles and descriptions suggests the pervasiveness of antiauthority themes in this era. Many of these films, in contrast with the Holmes stories, focus on the visual gullibility of police and detectives. In *An Interrupted Rehearsal* (1901), a policeman "mistakes rehearsing actors for murderers" (Gifford no. 00434). *The Bobby's Downfall* (1904) and *The Meddling Policeman* (1904) feature tramps who play tricks on sleeping policemen. In *The Misguided Bobby* (1905), a policeman "mistakes [a] fancy dress dancer for real burglar" (Gifford no. 01193). The title character from *The Defective Detective* (1913) attempts to trap a burglar, who turns out to be his fiancée's uncle.[23] *Our New Policeman* (1906) depicts an overzealous officer who interrupts a "burglary" being staged for a cinematographer; he becomes the butt of two girls' practical joke, and ends the movie with a bucket of paint over his head.[24] Many early films encourage an "us against them" collective mentality in the audience; Clarendon's *Everybody against the Policeman* (1908) depicts a boy, a woman, a man, and a sign-painter united in their ire against a policeman, who also ends the film with a bucket of paint over his head.[25] *The Eviction* (1904) similarly advocates collective opposition to authority: it depicts a landlord who evicts his tenants and summons the police to help get rid of them. The clumsy and incompetent police engage in a violent but comically slapstick battle with the tenants, who eventually drive the police off the property. Encouraging the audience to identify with the tenants rather than the agents of law, the film presents both the officers and the landlord as objects of working-class indignation.[26] Apparently, it was a crowd-pleaser: *The Eviction* was still being exhibited in Islington as late as 1909, five years after its initial release (Burrows, "Penny Pleasures II" 180).

As in *The Eviction,* police in early British film are generally the protectors of upper-class property, or metonymic stand-ins for the social order generally, as Thomas Sobchack has also argued (15). While crime fiction typically appeals to audience desire for containment of criminals and transgressors, crime film appeals to audience resentment of the class system and the authorities who uphold it. Indeed, crime film departs from fictional convention not only in humiliating police and detectives, but also by valorizing clever crooks. In the Sherlock Holmes stories, shrewd male criminals like Moriarty tend to be loathsome and biologically degenerate, and while Conan Doyle's and L. T. Meade's series both depict villainous women criminals as glamorous, they stop short of outright approbation of their behavior. In fiction, female criminals tend to be more appealing than their masculine counterparts, but in early film, female criminals can be overtly heroic.

B & C's film series *The Exploits of Three-Fingered Kate* is the most striking example of this trend in early British film. The series, which Alex Marlow-Mann calls "the first real example" of the series format in film (149), focuses on the "adventuress" Three-Fingered Kate, a master of larceny.[27] Her detective adversary is named "Sheerluck," and he is as inept as his name implies. Sheerluck lives on Baker Street, wears a bowler hat, and carries a cane.[28] Parodying Sherlock Holmes in this way, the film demythologizes the image of the detective constructed in Conan Doyle's stories. Instead of representing omnipotent social control via expert surveillance and systematic criminological method, the great detective's investigative power is "sheerly" based on "luck." The film series documents a strong intertextual relationship between late-Victorian magazine culture and early film, but also indicates a cultural gap between the two media. Holmes—a protector of bourgeois property, clients, and values—appears to be a less attractive subject for working-class audiences than has hitherto been appreciated.

The first film in the series, released in 1909, was called *The Exploits of Three-Fingered Kate*. According to a description in the contemporary trade journal *Bioscope,* the film depicts Kate successfully robbing a jeweler and eluding Sheerluck through disguise: she "takes refuge in the public baths, gets into a cabin, exchanges her garments, and walks out— her disguise being so complete that Sheerluck does not recognize her. He arrests the woman who comes out of the baths in Kate's clothes, but discovers that his captive has five fingers, and is a negress. There is general consternation."[29] Like Irene Adler in "Scandal in Bohemia," Kate eludes detection by cross-dressing; in depicting a specifically *racial* form of cross-dressing, however, the film counters not only the myth of the detective's all-seeing eye, but racialized theories of criminal typography as well. In the second film of the series, *Three-Fingered Kate—Her Second Victim, the Art Dealer* (1909), Kate and her sister rob a baron's art gallery, and in the third film, *Three-Fingered Kate—Her Victim the Banker* (1910), Kate again uses cross-dressing to circumvent arrest. A contemporary review says *Her Victim the Banker* "is by far the best of the films so far issued dealing with the adventures of this character, and, popular as the earlier ones were, we anticipate a still greater demand for this."[30] The film shows Kate "passing" forged banknotes and also "passing" to elude detective Rickshaw, who faces off against her in this film: "examining the notes, [he] finds on the back of one the imprint of three fingers, which tells him that his old enemy is concerned in the latest crime" (ibid). Rickshaw's criminological gaze identifies Kate's fingerprints, but still he cannot penetrate her cross-class disguise: this time, she changes clothes with a flower girl to elude detection.

In the fourth episode of the series, *Three-Fingered Kate—The Episode of the Sacred Elephants* (1910), Rickshaw and Sheerluck join forces against Kate, and this is the only film of the series in which she is caught. The arrest won't permanently deter her, however, as a contemporary review notes: "For the first time Kate, in this subject, suffers a reverse, although probably only a temporary one, in her struggle with law and authority."[31] The film shows Kate robbing a retired colonel from India "who has brought home with him from a native temple two priceless images of the 'sacred elephants,' worshipped by the natives" (ibid). Kate easily relieves the colonel of his colonial plunder, and initially deters Sheerluck and Rickshaw by cross-dressing as a male antique dealer. In the end, however, "the handcuffs are put upon her wrists for the first time." Remarkably, Kate's capture is not the end of the series, but the midpoint; three more films follow the fourth episode, and in all of them Kate escapes without arrest.

The only film of the series to survive is the fifth, *Three-Fingered Kate—Kate Purloins the Wedding Presents* (1912), which I discuss in detail in the next section of the chapter; it was followed by *Three Fingered-Kate—The Case of the Chemical Fumes* (1912), and *Three-Fingered Kate—The Pseudo-Quartette* (1912). In *Chemical Fumes,* Kate robs a baron's house party. A fictionalization of the film in the fanzine *The Pictures* describes the baron as "a man of wealth unbounded. Kings and cabinet ministers, statesmen and members of Parliament, those who look so big to us, looked nothing at all to him . . . he looked upon ordinary men, upon their labours and joys and sorrows, as ordinary men look upon cats and flies" (Norman 16–17). To rob such a man, for working-class audiences, would be hardly a crime at all. The baron hires Sheerluck to guard his home during his house party, but according to *The Pictures,* Sheerluck is flirting in the garden during the robbery and misses the whole thing. In the final film of the series, *Pseudo-Quartette,* Kate and her gang rob the house party of another wealthy aristocrat by posing as hired musicians. Lord Malcolm's guests are "wealthy" and "be-jewelled," so Kate makes quite a haul.[32] Sheerluck again fails to capture his nemesis in this final episode: "Kate's car breaks down, and she leads her pursuers through the bushes in almost a circle until emerging at practically the same spot she annexes their car, leaving 'Sheerluck' and his companions to their own reflections on the road, with a broken-down car on their hands."[33]

All of these films pit Kate against the wealthiest and most privileged members of her society: bankers, barons, colonels, and lords. The goods she steals are luxury items of the rich: jewelry, art, and priceless colonial loot. In the tradition of the populist outlaw, Kate's crimes do not alienate audiences, but attract them. She was played by the actress Ivy Martinek, who drew legions of fans among moviegoers for her work in the Three-Fingered Kate series, as contemporary film periodicals indicate. *The Cinema,* a fanzine, printed portrait-cards of Martinek that could be clipped and traded, as part of their "People's Popular Players" series.[34] Figure 19 shows a photograph and profile, which says she has "worked her way into the hearts of thousands of picture theatre patrons." In figure 20, Martinek graces the cover of the fanzine *The Pictures. The Pictures* also advertised postcards with Martinek's image, available for a penny, and answered readers' questions about the actress in its "Our Postbag" column.[35] In an article entitled "How to Become a Cinema Star: A Warning to Would-Be Picture-Actresses," the magazine cautioned readers against fantasizing that they could play Three-Fingered Kate:

> Imagine it . . . a young lady knowing nothing about acting or making up, or all the thousand and fifty things that a picture play actress has to know, manages in one single month to freeze out a leading lady . . . we are requested to believe that the Director unceremoniously dispensed with Miss Dorothy Foster or Miss Ivy Martinek, for what? For the sake of putting in a practically unknown lady, a stranger to the public. . . . Our fisher maiden of Cornwall and our precious Three-Fingered Kate are replaced by someone who could only have a spectators' knowledge of these characters.[36]

Possessed of a remarkable love of daring, Miss Ivy Martinek has worked her way into the hearts of thousands of picture theatre patrons in her various appearances in the British and Colonial films. She was the first leading lady of the B. and C., and appeared in their first success, an historical drama en-

MISS IVY MARTINEK.

titled "Her Lover's Honour." She is also the original "Three Fingered Kate" who caused such a furore in the picture world three years ago, while in that splendid production, "The Puritan Maid," she took the title role.

A thoroughly versatile woman, Miss Martinek can ride, swim, cycle, drive, fence, shoot, and is entirely without fear, and therefore a decided asset to the B. and C. stock companies.

Miss Martinek is a great traveller, having visited all the countries of Europe, also through the United States and Asia Minor, and apart from this speaks five languages.

Fig. 19. From *The Film Censor*, 14 August 1912, 3

Fig. 20. Cover from *The Pictures*, 24 August 1912)

If a mainstream film magazine could refer to an unrepentant thief as "our precious Three-Fingered Kate," popular film culture obviously had decidedly different norms of narrative liability than we see in contemporaneous crime fiction.

Three-Fingered Kate also appears in Jean Rhys's autobiographical novel *Voyage in the Dark,* indicating Kate's resonance among early-twentieth-century audiences. Rhys's novel was published in 1934, but she wrote it about twenty years earlier as a memoir of her life in London 1909 to 1910 (Athill ix). In the novel, the narrator, Anna Morgan, attends a Three-Fingered Kate film, and while the description of the film is completely inaccurate, it provides a fascinating window into Kate's cultural significance. Rhys describes two Three-Fingered Kate films that never actually existed, *Three-Fingered Kate, Episode 5: Lady Chichester's Necklace* and *Three-Fingered Kate, Episode 6: Five Years Hard,* and presents the series as conservative and moralizing, which it wasn't. Like Rhys's novel, the Three-Fingered Kate films are stories of overzealous female consumption, but Rhys reimagines the films to accentuate her society's penchant for punishing wayward women. Kate thus becomes an exaggerated version of Rhys's victimized protagonist, who, in the course of the novel, has an abortion after being abandoned by her wealthy lover. The fictional film audience's pleasure in Kate's punishment mirrors the casual sadism that Anna faces from men, landladies, and society at large:

> On the screen a pretty girl was pointing a revolver at a group of guests. They backed away with their arms held high above their heads and expressions of terror on their faces. The pretty girl's lips moved. The fat hostess unclasped a necklace of huge pearls and fell, fainting, into the arms of a footman. The pretty girl, holding the revolver so that the audience could see that two of her fingers were missing, walked backwards towards the door. Her lips moved again. You could see what she was saying. 'Keep 'em up. . . .' When the police appeared everybody clapped. When Three-Fingered Kate was caught everybody clapped louder still. (67; Rhys's ellipses)

The audience roots for the wealthy, aristocratic victims and the police who protect them rather than for Three-Fingered Kate; Rhys emphasizes the irony of this response, given that the "cinema smelt of poor people, and on the screen ladies and gentlemen in evening dress walked about with strained smiles." The irony is not lost on Anna, who complains, "Damned fools. . . . Aren't they damned fools? Don't you hate them? They always clap in the wrong places and laugh in the wrong places" (67). Rhys uses Three-Fingered Kate to illustrate British society's clamoring eagerness to discipline "bad" women, but it is important to realize that the actual *films* were firmly on the side of Kate rather than the police.

NEW WOMAN CRIMINAL: *KATE PURLOINS THE WEDDING PRESENTS*

It is a great disappointment that only one of the Three-Fingered Kate films has survived, for *Kate Purloins the Wedding Presents* is a brilliant satire and a fascinating film. The episode of the series released just before *Wedding Presents* depicted Kate's arrest, but here she returns to crime with a vengeance. Advertisements for the film emphasize that Kate was in no way chastened by her capture: "Do you remember 'Three-Fingered Kate'? She's up to her little games again. After lying low for nearly two years she has resumed her criminal career and stolen £1,000 worth of 'WEDDING PRESENTS.' The ingenious way in which the burglary was executed is shown in a new B. and C. film bearing the above title. LOOK OUT FOR IT."[37] The long gap between *Wedding Presents* and the film preceding it may indicate that the filmmakers had intended Kate's arrest to conclude the series, but ultimately depicted her return to crime, in a manner resembling Sherlock Holmes's return to detection after his ostensible death at Reichenbach Falls. With Three-Fingered Kate, however, the potentially endless chronology offered by the series as a narrative format—a format that demands no conclusion—corresponds with the films' challenge to narratives of legal containment. For Kate is not only as audacious as Madame Sara or any of the worst female villains of crime fiction, she pointedly lacks the regulating influence of a competent male adversary. Late-Victorian crime stories correlate the female criminal with the New Woman and first-wave feminism, as the Kate series does, but never depict criminal women as so obviously superior to male authority as we see here. In keeping with early crime film's class politics, Kate's association with New Women and independent femininity also correlates feminist objections to patriarchal authority with working-class resentment toward the wealthy ruling class.

Like many female criminals in crime fiction, Kate's thievery is motivated by a desire for consumer goods. She is the unintended consequence, or logical outcome, of London's new consumer economy and its ever more shrill appeals to female shoppers. As discussed in chapter 2, this economy was characterized by a saturation of advertising, department stores with prominent visual display, and other means of provoking consumer desire for unnecessary or luxury commodities. Kate's thieving tends to involve luxury items appealing to women, such as jewelry or domestic embellishments. She is the female consumer gone criminal, the lady shopper gone mad. Tammy Whitlock has described a nineteenth-century "scourge of light-fingered ladies" as expanding opportunities to consume offered expanding opportunities to shoplift (*Crime* 127). The invention of kleptomania in the second half of the century—a diagnosis "exclusively used for middle and upper-class women" (208)—signifies a widespread effort to pathologize women's insatiable consumer desires. *Wedding Presents* does not, however, use Kate to deride the excesses of female consumption. Instead, Kate's single-minded pursuit of material rewards, no matter what laws she must break, celebrates the pleasures of subverting paternalistic authority. Thus the film is ideologically feminist and antipatriarchal, but not necessarily anticapitalist. As with L. T. Meade's Madame Sara series, the film imagines female consumption as a means of feminist expression.

The first two scenes of *Wedding Presents* form a striking juxtaposition, pitting Kate not only against legal authority but against paternal power more generally. The film begins with a bride- and groom-to-be presenting an armful of wedding presents to the bride's father, Douglas Carrington. Carrington opens the gifts, suggesting his unusually central role in his daughter's wedding, as though he is the beneficiary in this ritual exchange of property. Spatially, his daughter is the literal and figurative channel of exchange between the men: as her father unwraps the packages, she has her arm around her father's shoulder, and the groom has his arm around her. Afterward, the men shake hands as though completing a transaction. The daughter's unusual name, Evadne, signals her deference to male authority: in Greek mythology, Evadne threw herself on the funeral pyre of her husband, committing suttee-like suicide after his death. In her popular 1893 New Woman novel *The Heavenly Twins,* Sarah Grand employed this name ironically for her heroine, Evadne Frayling, who deserts her husband within minutes of their wedding after learning the truth about his lewd sexual past. Facing fierce opposition from her parents—her mother laments, "all your beautiful presents, and such a trousseau!" (105)—Evadne consents to live in her husband's house, but not to consummate the marriage. As her childhood friend Diavolo observes, Evadne's marriage to the colonel little resembles that of her classical antecedent: "Evadne—classical Evadne—was noted for her devotion to her husband, and distinguished herself finally on his funeral pyre . . . wouldn't it be fun to burn the colonel, and see Evadne do suttee on his body—only I doubt if she would!" (603). In *Kate Purloins the Wedding Presents,* the name Evadne associates the film's bride not only with a feminine tradition of self-renunciation, but with Grand's widely read feminist attack on this tradition. At the same time, the film's focus on Evadne's wedding presents, worth a thousand pounds, symbolizes the substantial social rewards of sexual normativity for women as well as men.

In contrast to the opening scene's depiction of patriarchal and bourgeois domesticity, the next shot presents Three-Fingered Kate at home. An intertitle separates the scenes, simply stating: "Kate and her sister Mary." The brief text introduces a family made up of only two sisters. Lacking both men and parents, it is a family without a traditional figure of authority, unlike the Carrington family. The appearance of Kate and her sister, sitting in their parlor, is likewise a striking juxtaposition to the Carringtons: the two women smoke cigarettes and have short "bob" haircuts, associating them with New Women, bohemianism, and an early "flapper" style of femininity. Kate is lost in thought while Mary reads. The tableau accommodates various stereotypical images of modern women, dressed in "fast" styles, smoking, and engaged in intellectual pursuits. The style of the women's home likewise connects Kate and Mary with the "modern" or the "new." An art nouveau mirror, with contours reminiscent of Aubrey Beardsley's languorous curlicues, hangs above Kate's fireplace. Her mantel is adorned with a small statue of a naked woman, suggesting that Kate's aesthetic tastes are unorthodox, if not avant-garde. The scene's costumes, props, and mise-en-scène serve to distinguish between the Carringtons' patriarchal domesticity and Kate and Mary's independent femininity.

Such external differences are sharpened by the parallel actions of the characters. Shortly into the second scene, Mary gets up and sits on the arm of Kate's chair, putting her arm around Kate as the two women laugh. The actresses' positions and laughter mimic the body movements, blocking, and action of the first scene, but with two women rather than one woman and two men. The second scene is a mirrored reversal of the first, suggesting that the opposition between Kate and the Carrington family is more than an opposition between criminal and noncriminal: it is an opposition between traditional and new conceptions of family, gender, and domesticity. Indeed, Kate's and Mary's behavior during their comfortable domestic scene implies an even deeper dimension of familial unorthodoxy. After their maid leaves the room, Mary strokes Kate's hair, and Kate embraces and kisses Mary before leaving the house. Their kiss, rather long and passionate, may not prove that Kate and Mary are "sisters" in the metaphorical nineteenth-century sense of lesbianism, but it signals at least a heightened degree of sisterly intimacy. Regardless of the scene's specific sexual implications, Kate and Mary's sororal bond contests the hegemony of male authority, as in Christina Rossetti's poem "Goblin Market." They represent an alternative to the heteronormative, patriarchal family structure embodied by the Carringtons.

Kate's bodily disfigurement—her right hand has only three fingers—provides a context for viewing her as lesbian.[38] In the decades preceding this film, Havelock Ellis and Richard Von Krafft-Ebing had argued that homosexuality was symptomatic of bodily degeneracy, and associated lesbianism with physical pathology. Prior to this, a tradition of associating lesbianism with bodily defects is apparent, for example, in Wilkie Collins's 1868 novel *The Moonstone:* hunchbacked Rosanna Spearman and deformed Limping Lucy plan to move to London together and live "like sisters" (184). Likewise, George Moore's 1886 novel *A Drama in Muslin* has a hunchbacked character, Cecilia Cullen, whose desires are pointedly lesbian. Kate's deformed hand may be the physical manifestation of a similar sexual "pathology."

If Kate is physically deformed and sexually pathologized, she fits Lombroso's and Ellis's female criminal "type," but the film emphatically avoids offering a criminological perspective on deviance. Rather than casting the expert gaze of social authority upon Kate, *Wedding Presents* reverses crime fiction convention by disrupting viewers' allegiance to representatives of social control. It asks us to identify more closely with the criminal "other" than with the detective or victim. Marie-Christine Leps has argued that an opposition between the noncriminal "reader" and the criminal "other" developed in late-nineteenth-century newspapers and print media, providing the underlying discursive structure for detective fiction as a genre, but *Wedding Presents* rejects such a structure. Most scenes focus on Kate, rather than the detective or the victims, and the arc of the story revolves around her enactment of the crime rather than Sheerluck's attempt to solve it or the Carringtons' marriage plot. The film also highlights Kate's skill and distinction as a criminal, encouraging the audience to admire her. She has a gang of "confederates," who report to her "to receive their daily instructions." Her two male henchmen do the criminal dirty work—digging out a tunnel between Kate's fireplace and the Carringtons' fireplace next door—but Kate plots the crime and performs the theft on her own. A hero in the tradition of Odysseus, Kate is crafty rather than honorable. She eavesdrops on the Carringtons, steals a letter from a little girl by pretending to help her mail it, and steams open the letter to access its content surreptitiously. Even the "good" characters in the film obliquely celebrate her criminal ingeniousness: in a particularly ironic use of editing, the twenty-seventh shot of the film depicts Kate's celebratory return home after completing the theft, which is juxtaposed, in the twenty-eighth shot, with an image of the wedding guests' champagne toast. The effect of the montage is that guests appear to toast the success of Kate's crime.

Indeed, a significant portion of the film consists of ironic cross-cutting between Kate's theft and Evadne's wedding celebration, associating the two events. The dialectical editing likens the marriage to a crime, and likens the crime to a surrogate marriage ceremony for Kate. That Kate has all the presents at the end of the film supports such a reading; her haul of wedding gifts ironically suggests that she has undergone a nuptial rite of passage in enacting the theft. The end of the film juxtaposes Evadne's tears in the penultimate shot with Kate's gleeful laughter in the final shot. The contrast asks viewers not to sympathize with the woman who has submitted to male authority and expects the social rewards of complicity (symbolized by the presents), but to admire the woman who has taken those rewards for herself without undergoing the social transaction meant to precede them. An earlier scene in which the wedding guests admire the gifts supports such a reading: one present that gets particularly appreciative attention is a wide necklace that looks very much like a chain.

Perhaps Kate's most appealing characteristic is her gratuitous and audacious antagonism toward figures of authority. After stealing the Carringtons' wedding presents, for example, she sets an alarm clock to ring in the room where the presents are stored. When it rings, the alarm alerts Sheerluck's assistant, standing guard outside the locked room, that she has stolen the gifts. Why would Kate purposely leave herself just twenty minutes to escape? An intertitle explains that she does it "out of bravado." Further, after climbing back through the tunnel in the fireplace, Kate leaves a note for Sheerluck in her drawing room. He finds the message after she has escaped: "Compliments to 'Detective Sheerluck' from Three fingered Kate." Kate is so certain of his inability to catch her that she claims responsibility for the crime. The last shot of the film highlights this audacity: turning her rebellious bravado onto the

Three Fingered Kate, foundress and first president
of The Help Yourself Society.

Fig. 21. From *The Pictures,* 20 July 1912, 14

viewer, she faces the camera directly, holds up her three-fingered hand, and laughs in the viewer's face, apparently flipping the audience off with an obscene gesture *and* defiantly brandishing the physical marker of her criminal deformity. The shot is unsettling not only for its lack of attention to the fourth wall, but for the aggressiveness of Kate's appeal. She escapes uncaught, and is apparently quite proud of it, as well as of her malformed hand. Figure 21 shows a promotional still of Kate in this trademark pose, though in the film, Kate's flaunting of her hand appears more disconcerting since she is standing and laughing rather than sitting and smiling.

In the detective series discussed in the first two chapters, the detective's point of view is always prevalent, but *Wedding Presents* not only takes Kate's side, it takes seemingly excessive delight in subverting the efforts of the detective. Because Sheerluck stands in parodic relation to Sherlock Holmes, the film's pleasure in Kate's coup is also pleasure in undoing the vision of modernity that Conan Doyle's stories construct, characterized by the possibility of omnipotent social control. If we believe the film, Holmes's investigative triumphs are the result of "sheer luck," not panoptical vision. Conan Doyle's detective stories and late-Victorian criminology educe a fantasy of perfect legal surveillance, but in questioning the legitimacy of legal authority and in portraying outlaws sympathetically, the Kate films engage a very different set of desires. In chapter 1, I argue that female criminals disrupt Holmes's otherwise infallible system of visual detection; Three-Fingered Kate performs the same office far more deliberately. Sherlock and Sheerluck exemplify the intertextual relationship between magazine series and early film, but their differences indicate that Holmes was less attractive to film's working-class audiences, except in parodied form, than to the middle-class audience of the *Strand*.[39]

CLASS, GENDER, AND FILMIC FEMALE CRIMINALS

Other early crime films likewise employ the female criminal to demystify modern social authority, but the gender politics of such films are rarely as radical as *The Exploits of Three-Fingered Kate*. Four years before the first Three-Fingered Kate film, Cecil Hepworth's *An Interrupted Honeymoon* (1905) depicted a crafty and appealing female criminal who faces off against inept enforcers of the law.[40] The film, like *Wedding Presents,* includes both a wedding and crime, but here it is two criminals who marry. As its title suggests, *An Interrupted Honeymoon* ingeniously pits the marriage plot against the detection plot, so that viewers must choose between the criminal honeymooners and the police on their trail. Because a policeman literally *interrupts* the honeymoon, also interrupting consummation of the marriage, the film uses the conventional dramatic device of the blocking figure to generate audience resentment against the interfering officer. Rather than challenging familial, domestic, and sexual norms, as the Kate film did, this film draws on audience investment in such norms to generate support for the outlaws.

The film opens with a juxtaposition between two disparate scenarios: after a prototypically romantic proposal scene, the groom-to-be robs a jeweler. The first scene shows a couple punting on a river, where the groom proposes to the bride. The sentimental scene entangles viewers' sympathies in the love story before the crime occurs, and desire for the marriage plot's fulfillment takes precedence over the desire for containment and comeuppance that crime stories typically elicit. Indeed, the marriage almost seems to depend upon the crime, since the groom gives the bride stolen jewelry as a wedding gift. As in *Kate Purloins the Wedding Presents, An Interrupted Honeymoon* strips away the sentimentality of wedding gifts, which become subject to theft and appropriation like any other property. In this case, the bride doesn't commit the robbery, but as with Kate, her acquisitive desire for jewelry is the implicit catalyst for the crime.

Directly after the couple leave the church where they have wed, a policeman arrives looking for the jewel thief. Spectators of the wedding appear to point him in the wrong direction, indicating that the audience within the film has taken the couple's side against the police, just as the film's audience is expected to do. As in *Wedding Presents, An Interrupted Honeymoon* cross-cuts between scenes of a wedding and scenes of a criminal investigation; whether or not the newlyweds will be caught is its central narrative tension. As the bride and groom toast their honeymoon, the groom sees the authorities approaching outside the window. He removes the jewelry from the bride, hides it, and pleads her forgiveness on his knees. After a brief remonstrance, the wife quickly metamorphoses into a cunning criminal. She hatches a plan to avoid detection, and like Irene Adler and Three-Fingered Kate, her plan involves crossdressing. The bride dresses in her husband's suit and top hat, while he dons her dress and a wig. The woman is much shorter than the man, so they make a comical drag couple in ill-fitting clothes at the end of the transaction.

When the policeman and jeweler enter the drawing room where the bride and groom had been sitting, they find the couple's leftover champagne, and the officer convinces the jeweler to have a drink with him. Earlier in the film, the groom had been able to steal the jewelry in the first place because the jeweler was drunk; in both scenes, emphasis on the jeweler's drinking detracts from his victimization. In yet another filmic example of drunk and incompetent policing, the officer is evidently intoxicated in the scene that follows: after downing a drink and hitting his chest with his fist, he pries open the door to the adjoining bedroom.[41] The wife (dressed as a man) approaches the officer, puffs out her chest with bravado, and assumes an indignant attitude. The officer is about to hit her with a stick, but notices how small she is, and gathers that this is the wrong man. He checks his description and measures her with tape, while the husband (dressed as a woman) hangs back shyly and weeps into his handkerchief, thereby avoiding the policeman's gaze. In a similarly exaggerated affectation of gender roles, the bride stands with her legs wide apart and hands on her hips, dominating the space around her body. Amid the policeman's confusion, the "wife" faints on the bed and the "husband" orders him out of the room; when he refuses to leave, they put a pillowcase over his head and tie him up. Binding the policeman to the bed and running out of the room, the couple escapes, presumably to finish their interrupted honeymoon. The last shot lingers over the officer's comic predicament, wriggling around helplessly and dragging the bed across the room with a pillowcase over his head.

An Interrupted Honeymoon's female offender is not the instigator of the theft, but exhibits a skillful criminal instinct in coming up with the idea to cross-dress. As in *Wedding Presents,* the film's narrative perspective is the criminal perspective; the police devolve into blocking figures for the marriage plot. In privileging the resolution of the love story above the resolution of the crime, the film perhaps merely reinforces one governing social institution over another, but its use of cross-dressing suggests that an overly rigid sense of gender roles prevents the officer from detecting the criminals. Such narratives—common in turn-of-the-century crime plots—can be read as a contribution, perhaps unintentional, to feminist arguments about androgyny and gender roles. The politics of *An Interrupted Honeymoon,* however, are most striking in their representation of class: the police represent an unjust and irrational force dedicated to preserving an unequal share of wealth, property, and luxury consumption.

Even films that follow a more formulaic criminal plot share this perspective toward police authority. The 1910 Hepworth film *A Woman's Treachery* moralistically punishes its female criminal, but resists conventional legal containment. The film, directed by Theo Bouwmeester, depicts a housemaid who is a thief and traitor, but in contrast to similar depictions of female domestic workers in crime fiction, it emphasizes her treachery toward her lover rather than her employer. The film is set in a wealthy household, where the butler James is in love with the beautiful maid.[42] The maid, tempted by vanity and acquisitiveness, steals one of her lady's necklaces; she is motivated, like other filmic female criminals, by desire for consumer commodities and luxury goods. When the lady realizes her necklace is missing and summons the police, James takes the blame for the theft and is imprisoned. An intertitle reads: "Three months later ~ On with the new love." The next two shots contrast the maid, kissing a new butler, with James, kissing the maid's photograph in prison. The film uses a fading effect to blend the two shots, highlighting the maid's betrayal. When James escapes from prison, she betrays him again by telling the police where he is. Eventually the maid is punished, but not by the law: in the last scene of the film, the maid and the second butler are just about to marry, when James arrives and denounces the maid, so that her new love rejects her. *A Woman's Treachery* thus punishes its female criminal for betraying her lover, but not for stealing the necklace. The maid is never disciplined for theft, and James's escape from prison indicates that the film has little attachment to legal institutions or procedure. In general, early crime films were not interested in reinforcing authoritarian narratives of social control, particularly when it would require taking the side of a wealthy woman with stolen jewels. The narrative of *A Woman's Treachery* reinforces "womanly" values of domestic fidelity, but not "citizenly" values of legal obedience.[43] Early British films are not always feminist, but almost never do they depict a woman criminal "caught" by police or detectives.[44]

Most filmic female criminals are motivated by the desire to consume, but just as in crime fiction, some early British films portray women criminals as avengers rather than consumers, acting from noble intentions rather than greedy, acquisitive desires. Such representations can serve to reinforce idealized notions of femininity, but can also establish women's capacity for just intervention into traditionally male social transactions. A 1913 film called *The Tube of Death* depicts a widow as suicide bomber: in a parodic inversion of the birth canal, she uses an explosive "tube of death" to blow up the anarchists who caused her husband's death, killing herself in the process.[45] The film was promoted as exceptionally shocking: "Enough of [*sic*] sensation is contained in the three reels to satisfy the most *blasé habitué* of a theatre."[46] Cricks and Sharp's *A Wife's Revenge; Or, the Gambler's End* (1904) also depicts a woman killing her husband's killer. As the film begins, she attempts to pull her husband—a compulsive gambler—from a game of cards, but is perfunctorily dismissed by the men in the game. The husband, continually losing, eventually realizes that he is being cheated, and challenges one of the cheaters to a duel. When he dies in the duel, his wife—obscured in a long cloak—demands to fight his killer. She throws off the cloak, picks up her husband's sword, and makes a beautiful spectacle dueling in a white lace dress with flowing sleeves. The fight is set outdoors, with high trees in the background; the film's sense of space and height gives a heroic and epic feel to the action, but ironically the wife rather than the husband becomes the hero. She wins the duel and kills the villain, wielding her husband's sword to greater effect than he did himself. As in Conan Doyle's story "Charles Augustus Milverton," the female avenger's weapon aligns her with a form of social power associated with the phallus.

FEMALE TROUBLE: SUFFRAGETTE TERROR ON FILM

With her mastery of the sword, the female dueler in *A Wife's Revenge* reflects an escalating narrative interest in female militancy, a trend that corresponds with the intensifying campaign for women's right to vote. During the early years of film, suffragettes were a serious threat to national security, and suffragette violence was an everyday reality in urban Britain.[47] Violent and encroaching upon traditionally male spheres, the militant suffragette embodied all of the fears and anxieties surrounding representations of female criminality. Nevertheless, suffragettes on film, whether committing crimes or not, differ markedly from other filmic female criminals. Villains like Three-Fingered Kate or the maid in *A Woman's Treachery* steal out of a greedy desire to consume goods, an impulse that essentially accords with the individualist and consumerist values of modern English capitalism. Militant suffragettes, in contrast, want to achieve social change through violent collective action, which at root was a far less tolerable offense than individual criminal deviance.

Because militant suffragettes posed a threat of collective feminine action, they were no less threatening to lower-class male filmgoers than middle-class male fiction readers. Even in the antiauthoritarian context of early British film, representations of suffragettes attract a great deal more vitriol than conventional female criminals. The 1898 comedy *Suffragette in the Barber Shop,* for example, depicts a suffragette infiltrating a space of "male privacy" and "the havoc wreaked by the woman who usurps the law of such a space" (Monaghan 27).[48] In *Sweet Suffragettes* (1906), a suffragette is punished for infiltrating male discourse: she is pelted with eggs after giving a speech. Other films satirize the suffrage movement as permanently hampered by women's vanity. *The Suffragettes and the Hobble Skirt* (1910) depicted a "persecuted man" who "gives women hobble skirts and they are jailed" (Gifford no. 02588). The hobble skirt, popular 1910–14, was so narrow that it impeded walking; the film suggests, like Max Beerbohm's essay discussed in the last chapter, how self-imposed fashion regimens can effectively "jail" women who might otherwise pursue liberation. *Scroggins as a Census Official* (Cricks and Martin, 1911) likewise depicts vain suffragettes who protest the census only because it requires them to reveal their age.[49]

Suffragettes were extremely common figures in early film, and in the era of first-wave feminism, this new medium served as a venue for reflecting upon and sometimes satirizing women's new political and social freedoms. As a specifically visual medium, film changed the way the feminist movement was represented and understood: early suffragette films anticipate visual mass media's profound effect on gender and on civil disobedience throughout the twentieth century. Antisuffrage narrative films, for example, often minimize suffragettes' visual markers of femininity, signifying the heightened attentiveness to surface manifestations of gender that accompanied the birth of visual mass media. The defeminization of suffragettes thus emerges as the filmic countermovement to the glamorization of female criminals. "Actuality" and newsreel films documenting militant suffrage action, meanwhile, focus not on suffragettes' individual bodies, but on the cumulative effect of en masse militancy on public space. These newsreels express how film could, in some cases, actually facilitate the suffrage campaign by realizing its public effects.

The campaign for suffrage in Britain was more militant than in other countries, and aroused particular derision in British popular culture. It included a faction of so-called guerrilla suffragettes who employed aggressive civil disobedience to further their cause, including arson, bombings, window-smashing, destruction of public and private property, and acts of self-violence such as hunger strikes. In 1912, a suffrage group in

Dublin (British at the time) even tried to burn down a theater by placing "a handbag containing gunpowder inside of the cinematograph box" and then tossing in a lighted match ("Irish Rush").[50] Filmic depictions of suffragettes, unsympathetic to such tactics, are often strongly informed by criminological theory, in sharp contrast to glamorous depictions of female thieves and killers. Criminologists argued that suffragette violence was pathologically antisocial, not socially or politically grounded, and Havelock Ellis argued against affording such acts tolerance on the basis of political commitment ("Letter"). Some thought suffragette militancy was prompted by "primitive" impulses toward crime and destruction: Hargrave Adam asked in 1912, "Would any male . . . reformers . . . allow themselves to be guilty of such tiresome and contemptible monkey-tricks[?]" (16). At a time when criminality was indexed to biological degeneration, the phrase "monkey-tricks" depicts suffragettes as not only underevolved, but essentially opposed to civil society.[51]

The prevalence of men dressed as suffragettes in early film exemplifies how some filmmakers belittled suffragists by drawing on a long-standing stereotype that feminist advocates were mannish or ugly, a stereotype that was supported by scientific theorists of gender. Eugenicist Karl Pearson, for example, wrote in 1894 that the women's movement was dominated by "asexual" women who lack a "normal" woman's "sex instinct" ("Woman and Labour" 234–38). Film took the type of the disgendered feminist to a new level simply by putting male actors in suffragette roles. The most famous example of this is Charlie Chaplin's *The Militant Suffragette,* a 1914 U.S. film starring Chaplin in drag, but several British films predating Chaplin's work also put male actors in drag to play ugly, disgendered suffragettes.[52] Cross-dressing often functions to critique ideologies of gender, but it does not always do so. Images of men cross-dressing as women do not inevitably denaturalize gender; sometimes, as Anne McClintock argues, cross-dressing can actually solidify existing inequalities by staging the "right to ambiguity" enjoyed by those in power (68).

Bamforth and Company's *Women's Rights* (1899) exhibits this kind of privileged ambiguity, depicting men in drag as suffragettes to burlesque the women's movement rather than gender itself.[53] In the first shot of the film, as figure 22 shows, two women played by male actors talk in front of a fence. In the second shot, two men sneak up behind them, eavesdrop, and nail their dresses to the fence (figure 23). The "women" catch the men but are too late, and the final shot of the film shows them flailing wildly attempting to escape (figure 24). Casting the suffragettes

Fig. 22. First shot from *Women's Rights* (1899)

with men means more than topsy-turvy, vaudevillian carnivalesque: it is antifeminist satire, positing a distinction between "suffragettes" and "women" and suggesting that suffrage advocates have nothing to say on "real" women's behalf. Depicting suffragettes' physiological grotesqueness and the gendered degeneracy of their bodies, *Women's Rights* disciplines gender by casting suffragettes with men: the actors' bodies are deterrents, signifying the absence of femininity in women who campaign for equality, and this is conveyed seemingly "immediately" through visual image, anticipating twentieth-century feminist theories about the power of visual, bodily manifestations of gender in image-saturated societies.

As the film constructs a gendered distinction between "women" and "suffragettes," it also orchestrates a sharp division between "men" on one side of the fence and "women" on the other. The formal arrangement of shots emphasizes the schism between the actors who play women and those who play men, and the choice to position the film's

Fig. 23. Second shot from *Women's Rights* (1899)

action on two sides of a fence exacerbates the divide between them. In this arrangement, men and women are literally on separate sides, and the rift between their perspectives is intensified by the chronological gap between the first two shots of the film. After showing the women speaking and gesturing angrily on their side of the fence, the camera cuts to the other side, showing the same span of time from the men's point of view. *Women's Rights* juxtaposes back-to-back scenes from two different perspectives of what we are to imagine as the same span of time. This method allowed filmmakers to evoke chronological simultaneity before the innovation of cross-cutting, but in *Women's Rights,* the curiously disparate simultaneity of this stylistic choice underscores the characters' formal separation. Without montage, there is no union between the two "sides" through visual form. Not only do the women and men inhabit different filmic spaces demarcated by the fence, they inhabit different filmic chronologies.

By successfully nailing the suffragettes to the fence, the men in *Women's Rights* literally demonstrate how to keep women in their

Fig. 24. Third shot from *Women's Rights* (1899)

metaphorical place. Fences typically serve to demarcate private space from public, so on an allegorical level, the film humorously advocates keeping women on "their" side of the fence and out of the public political sphere via voting. Moreover, the film's costuming pits against one another two social groups that were campaigning to get the vote: women and labor. The men in the film wear aprons, indicating that they—like most of the film's audience—are members of the working class. The "women," in contrast, have ladies' elaborate costumes and are identified as "ladies" in the alternate title of the film (see note 54). Anti-suffrage propaganda often targeted working-class men, in an effort to drum up fear about "petticoat government" among a sizable though not universally enfranchised demographic; this film similarly serves as a cautionary tale to working-class men who may fear that women's suffrage would put them in metaphorical dresses.

Suffragettes' Downfall; Or, Who Said Rats? (1911) does not stage the confinement of women to private space, like *Women's Rights,* nor use male actors to embody suffragettes, but instead specifies how the suffrage campaign infests domestic space. The film opens in a middle-class home where a "Votes for Women" sign, rather than a "Home Sweet Home" sign, hangs above the mantel. A bourgeois couple argues as the wife gestures toward the sign, indicating that their dispute is about suffrage. A maid comes in to serve tea, but trying to read a newspaper as she pours, she drops a dish on the husband. He yells and shakes his fist at the maid, but the wife comforts her, kisses her, and takes her part. The maid simulates a punch to the husband's face, and the wife grabs him by the ear and slaps him. In this home, the wife and the maid are overtly engaged in political discourse—via the suffrage campaign and the newspaper—to the detriment of their domestic roles. The wife has a greater allegiance to her maid (a member of her sex) than to her husband (a member of her class), and the husband is at the mercy of their physical domination.

In the next scene, the wife leaves with a friend to play golf, a sport that was associated with New Womanly athleticism as well as with militant suffragettes, who were known to sabotage golf courses as a form of political agitation (Tickner 135). The women are dressed in a masculine style, with neckties and severely tailored outfits; *The Suffragette's Downfall*'s action and iconography thus present the suffragettes as bodily disgendered, masculinized, athletic, and violent. The surviving copy of the film ends here, but is incomplete; descriptions of the film in contemporary trade journals describe its original conclusion:

> While the two ladies are busily making wild swings with their golf clubs, hitting the turf, caddies—in fact, everything but the ball—the good man is making the round of the shops, placing the articles he buys in the pram on top of the infant. His last call is at a pub, and here, detailing his wrongs, he is sold a cage containing a rat, and hides the latter under a dish cover on the table at home, and releases it when his wife begins to upbraid him on her return. The effect is marvelous. With her friend she flies to the table and gladly signs a declaration afterwards forswearing the suffrage movement for ever, and promising to attend to her own duties.[54]

In the film's missing segment, the husband is further emasculated by being forced into the feminine role of consuming shopper, but ultimately the film suggests that gender will trump politics and "order" will be restored.

Such a stance was common among antisuffrage narrative films. *Child of a Suffragette* (1913) presented militant feminism as a dangerous perversion of conventional family relationships. Here, a suffragette mother bombs a mailbox and a residence, but repents the error of her ways when her own daughter is nearly killed in trying to defuse one of her mother's bombs. The film no longer exists, but garnered positive reviews in the *Bioscope,* which praised the film—absurdly enough—for its realism: "as a study of militant methods, it is amazing in its intimacy."[55] The writer thought the film would "create wide interest amongst a public so morbidly fascinated by the doings of political women as ours."

The public appetite for suffragette films was not limited to narrative cinema, and "made-up" films were not alone in drumming up fear about suffragettes and the demolition of the home. A 1911 advertisement for Pathé, who produced many newsreels about the suffragettes, proclaimed the popularity of these topicals: "THE SUFFRAGETTES BREAK WINDOWS. WE BREAK RECORDS."[56] *St. Leonard's Outrage,* a 1913 Pathé newsreel, was not unlike *The Suffragette's Downfall* or *Child of a Suffragette* in pitting women's rights against domestic tranquility. Depicting the torched spectacle of a house severely damaged by recent suffragette militancy, the film presents suffragette political action as violence against the home and all it stands for. The opening frame reads: "Damage estimated at £10,000 was caused by suffragettes firing the residence of Mr. Arthur DuCros M.P." The newsreel does not show this Member of Parliament, nor does it show any suffragettes; it only surveys the ruined house and the onlookers who have come to gaze upon it. The first shot shows the front of the burned home and a crowd of thirty-two spectators gathered to see it. The camera's inclusion of the crowd in this shot reminds us that a private family home has become the object of public gawking. The film's second shot focuses on a workman, standing on a ladder and knocking burned debris from the roof. The final shot takes viewers inside the ruined house, still smoking and completely destroyed.

The film narrates the devastating effect of the suffrage campaign on the "home," stunningly portraying the force of suffrage action en masse. Obliquely, it may have served suffragette interests by emphasizing their power. Indeed, *St. Leonard's Outrage* expresses its own status as filmic documentation in ways that suggest film's unique capacity for furthering the suffrage cause. During the first shot, which takes in the outside of the house, the crowd of onlookers gradually becomes more interested in the camera than the house. As the shot lingers, spectators turn their gaze away from the wreckage to look at the camera, until eventually there are far more people looking at the camera than the house. This reminds viewers that film and other visual innovations of modernity require a reorganization of vision: not only *better* vision or *more* vision, but sometimes the withholding of vision to maintain the illusion that the camera does not exist. The meaning of this film changes when its subjects fail to sustain that illusion: their interest in the camera highlights the filmic nature of the scene, reminding us that the image of devastation will be projected to an incalculable number of observers, and suggesting how militancy is changed in the age of visual mass media.

Not only does *St. Leonard's Outrage* emphasize the expanded number of spectators that film creates, it also stresses how film offers a privileged view of the event. By moving ever closer into the damage, the camera provides a more intimate view of the devastation than on-site witnesses would see. The progression of shots is particularly important in this regard: the first shot shows the front of the house, which any random passerby could see; the second shot is high, giving viewers a close-up of the damage to the roof and paralleling the visual perspective of the man on the ladder, above the "crowd in the street" view of the first shot; the final shot goes into the wreckage of the home, not only taking spectators within private property, but to a position of some danger, since the fire continues to smolder and the house appears structurally unstable. As the newsreel progresses, it marks more and more insistently film's capacity for *realizing* the destructive activities of the suffragettes. Not only does it spread these images to a mass audience, it purports to give them a privileged view of the action. The camera sees what the crowd outside does not.

St. Leonard's Outrage depicts the power of suffragette violence as well as film's unique capacity for revealing that power. The suffragettes themselves were keenly aware that the new visual technology of film could be used to forward political ends. A 1908 article in *Kinematograph and Lantern Weekly* describes suffragettes giving exclusive rights to cinematographer W. Jeapes to document their "pictorial history" (Low 151), and Chanan describes the 1908 *Suffragette Film,* no longer surviving, made by suffragettes who intended it as propaganda (235).[57] Likewise, some seemingly "objective" newsreels hint at the suffragettes' savvy approach to the new medium. *The Suffragette Derby of 1913* appears at first to be a filmmaking accident: while covering the Epsom Derby, a cinematographer caught on film the death of suffragette Emily Davison, who ran onto the racetrack right in front of the king's horse. Historians are unsure whether Davison intended to commit suicide by this act; she had a suffrage banner in her pocket, which she may have merely planned to unfurl for the cameras.[58] The newsreel of the event shows her ducking under the fence and onto the course mere seconds before being tram-

Fig. 25. Photograph of Emily Davison's death, captured on film in *The Suffragette Derby of 1913*.

pled; by darting out directly in the path of the king's horse, Davison brought on her own demise, and managed to position herself center-stage for the newsreel camera. (See figure 25.)

Feminist historians have considered Davison's funeral procession, which drew several thousand spectators, as one of the great public spectacles of British feminism, "Davison's last gift to the movement she cared so passionately about" (Stanley 172). Davison's death, however, was a spectacle that reached even more viewers than her funeral; large audiences, including prominent members of Parliament, witnessed Davison's act on Gaumont's film. The extent to which Davison purposefully orchestrated the film's creation is not clear. The opening frame's title prepares us to view the film as completely accidental, not an orchestrated performance: "The Gaumont Graphic alone secured the thrilling incident at Tattenham Corner, resulting in the death of Miss Davidson [*sic*]." Gaumont frames the spectacle as exemplifying the power of film itself, not the power of suffragettes like Davison to manipulate it, but this filmic event nonetheless portends the powerful shift that visual mass media would have on activist politics, as organizers of political protest have steadily focused more and more on obtaining visual media coverage. *The Suffragette Derby of 1913* implies a sea-change in civil disobedience, with a newly vital emphasis on performance rather than demonstration.

The 1913 Pathé newsreel *Trafalgar Square Riot* similarly conveys the power of the new medium to communicate the disruptiveness of suffragette action. The opening frame notes that Sylvia Pankhurst, the infamous radical suffragette, participated in the riot, but the film itself does not focus on Pankhurst or any other individual body. Instead, it shows a group of suffragettes peaceably carrying banners, the crush of the crowd gathered to watch the event, and omnibuses struggling to navigate through the protest. The emphasis is on the suffragettes' capacity to disrupt the normal functioning of the city and its inhabitants. Likewise, *Suffragette Riots at Westminster,* a 1910 Pathé newsreel, shows footage of a London protest and focuses on the resulting urban commotion. The camera is positioned at the level of the crowd, not an elevated vantage point, thus few suffragettes are visible at all; the film lingers instead on masses of crowding people, there to watch rather than riot. We might contrast this approach with the popular 1897 films of Queen Victoria's Diamond Jubilee: at this early moment in filmmaking, the cameras were placed high above the crowd, to capture the procession as it "really" looked—not how it looked to the spectators—and to de-emphasize its status as a film-mediated event. As Barnes notes, "We are never shown the faces of the cheering crowd, the children, or the fluttering flags and decorations" (2:198). Thirteen years later, *Suffragette Riots at Westminster* stresses the mass spectatorship of suffragette action rather than the "action" itself. As more and more of the crowd—including the police—turn to look at the cinematographer, watchers of the riot become watchers of the camera, underscoring the event's status as filmic spectacle.

On screen and off, suffragette newsreels quite literally provided suffragette militancy with an audience. A century before reality television, "actuality films" of suffragette activism indicate that political theater and "film-friendly" news were already intertwined. In his memoir of the early years of British cinema, cartoonist and screenwriter Harry Furniss describes an event in which a suffragette kidnapping was staged for filmic representation. Spectators of the event, confused, moved to rescue the male "victim," only to learn that the filmmakers were simply trying "to obtain realistic pictures of a suffragette demonstration" (*Our Lady* 136). As this anecdote suggests, early film responded to suffragette militancy in ways that echo other forms, but film as a medium also changed the way that contemporaries understood the suffrage movement. Suffragette films reveal the conflicting consequences of modernity's visual innovations: some enact a criminological gaze that works to discipline gender, but others enhance the legitimacy of mass political action by proffering visual proof of its clout.

Most films about suffragettes do not fit the genre of "crime film," but nevertheless highlight the surprising contrast between representations of glamorous, individual female criminals in crime film, and representations of en masse female militancy in films about suffragettes. Crime film risked a far more radical narrative perspective than crime fiction toward class, authority, and power, but such radicalism breaks down when film touches upon collective feminist movements for social change. The suffragette films help us make sense of crime film's anti-disciplinary accounts of female criminality: films about female criminals, as we have seen, naturalize women's desire for consumption, possession, and material gain; insofar as they encourage viewers to value and desire luxury-level consumption, such films are hand-in-hand with the individualist and consumerist values of capitalism. But just as *Three-Fingered Kate* valorizes consumption to make a feminist point, many early films about female criminals valorize consumption to make a *democratic* point: that all viewers deserve to—and ought to be able to—consume abundantly. This hyperconsumerist message occurs at the expense of conventional authority figures, whose function in such films is to police consumption in favor of a plutocratic class order. Films about female criminality thus reinforce the idea that consumer capitalism has an implicit democratic sensibility: a "utopian vision," as Thomas Richards has put it, in which everyone is "equal in the sight of things" (61). These films depict the female criminal as the emblem of modern, democratic, individualist, *and* consumerist values.

British crime film's early marginality and lower-class audience meant that it celebrated different values than crime fiction and engaged a diverging set of desires: it questioned the legitimacy of legal authority and portrayed outlaws sympathetically; as a visual medium, it intensified the glamour of female criminality; and as a lower-class medium, it was resistant to containing criminal women via forces of social control. Prior to 1913, film's decentralized production and distribution allowed a surprisingly heterodox crime film tradition to flourish, which challenges critical presumptions about the disciplinary prerogative of mass culture. Critics following Theodor Adorno and Max Horkheimer have viewed mass-cultural escapism as a force of class complacency, but in the early days of cinema, conservative voices considered film to be dangerous to the status quo precisely *because* it encouraged film viewers to aspire to middle-class lifestyles and consumption patterns.

When cultural conservatives claimed that crime films would encourage "thieving" among the lower classes, they were essentially protesting film's hyperconsumerist ideology, since attempts to legislate against crime film stemmed from the idea that such films incite criminal behavior by valorizing it.[59] Film was accused of encouraging antisocial behavior in "sensitive" populations—especially youth, women, and the working classes—and early opponents considered it a degenerative and dangerous cultural force. It was practically synonymous with the "modern," and largely because of its depictions of crime, became a target for reactions against social change. Film seemed to erode traditional social distinctions, and not only those based on class and consumption: the cinema itself sat somewhere between public and private space, public because the spectators are strangers to one another, but private in the intimacy imposed by the absence of light.[60] Associations with darkness and illicit sexual activity meant that female filmgoers were a cause of anxiety, but accompanying fears about moral corruption was a fear that cinema might actually cause physiological corruption in its audience.[61]

Even among proponents of cinema, such rhetoric was common. Furniss wrote that when audiences leave the movies, "they rush, they struggle, they run. What they have seen has entered into their being. . . . The never-ceasing movement of the pictures so inoculates the spectators, that they are prone to carry out in real life what they see upon the screen" (*Our Lady* 30). Here, the modern shock of moving pictures is akin to hypnosis or subliminal influence.[62] According to a 1912 article, some doctors did believe in the "curious effect which the motion picture has upon many spectators in the matter of hypnotic suggestion" ("Cinema and Hypnotic Suggestion" 3), and in "The Craze for Sensation," a trade journal bemoaned the "orgy of sensationalism" in contemporary film: "many producers labour under the delusion that it is necessary nowadays to tickle the public palate with as many nerve-racking sensations as can be crowded into a limited number of feet of film" (1). Fears about early cinema's shocking, nerve-racking, and hypnotic effects echo earlier reactions against penny dreadfuls, sensation fiction, detective fiction, and dynamite fiction. This parallel was not lost on Furniss, who wrote in a procensorship piece, "in the past the juvenile criminal was wont to tearfully allege in the dock of the police-court that it was the perusual [*sic*] of cheap-and-nasty sensational literature that caused his lapse from the path of virtue. Now his secession from the straight and narrow way is attributed to what he sees on the cinematograph screen" ("Wanted—A Censor" 81).[63]

As film producers and exhibitors strove to attract middle-class audiences, many of early film's unconventional narrative tendencies were suppressed in an attempt to snuff out film's reputation as an inciter of crime. The film industry believed greater profits were to be found in higher-class audiences, so they engaged in a campaign to raise the status of cinema. An article called "Penny Shows Must Go!" in the *Bioscope* argued: "The opening of so many theatres de luxe, with their comfortable seats, cosy appearance, and high-class show of films, has sounded the death-knell of the penny picture show, which will, except in the very poorest districts, be soon as dead as a door-nail" (4). By appealing to higher-class customers, this piece argued, an exhibitor might "charge double the former price of admission": "The penny showman is going the wrong way to work. That is, he is making himself and his show too cheap, with the result that the majority of his patrons are riotous children and illiterate aliens who cannot understand and appreciate the difference between good shows and bad. And whereas he should and can make pounds a week profit, he is only making shillings" (4). This is a running theme in cinema trade journals of the era; they presume that the advancement of film as an art and a business will entail its gentrification. Beyond purpose-built theaters, other practices instituted in the 1910s to gentrify the British film audience included tiered pricing, longer films unsuitable for the variety show format, and adaptations of "respectable" literary classics.[64] Censorship was a key part of the gentrification project: the British Board of Censorship was established in January 1913 by the film industry itself as a means of boosting its own respectability. Official criteria for censoring a film included "scenes tending to disparage public characters and institutions," and "scenes calculated as incentive to crime" (Low 91). Unsurprisingly, such developments curtailed the antiauthority tradition in early British film, as well as the appreciative and admiring depictions of female criminals like Three-Fingered Kate.

PART THREE

DYNAMITE NARRATIVE

DYNAMITE, INTERRUPTED

FOUR

*Gender in James's and Conrad's Novels
of Failed Terror*

Henry James's 1886 novel *The Princess Casamassima* and Joseph Conrad's 1907 novel *The Secret Agent* are in many ways two very different works—different in tone, style, and narrative voice—but both participate in a popular genre of crime narrative that emerged in 1880s Britain: the "dynamite novel." Dynamite narrative treats the characteristically modern topic of political terror; it doesn't always include literal dynamite—the mode of terror may be an explosion, an assassination, or some other threat to the social order—but always depicts a politically motivated criminal plot.[1] Both James's and Conrad's dynamite novels are set in 1880s London and concern the same constellation of issues regarding gender, terrorism, and individual liberty within modern economic and political systems. As with other crime narratives that I discuss in this project, female criminality plays a central role in their investigations of these issues. James and Conrad imagine the impulse to "terrorize"—to threaten the destruction of civilization—in feminine terms, and present a feminized culture of consumerism as an anarchic force threatening civilization. In both novels, masculinity and femininity are central thematic concerns, and changing gender roles represent and convey broader changes in the organization of modern society.[2]

In this chapter, I explore the relationship among three seemingly distinct facets of late-Victorian society that both James and Conrad link to the proliferation of political terrorism in London: the rise of first-wave feminism, the social-scientific theorization of masculine degeneracy, and the emergence of late-capitalist consumer culture.[3] Both novels insist on the interrelation of these issues, and make a case for such an interrelation by means of a shared literary premise: the fictionalization of failed historical attempts at political violence, mounted by radical political groups in late-Victorian London. Given all of the successful terrorist attacks undertaken in 1880s London, such as the dynamiting of two underground railways in October 1883, the 1884 bombings of Victoria Station in February and Scotland Yard in May, or the near-simultaneous attacks on the House of Commons, Westminster Hall, and the Tower of London on 24 January 1885, it is surprising that the two most canonical literary representations of late-Victorian terror should use futile attempts at political violence as their climactic, or anticlimactic, events. According to an 1894 report in London's *Strand Magazine,* without counting "minor explosions," there were eighty-six "important dynamitic efforts" in Britain between 1881 (the year of the first such attack, which occurred in Salford on 14 January) and 1892, in addition to a number of assassinations ("Dynamite" 120).[4] Rather than documenting how terrorism had traumatized the national psyche during the final decades of the nineteenth century, however, James and Conrad depict societies seemingly impervious to it.

If terrorism is defined as a strategy of desperation on the part of an individual, or small minority of individuals, to produce an effect upon otherwise untouchable structures of power, then these narratives—depicting *failed* terror—seem to question all individual efficacy in the face of monolithic institutions. On the surface, this seems an odd conclusion for Conrad and James to reach, since they lived in a society so frequently disrupted by terror. The late-nineteenth-century rise in weapons of mass destruction such as dynamite would appear to make lone individuals *more* capable of influence through large-scale violence: certainly, many radical revolutionists of the time imagined this to be the case.[5] Instead, Conrad and James use terrorist acts to symbolize the negligible power individuals actually have to effect social change in the modern world: to wreak destruction may be possible, they suggest, but to modify social conditions is not. In the period of Britain's history with which James and Conrad are concerned, the consolidation of consumer capitalism and the expansion of legal interventionism provide a context for such a reading. Lauren Goodlad has argued that John Stuart Mill, for example, came in his later work "increasingly to believe that the diminished power of individuals was an inevitable product of modern historical conditions" (224); James and Conrad likewise represent, through the vocabulary of masculine degeneration, diminished individual freedom in the face of late-capitalist consumerism and newly consolidated state control over individuals.

In a political and cultural climate steeped in the language and ideals of personal liberty, James and Conrad attempt to delineate this historical condition in individual rather than systemic terms; they imagine the individual's new relation to economic and political structures in the terms provided by late-Victorian gender discourse. Theories of gender gave them a model for conceptualizing the modern individual's complex relationship to power. Terrorism functions in both novels as a metaphor for individual efficacy within a dauntingly complex and crowded society, but gender comes to symbolize one's access to power within that society. The two novels are deeply interested in the significance of contemporary controversies surrounding gender and sex roles, such as the scientific theorization of degenerative masculinity, the rise of first-wave feminism, and the perceived feminization of public culture via the expansion of consumerism. By interlacing topics central to these gender debates with narratives of failed terror, I argue, James and Conrad pinpoint the particular use-value of gender ideology in the political imaginary at this time.

In other words, both novels show that the reassessment of conventional Victorian gender ideology in the last two decades of the nineteenth century was a central component in the way that the new political and economic conditions of modern society were imagined and understood. Categories of masculinity and femininity were useful metaphors to make sense of the individual's changing relation to power, and gender roles function in these novels to signify an emerging conception of the individual within the modern nation-state. James and Conrad suggest that the prototypically modern subject—hemmed in by over-civilization—inhabits a feminine role of pliant consumption. Conventional anxiety about degenerative masculinity thus functions, in these texts, to convey individual powerlessness within apparently monolithic structures of power. As we have seen in other texts, however, female criminals in crime fiction of this period are not so easily relegated to pliant or disciplined symbolic roles. While the novels' male characters are tragically relegated to positions of "feminine" submission, the female characters are subversively criminal, modeling the peculiarly feminine and necessarily consumerist means by which agency is enacted in modern society.

James's and Conrad's means of representing terror strikes a dissonant note in the context of late-nineteenth-century dynamite fiction. Far more common were narratives that exploited fear of terrorist attacks for sensational effect, emphasizing the fragility rather than the imperviousness of the social order. In Grant Allen's 1894 story "The Dynamiter's Sweetheart," for example, a young American woman in Paris, Essie, falls in love with a fiery, hypermasculine, daredevil revolutionist who attempts a terrorist explosion. Allen sets the story in France rather than Britain, but presents a vast underworld of organized terrorists across Europe. The group is advanced and proficient beyond Essie's imagination: "Her simple little New England mind could not grasp the full awesomeness of Continental Anarchy" (146). Clearly, for English readers, the prospect of such a sophisticated movement only a channel away would be unsettling. A whole subgenre of fiction organized around a similar economy of fear and sensation emerged in England in the 1880s, and remained popular in the decades prior to World War I. It was not uncommon for such narratives to depict foiled acts of terror, as James and Conrad do; dynamite, bombs, and "infernal machines" were, after all, quite unreliable technology. *The Princess* and *The Secret Agent* are nevertheless unusual, however, in the extreme ineffectiveness that plagues their radical groups. In these novels, radical inefficacy actually becomes a source of terror in itself. James and Conrad were obviously influenced by Robert Louis and Fanny Van de Grift Stevenson's immensely popular 1885 burlesque of the dynamite genre, *The Dynamiter,* which I discuss in the next chapter, but *The Princess*'s and *The Secret Agent*'s elements of generic parody serve a much different function.[6] Both novels clearly evoke the dynamite genre, and both authors' letters indicate that they hoped the novels would be popular, but their focus on inept terrorists and unthreatening political crime make them uniquely skeptical participants in this popular fictional discourse.[7]

James gleaned the idea for the plot of *The Princess Casamassima* from an 1884 conspiracy to assassinate the German emperor during a state visit to England, a plan that fell apart when a key collaborator withdrew.[8] This collaborator became the inspiration for Hyacinth Robinson, James's protagonist, who ends the novel by killing himself with the gun intended for the assassination. Similarly, Conrad's novel is based on Martial Bourdin's abortive and self-destructive endeavor to blow up the Greenwich Observatory in 1894 (though *The Secret Agent* is set in 1886). In Conrad's

FIG. 2.—"BABY'S BOTTLE?"   FIG. 3.—EXPLOSIVE COAL.

Fig. 26. From "Dynamite and Dynamiters" (120)

novel, the bomber's brother-in-law is the agent provocateur of an anonymous Eastern European embassy with a mandate to scare Britain into undercutting civil liberties in favor of stricter legislation against political radicalism.[9] (Under the Extradition Act of 1870, Britain had extended a liberal policy of asylum toward political criminals, much to the annoyance of other European governments.) *The Secret Agent* is thus doubly skeptical of the putative threat implied by the idea of "terrorism": not only is the attack bungled, so the only casualty is the bomber himself, but an official state government actually authorizes the undertaking.[10] Conrad undercuts conventional depictions of terror as an individual, rather than governmental or collective, category of crime. Moreover, both Conrad and James challenge the central message at the heart of contemporary accounts of terror: that terrorism should be a persistent source of fear, cementing the appeal of state protectionism.

An 1894 article in the *Strand* called "Dynamite and Dynamiters" is typical of the discourse surrounding terror from which James and Conrad depart. This piece is the first in a series called "Crime and Criminals," which provided readers with documentary reports about various kinds of crime. The author warns of the dangers of "dynamiters" and catalogs, James Bond style, various weapons and devices a terrorist might use. A total of twenty-six photographs accompany the article, so readers can visualize the effects of terrorism as well as the "infernal devices" themselves. Most of the weapons appear eerily innocuous: one bomb, for example, is disguised as a baby bottle (figure 26). Some of the images depict

FIG. 21.—EXPLOSION AT SCOTLAND YARD.

Fig. 27. From "Dynamite and Dynamiters" (130)

contraptions used in notorious bombings, or pistols from infamous assassinations; others portray the damage incurred in various attacks, such as the 1884 bombing of Scotland Yard (figure 27) or the 1885 bombing of the Tower of London (figure 28). Citing Colonel Majendie, chief inspector of explosives, the article describes how state authorities combat and defuse terrorist threats, but insists that the public at large needs to be more aware of how bombings are accomplished in order to prevent them. The article presents terrorism as an imminent, persistent danger, and focuses on how dynamite technology allows a lone individual to create the kind of mass destruction previously limited to government militaries: "it is only by becoming on a more familiar footing with the manners and customs of those enterprising individuals who seek to shatter anything between our nerves and our residences, either by relieving us of our purse or planting a dangerous species of explosive at our front doors, that we are the better able to take care of ourselves, our relatives, and our belongings" (119). These terrorists are free agents—"enterpris-

FIG. 24.—EXPLOSION AT TOWER OF LONDON—THE BANQUETING HALL.

Fig. 28. From "Dynamite and Dynamiters" (131)

ing individuals"—whose motivations are comparable to a purse thief. The article also suggests that terrorists are frightening and unpredictable in their choice of targets. Any harmless citizen may, for example, become the victim of a dynamiter with an explosive cigar:

> A gentleman who has no great love for you, and who fully appreciates the weakness of human nature of the male persuasion in seldom refusing a cigar, offers you one out of his case:—
>
> "Something very choice, sir, I assure you," he says. He is a perfect stranger to you, but—well, a cigar's a cigar, and you accept the kind offer. The benevolent cigar proprietor sees you light up, and you puff away in peace. He is suddenly called away. The cigar explodes! (121–22)

In this account, dynamiters are savvy, pervasive, independent, and utterly volatile, a depiction that stands in sharp contrast to the terrorists of *The Princess* and *The Secret Agent,* who are confused, incompetent, and altogether less scary. Unlike the article in the *Strand,* and unlike the bulk of dynamite fiction, a reader is not likely to emerge from these novels fearing imminent, indeterminate danger from terrorists. In Conrad's depiction of his bomber's target, for example, he emphasizes the hopelessness of the terrorist enterprise rather than its menace; the Greenwich Observatory represents that which is most indifferent to human intervention: time, astronomy, and the inexorable laws of nature.

James's and Conrad's departure from their contemporaries, in focusing on abortive attempts to engender terror and on the unfeasibility of the terrorist enterprise, perhaps accounts for another remarkable similarity between the two novels: both sidestep the topic of Ireland and Home Rule. This is a striking omission, as Barbara Melchiori and Eileen Sypher also discuss, considering that Fenians committed nearly all of the terrorist acts in late-Victorian Britain.[11] Avoiding the "Irish question" altogether, James and Conrad make their terrorists anarchists, socialists, and nihilists, a surprising choice considering that these groups produced very little "terror" in Britain, and since neither novel has a sincere interest in exploring these political philosophies. Indeed, James's slippage between the terms *anarchism, nihilism,* and *socialism* suggests a confusion on the part of the characters—or, some would say, the author—about their motivating ideology.[12] Conrad's novel, meanwhile, features a militant group "open to all shades of revolutionary opinion" (62), but if its members operate from various ideological perspectives, they share a tendency toward inconsistency of belief. James's and Conrad's neglect of Irish nationalism and their disengagement from radical political discourse powerfully inflect a key theme that the two novels share: masculine degeneration. Rather than representing terrorism's failure as reassurance of Britain's prowess in exterminating political crime or in defusing radical political ideas, the novels instead render abortive terror as symptomatic of a national crisis in masculinity. The attempts at political violence, sublimated in both novels into acts of self-destruction, signify nothing so much as the terrifying combustion of the individual masculine body.

Debates about a degeneration of masculinity surfaced in scientific and cultural discourse in the 1880s and persisted at least until World War I.[13] These debates were informed by a widespread public sense, during the period in which James and Conrad were writing, of Britain's imperial and economic weakening after a century in which it had been the most powerful nation in the world. In an 1885 letter to Grace Norton, James wrote of his adopted homeland, "the 'decline,' in a word, of old England, go[es] to my heart," and imagined that he would be alive to see "this great precarious, artificial empire . . . expended, struggling with forces which, perhaps, in the long run will prove too many for it" (*Letters* 67). James's and Conrad's contemporaries often attributed Britain's national decline to a host of concerns about gender, as Elaine Showalter has discussed, focusing on a fear that British men were becoming degenerate and effeminate while British women were becoming deviant and masculine. In 1904, alarmed by more than a decade of disproportionately unfit military recruits, the British government formed the Inter-Departmental Committee on Physical Deterioration to address the perceived crisis in masculinity. The Boy Scouts is one enduring legacy of this cultural moment.

Critics have uncovered a fixation on the degenerate masculine body and on eroding masculinity in a number of late-Victorian genres, including aestheticism, decadence, and New Woman fiction. The colonialist adventure stories of authors like Conrad, Rider Haggard, Rudyard Kipling, and Robert Louis Stevenson have likewise been read as a "male romance" genre depicting the regeneration of English masculinity in the invigorating lawlessness of the colonial frontier.[14] Amid this cultural context, the diminished agency of the male revolutionaries in James's and Conrad's novels is particularly evocative: each has a cast of enervated and ineffectual male radicals whose representation is steeped in the language of degeneration. The revolutionists are threatening not because of their action, but because of their inability to act; the menace that they represent is not one of anarchic violence, but submissive debility. As imagined by James and Conrad, feminine—rather than masculine—qualities constitute the heart of the terrorists' physical corruption; both novels use the rhetoric of gender, body, and sexuality to describe a condition of political inaction and paralysis.

The Princess's revolutionaries are notably passive and sedentary. They are, as a contemporary critic wrote in the *Athenaeum,* "a set of people who . . . had not among them so much purpose as would be required to drown a kitten" (Hayes 175). Their regular meetings at the Sun and Moon pub have "plenty of palaver," but never any action (280). Predictably, James imagines their "palaver" as rubbish: "there were nights when a blast of imbecility seemed to blow over the place, and one felt ashamed to be associated with so much insistent ignorance and flat-faced vanity" (280). Regenia Gagnier has argued that James's working-class characters in *The Princess* tend to "grotesque stereotyping" (*Subjectivities* 112) and "objectification" (114), but in a sense his characterization goes beyond stereotyping to create an altogether new form of deprecation. It is customary to depict proletarian rhetoric against the establishment as "ignorant" or "flat-faced," but James more unusually depicts the meetings as entirely lacking in active, physical menace. This is not Edmund Burke's rough, brutish mob; this is a group with bodily as well as mental inertia. Even amid what James calls "the deep perpetual groan of London misery," which "seemed to swell and swell and form the whole undertone of life" (283), the talk at the Sun and Moon remains "loud, contradictory, vain, unpractical babble" (291). Hyacinth, the novel's protagonist, begins to feel that the "blundering, divided counsels he had been listening to only made the helplessness of every one concerned more abject" (293). The emasculation of this "helpless" group is obvious when one member compares his comrades to "a collection of pettifogging old women" (291); at another point, the narrator describes one participant as a closet hairdresser with a "high, lustrous curl" atop his head (290), and continual references to the group members' "vanity" (280, 291) associate them with a characteristically feminine weakness.

James also associates Hyacinth, initially an enthusiastic advocate of these meetings, with effeminacy and masculine degeneracy. Hyacinth believes, following conventional scientific wisdom, that his "natural portion" is "an inherited disposition to crime" (371), handed down from his mother who murdered his father. He is referred to as "a thin-skinned, morbid, mooning little beggar, with a good deal of imagination and not much perseverance" (72). The term "morbid" connotes possession of a corrupt physical trait, and if Hyacinth lacks "perseverance," he lacks one of the most valued characteristics of Victorian masculinity. Hyacinth's physicality, as Wendy Graham also discusses, matches the androgynous quality of his name: James writes, "he had never got his growth. . . . His bones were small, his chest was narrow . . . his whole figure almost child-ishly slight" (104). As a child, early in the novel, he is "exceedingly diminutive," and his "features were smooth and pretty; his head was set upon a slim little neck" (62–63).[15]

The men of *The Secret Agent* are also physiologically inferior, and in describing them, Conrad makes overt reference to scientific theories of degeneracy. Stevie, would-be bomber of the Greenwich Observatory, is practically a poster child for degeneration. Son of an alcoholic and brother of a murderess, he has a "vacant droop of his lower lip" (49), and his address is sewn inside his coat so he won't get lost. The novel presents Stevie's debility, as well as his sister Winnie's tendency toward criminal-ity, as metaphorical assaults on patriarchy and male authority: Stevie's abusive father was "a man wounded in his paternal pride . . . since one of his kids was a 'slobbering idjut and the other a wicked she-devil'" (220). Degenerative masculinity and unruly femininity are here corre-lated with the failure and breakdown of paternal rule over the home—a salient topic of the day, in the context of debates about interventionist legislation and the sanctity of domestic patriarchy. Though his sister and mother describe Stevie with euphemisms such as "delicate" or "queer," Alexander Ossipon explicitly associates him with the theories of Cesare Lombroso: "Very good type, too . . . of that sort of degenerate. It's good enough to glance at the lobes of his ears. If you read Lombroso" (77). Ossipon functions as *The Secret Agent*'s parody of scientific socialists such as the eugenicist Karl Pearson. An ex-medical student who goes by the nickname of "the Doctor," he is a disciple of Lombroso who has au-thored a "popular quasi-medical study . . . entitled *The Corroding Vices of the Middle Classes*" (77). He is ironically described, however, as "cast in the rough mould of the Negro type" (75). Degeneracy, as I discuss in chapter 1, was thought to manifest in atavistic, "primitive" features—in other words, features similar to non-European races. The narrator's de-scription thus implicates "the Doctor" in the same racist system of typol-ogy that he projects onto others.[16]

The novel's other revolutionists are as inconsistent as Ossipon and even less effectual than Stevie. Michaelis, a Marxist materialist, finds so much comfort in the inevitability of the historical dialectic that he feels no need to act in the revolutionary cause: "he saw already the end of all private property coming along logically, unavoidably" (74). Consequently, he has no qualms about living fat off the patronage of a wealthy aristocratic woman. His ineffectiveness as a "voice" against capitalism is implied by his dampened speech: he has "a voice that wheezed as if deadened and oppressed by the layer of fat on his chest" (73). Karl Yundt, another anticapitalist rhetorician, is similarly ineffectual. Though he self-identifies as a "terrorist," he is ironically afflicted with gout, the disease of wealthy decadence (74). Like an aristocrat, he enjoys a leisured existence: "The famous terrorist had never in his life raised personally as much as his little finger against the social edifice" (78). The Professor, an associate of the group who makes bombs, is likewise weak and sickly. He serves as the novel's mouthpiece for Nietzschean individualism, but is apparently no Übermensch: "The lamentable inferiority of the whole physique was made ludicrous by the supremely self-confident bearing of the individual" (88).

Meanwhile, the novel's titular secret *agent,* Adolph Verloc, shows no penchant for agency: he has "an air of having wallowed, fully dressed, all day on an unmade bed" (46), and holds a "philosophical unbelief in the effectiveness of every human effort" (52). The narrator refers to Verloc as "burly in a fat-pig style" (52), and here, as in *Heart of Darkness,* Conrad uses obesity to signify a repudiation of the militaristic restraint with which he had lived during his years at sea. Conrad typically depicts such discipline and efficiency as the hallmark of masculine productivity; thus the narrator's denunciation of the anarchists' obese and lethargic bodies illustrates the distinctively physiological way that the novel conceptualizes and represents male dissipation. In both novels, the failings of the men are identified as failings in their bodily productivity and physiology.[17]

This focus on the degenerate male body extends to the novels' depiction of male sexuality: the men cannot produce, nor can they reproduce. Throughout *The Princess,* Hyacinth's desultory attempts at sexual intimacy prevent him from cementing his masculinity through heterosexual conquest. He pursues two women from vastly different backgrounds, but in the end, both reject him for another man. Hyacinth explicitly links his sexual unproductiveness to what he sees as a biological defect—his criminal inheritance: "He would never marry at all—to that his mind was absolutely made up; he would never hand on to another . . . the inheritance which had darkened the whole threshold of his manhood" (105). His only "bedroom scene" involving a woman occurs at the novel's conclusion, when the Princess finds him in bed, dead, with a pistol: "she flung herself beside the bed, upon her knees. Hyacinth lay there as if he were asleep, but there was a horrible thing, a mess of blood, on the bed, in his side, in his heart. His arm hung limp beside him, downwards" (590). The sexualized quality of this suicidal tableau suggests a latent morbidity in Hyacinth's sexual makeup.

Earlier in the novel, Hyacinth has a different kind of "bedroom scene" that parodies a ceremony of marriage, but rather than making his vow to a wife, he pledges himself to the great socialist leader Hoffendahl.[18] The scene provides a brief glimpse into the revolutionary organization, which is structured around a patriarchal hierarchy, excluding women to maintain a homoerotic dynamic and a male familial bond. Hyacinth compares his oath, for example, to the "vow of blind obedience" taken by "the Jesuit fathers . . . to the head of their order" (333). As Deborah Esch also points out, Hyacinth's bedroom vow to Hoffendahl closely resembles a man-to-man wedding ritual. Calling the ceremony "the most important event of his life," Hyacinth says, "I pledged myself, by everything that is sacred . . . I took a vow—a tremendous, terrible vow—in the presence of four witnesses" (327). He calls Hoffendahl "the very remarkable individual with whom I entered into that engagement" (329). When the Princess asks about the nature of his vow, Hyacinth says, "I gave my life away" (327); Hoffendahl "will require my poor little carcass" (329). The ceremony thus celebrates Hyacinth's yielding of his body to another man, parodying the origin of the wedding ritual—the passing of the woman's body from the father to the husband—and creating a nonprocreative union. During the ceremony, three men witness the vow, including Hyacinth's surrogate father Poupin.

In *The Secret Agent,* persistent motifs of masturbation and pornography likewise underscore the novel's emphasis on what was at the time considered male sexual perversion.[19] The anarchists of *The Secret Agent* meet in the back room of Verloc's pornography shop and are frequently associated with the sexual perversion of nonprocreative autoeroticism: the Professor, for example, wanders the streets of London like a masturbatory suicide bomber, "keeping his hand in the left pocket of his trousers, grasping lightly the indiarubber ball" that will detonate the bomb he keeps on his person (102). Onanism is imagined here as not only nonprocreative, but downright destructive.[20] The Professor's "frenzied puritanism of ambition" (102) is sublimated through the stroking of his "detonator," which resembles "a slender brown worm" (91). Similarly, the narrator links Yundt's unproductiveness as a terrorist to his sexual inadequacies: he is characterized by a "worn-out passion, resembling in its impotent fierceness the excitement of a senile sensualist" (74). None of the men in the novel has any children. By focusing on the non-reproductive sexuality of the anarchists, Conrad emphasizes the dissipated morbidity of their bodies. In both novels, male sexual fruitlessness explicitly parallels male terrorist fruitlessness.

SEXUAL TERROR: ANARCHIC
FEMALE CRIMINALITY

In James's and Conrad's portrayal of impotent and unproductive male terrorists, we can recognize a broader shift in the cultural understanding of criminal deviance. Martin Weiner, among others, has outlined this development: the focus of social anxiety about deviant behavior, he claims, underwent a sea-change at the end of the Victorian period, wherein "fears of a dam-bursting anarchy began to be replaced by opposing fears of a disabled society of ineffectual, devitalized, and overcontrolled individuals molded by environmental and biological forces beyond their control" (12). *The Princess* and *The Secret Agent* develop this new concept of social deviance in their treatment of masculinity, and both novels attribute such "overcontrolled" individuals to a political, social, and economic organization that has become too large, too complex, or too sophisticated to register the existence or resistance of the individual actor. I would also argue, however, that this new understanding of criminality is really only apparent in the novels' *male* criminals. Like other authors from this period, James and Conrad draw on an alternative conception of social menace in their portrayal of female deviance, which indeed constitutes a potential "dam-bursting anarchy" in the texts. The incapacity of the novels' men is set against the violent energy of the women, so that although James and Conrad depict male criminals as effeminate to indicate their paralyzed political agency, the female characters simultaneously challenge this association of femininity and inaction.

The precipitating event of *The Princess*'s plot, for example, is when Hyacinth's mother murders his father, while the climactic action of *The Secret Agent*'s plot is when Winnie Verloc murders her husband. These two emblematic scenarios are both stabbings committed with long knives and are both crimes of passion (unlike most murders by real Victorian women, which were typically premeditated, according to Judith Knelman and Lucia Zedner). Both murders result, too, from a denial of agency on the part of the male victim. Lord Frederick disputes that he is Hyacinth's father, abjuring his sexual agency or potency.[21] Similarly, Verloc disavows his responsibility for Stevie's death, imagining himself a passive player in a chain of causation beyond anyone's foresight or control: he "accepted the blow in the spirit of a convinced fatalist. The position was gone through no one's fault really. A small, tiny fact had done it. It was like slipping on a bit of orange peel in the dark and breaking your leg" (215). The novels thus share, at their narrative cores, men who deny their own capacity for productive or effective action, and are consequently killed by murderous women brandishing phallic knives. Enervated masculinity and female criminality don't just coexist in these novels, but mutually constitute one another.

The Princess's central concern with female criminality is apparent from its opening scene, when Mrs. Bowerbank, warden of the Millbank women's prison, visits Amanda Pynsent ("Pinnie"), the guardian of young Hyacinth. Millbank is the prison where Hyacinth's mother is serving her sentence for the murder of Lord Frederick, and Bowerbank visits to ask if Florentine Vivier, now on her deathbed, can see her son before she dies. This opening scene provides readers with a synopsis of the crime at the heart of Hyacinth's existential dilemma: as Bowerbank describes it, "nothing was proved except that she stabbed his lordship in the back with a very long knife, that he died of the blow, and that she got the full sentence" (57). In many ways, Florentine's murder of Lord Frederick resembles a revolutionary political assassination. The murderer is lower class and French, while the victim is an aristocrat; besides the obvious allusion to the Revolutions of 1789 and 1848, as well as the 1871 Paris Commune, France remained a hotbed of radical activity at the time The Princess was published.[22] We learn, too, that Florentine's father, whom Hyacinth is named after, was himself an ardent French radical. Florentine's method of killing Lord Frederick—stabbing him in the back with a very long knife—is likewise reminiscent of a stealthy assassination rather than the impassioned intimacy of a face-to-face impulse. The novel thus begins with a successful assassination by a woman, and ends, in contrast, with Hyacinth's suicidal desertion of his own mission to assassinate the duke. James depicts Hyacinth's decision as a rejection of his maternal "criminal inheritance," but the link between gender and politics at the heart of the narrative is nevertheless explicit in this juxtaposition: of the two contrasting assassinations that bookend the novel, the one that is accomplished is feminine and subversive, while the aborted attack is degenerately masculine.

Against the backdrop of Florentine's crime, the beginning of *The Princess* presents other images of criminalized women, and even harmless Pinnie begins to imagine herself an offender in the presence of the prison warden. Pinnie sees Bowerbank as "an emissary of the law" (58), and during her visit Pinnie is "unable to rid herself of the impression that . . . somehow the arm of the law . . . was stretched out to touch her" (59). Bowerbank is described as a "big, square-faced, deep-voiced lady who took up, as it were, all that side of the room" (61), and as "a high-shouldered, towering woman, [who] suggested squareness as well as a pervasion of the upper air" (55). Representing, in Pinnie's mind, a vast, undivided system of law and imprisonment—"square" in its unaccommodating indifference—Bowerbank intimidates her listener: Pinnie "felt herself to be, in an alarming degree, in the eye of the law; for who could be more closely connected with the administration of justice than a female turnkey, especially so big and majestic a one?" (56). After Bowerbank's visit, Pinnie describes to her neighbor Mr. Vetch how she came to adopt Hyacinth, and "defended herself as earnestly as if her inconsistency had been of a criminal cast" (71).

Pinnie's rigorous internalization of her society's legal institutions may make her the paradigmatic Foucauldian subject, as Mark Seltzer has argued, but Seltzer does not account for the fact that in this novel, Pinnie's sense of her own criminality is inseparable from her gender. The book's initial chapters present a peculiarly feminized scenario of social order, enforced by Bowerbank (particularly remarkable since female prison wardens didn't even exist in Britain at the time in which the novel is set), internalized by Pinnie, with Florentine as the disciplined violator.[23] Seltzer notes that Millbank Prison, where Bowerbank is a warden and Florentine a prisoner, was built according to Jeremy Bentham's panoptical scheme, and that James visited the prison in preparing to write the novel, but he neglects the significant fact that it is a woman's prison. James presents the modern "justice" system as quite conspicuously feminine: maternal in its control over the person—Bowerbank, unsurprisingly, has seven children of her own (55)—and feminizing in the submission it induces in Pinnie and in the confinement it confers on Florentine. Social order is maintained, the novel suggests, through systematic effeminization at every level of organization, and femininity functions here as a metaphor for the kind of individuality demanded by modern social systems and highly structured "maternalistic" bureaucratic institutions. Just as we saw in the Sherlock Holmes stories, new social controls in modern society are depicted as emblematic of women's increasing public power.

Pinnie's fantasies of criminal culpability are soon literalized in a stay (however short) at the women's prison, for she and Hyacinth do ultimately visit Florentine at Millbank, and the symbolic value of this institution looms large in the novel. In a narrative focused on a group of male revolutionaries plotting a political crime, it is striking that the only actual prisoners are female, reinforcing the novel's depiction of antisocial agency as feminine, but also portraying incarceration as an inherently feminine condition. The trip to the prison aggravates Pinnie's internal sense of perpetual wrongdoing, and she has "no confidence that once she passed through the door of the prison she should ever be restored to liberty and her customers" (78). Strangely enough, however, the female criminals inhabiting the prison seem to be hardly women at all. They are "dreadful figures, scarcely female . . . of lumpish aspect" (82). Pinnie remembers Florentine Vivier as the lively woman that her name suggests, "pretty" and "her idea of personal . . . brilliancy," but now "there was no beauty left in the hollow, bloodless mask that presented itself. . . . She looked unnatural. . . . Above all she seemed disfigured and ugly, cruelly misrepresented by her coarse cap and short, rough hair" (84).[24] That *The Princess* presents female prisoners as unwomanly may seem to contradict the assertion that the novel depicts imprisonment as inherently feminine, but the androgyny of the female prisoners suggests here that they have lost their identity or personhood through institutionalization; they are now merely "lumpish" with faces like "masks." James describes an exhaustion of identity within modern institutions, and uses femininity to indicate the pliancy, confinement, and submission that institutionalization entails.

In a novel riddled with women criminals, beginning with a dramatic scene in a women's prison, *The Princess*'s title character is nevertheless its most subtly worked-out study in female transgression, and she is a far more effective antisocial force than the women of Millbank. Few critics have remarked how odd it is that James named the book after the Princess Casamassima, formerly Christina Light of his 1875 novel *Roderick Hudson*. In the novel that bears her name, she is completely absent from the first third of the text, and Hyacinth remains the focus throughout. Possibly, James was influenced by Ouida's 1884 novel *Princess Napraxine*, which features an eponymous protagonist who closely resembles James's princess.[25] In any case, James's title plainly acknowledges the Princess Casamassima's symbolic import in his novel: a revolutionary and a would-be terrorist who yearns to destroy civilization, she is the heart of James's investigation into gender, modern subjectivity, and social order.

Through the course of the narrative, the Princess follows a trajectory of opinion that is opposite from that of Hyacinth and the other male characters in the book; as Hyacinth, Vetch, and even Paul Muniment become gradually reconciled to the status quo, the Princess's opinions become more and more militant.[26] In a novel about political radicalism, she is the most militant character: she divests herself of her wealth in the second half of the book, and toward the end, tries to usurp Hyacinth's mission to assassinate the duke.[27] Despite her profound revolutionary commitment, however, her male co-conspirators remain suspicious of her desperation to "go deep" in the movement. Even her lover Paul tells her: "I don't trust women—I don't trust women!" (456).[28]

The Princess's attempts to enter into the radical underworld are frustrated again and again in the course of the novel, primarily due to her sex. Her difficulty in becoming involved in the revolution led to her meeting Hyacinth in the first place. She calls him up to her box at the theater, she says, "to ascertain what really is going on; and for a woman everything of that sort is so difficult" (197). Despite all her attempts, however, the Princess is never really accepted into the revolution's inner ranks. After she donates much of her fortune to the cause, Paul tells her: "I should let you know that I *do* consider that in giving your money— or, rather, your husband's—to our business you gave the most valuable thing you had to contribute." The Princess asks: "You don't count then any devotion, any intelligence, that I may have placed at your service[?]" Paul responds: "You are not trusted at headquarters." "Not trusted! . . . I thought I could be hanged to-morrow!" "They may let you hang, perfectly, without letting you act" (579). The Princess's fervor to act for the cause is inhibited by the male revolutionaries, although none of them, ironically, can act on their own. At one point, inspired by Hyacinth's vow to Hoffendahl, the Princess asks: "Don't they also want, by chance, an obliging young woman?" Hyacinth replies: "I happen to know [Hoffendahl] doesn't think much of women. . . . He doesn't trust them" (329). Given the outcome of the novel, this statement is laden with dramatic irony: the Princess would have been a far more effective assassin than Hyacinth, as she herself is perfectly aware. As radical as the revolutionary brotherhood's opinions are about class, government, economics, and property, they see these as having nothing to do with women's interests. In contrast, the novel itself insists on the significance of gender in conceptualizing politics.

The Princess's interest in the cause began, in fact, as a way to escape the patriarchal hegemony that she also encounters among the revolutionists. Speaking of her marriage to Prince Casamassima, she tells Hy-acinth (as the narrator summarizes): "If he could have seen her life . . . the evolution of her opinions . . . would strike him as perfectly logical. She had been humiliated, outraged, tortured; she considered that she too was one of the numerous class who could be put on a tolerable footing only by a revolution" (250). Hyacinth gleans that her unhappy marriage had made her "modern and democratic and heretical" (251). Indeed, the root of the Princess's personal animosity toward the social order is not only the disparity between rich and poor—as with other members of the group—but the economic restrictions on women that forced her into a prostitutional marriage: "in the darkest hour of her life she sold herself for a title and a fortune" (259). The source of her revolutionary fervor is a deep reservoir of rage against the society in which she "had been mar-ried by her people, in a mercenary way, for the sake of a fortune and a title, and it had turned out as badly as her worst enemy could wish" (249). The Princess has become conscious of her objectification within a marriage that amounted to an economic exchange. Being objectified and prostituted in this way gives her common ground with socialist laborers who are subject to the instrumental logic of capitalism.

The Princess thus becomes involved in the revolutionary movement largely because she believes, in the tradition of Marxist feminism, that socialism alone has the capacity to improve the condition of women. She says to Paul: "Don't you consider that the changes you look for will be also for [women's] benefit? . . . If I didn't hope for that, I wouldn't do anything" (498). This was also the hope of late-Victorian feminists like Eleanor Marx, who thought socialism was more likely to meet feminist goals than the bourgeois women's movement of the day. If the Princess believes socialism will answer "the woman question," however, the male revolutionaries in her circle are much less interested in ameliorating sex-ist oppression. Paul tells her: "I don't think [the changes] will alter your position" (498); even his sister Rosy, he says, "will continue to be, like all the most amiable women, just a kind of ornament to life" (499). In-deed, Paul does not seem to believe sexist oppression exists at all; when the Princess says, "It's far better, of course, when one is a man," he re-sponds, "I don't know. Women do pretty well what they like" (451–52).[29]

Thwarted, the Princess attempts to build a homosocial, familial al-liance of her own with another female revolutionist. When she meets Lady Aurora Langrish, an aristocratic woman who also wants to level the class system, the two women immediately connect. Lady Aurora tells

Hyacinth: "If I were a man, I should be in love with her" (429), and the Princess says, "dear lady, we must make a little family together" (433). Lady Aurora responds to her advances, "indulging in the free gesture of laying her hand upon that of the Princess" (435), and soon the Princess is "always inhaling Lady Aurora's fragrance, always kissing her and holding her hand" (483). Some critics have interpreted the Princess's attraction to Lady Aurora as an example of her fickleness or whimsicality, as though she temporarily abandons the revolution to fraternize with Lady Aurora in the slums. I view this relationship instead as an extension of her revolutionary spirit. Denied a role in the "official" movement to bring down the social order, the Princess's antisocial rebellion begins to manifest in other arenas, including the sexual. The Princess and Aurora's sexually charged friendship suggests a connection between political and sexual dissidence, also apparent in the novel's male characters.[30] Both women are sexual threats within their society because of their unwillingness to fulfill "normal" sexual expectations. The Princess has abandoned her husband and developed the reputation of being "a bedizened jade" (207), whose "own husband has had to turn her out of the house" (204). Paul calls her "a monster" (227) who reels in unsuspecting, lower-class men and "swallows 'em down" (226). Lady Aurora also opts out of the sexual script. One of seven unmarried daughters born to a man with a title but little wealth, she has declassed herself: "I do as I like, though it has been rather a struggle. I have my liberty, and that is the greatest blessing in life, except the reputation of being queer, and even a little mad, which is a greater advantage still" (221). Hyacinth admires her, and believes she "was not a person to spare, wherever she could prick them, the institutions among which she had been brought up and against which she had violently reacted. . . . she appeared to have been driven to her present excesses by . . . the conservative influences of that upper-class British home" (222).

In depicting Lady Aurora and the Princess, James gestures toward lesbianism as an avenue of political and sexual rebellion, but ultimately retreats from this line of contention. The Princess's revolutionary deployment of her sexuality remains a key focus of the text, but shifts from same-sex desire to cross-class desire. Aurora and the Princess share a fascination for working-class men, and both women are attracted to Paul. For a while, nonetheless, their alliance is a success: they work in the slums together, and the "two ladies had liked each other more, almost, than they liked any one" (438). As Paul's relationship with the Princess develops, however, the union between the women fades. When Hyacinth goes to see Aurora near the end of the novel, each recognizes that "the Princess had . . . combined with [Paul] in that manner which made [Hyacinth's] heart sink and produced an effect exactly corresponding upon that of Lady Aurora" (540).

The Princess fails to establish a female familial revolutionary association structured according to homosocial bonds like that of the men, but she remains a sexual radical: Paul, not Lady Aurora, becomes the new object of her monstrous desires. Paul is far below the Princess in social rank, but their relationship is marked by a deployment of power on his part, enjoyed by the Princess in a way that can only be described as masochistic. When Paul speaks rudely to her, she "blushed on hearing these words, but not with shame or with pain; rather with the happy excitement of being spoken to in a manner so fresh and original" (449–50). She decides this "very different type of man appeared to have his thoughts fixed on anything but sweetness; she felt the liveliest hope that he would move further and further away from it" (450). The Princess encourages Paul's sadistic impulses—telling him, "you are the sort of man who ought to know how to use [women]" (453)—as a means, it seems, of gratifying masochistic desires.[31]

The Princess's masochism sexualizes her political efforts for the revolution, suggesting that her seemingly politically motivated degradation is actually pleasurable. When she gives up her large country house to move to a "mean and meagre and fourth-rate" section of London, Hyacinth believes she "wished to mortify the flesh" (417). Her new eating habits, devoid of past luxury, are also called "mortifications" (422). In pathologizing the Princess's sacrifices for the cause, the novel appears to dull the impact of her pleas for class equality and women's rights; but in the context of James's broader treatment of political agency, the Princess's complex relationship to power actually better suits her for revolutionary political action in the modern capitalist state. In divesting herself (and the royal family of the Prince) of inherited wealth, she is the only revolutionist in the novel who enacts positive action for political change—and it is clear that she is willing to sacrifice much more than money. She is of course much wealthier than most characters in the novel, but other socialists such as Paul and Hyacinth repeatedly say that if they had wealth, they would enjoy it rather than give it away. When Hyacinth receives a small inheritance from Pinnie and Vetch, he promptly splurges on a trip to the Continent, where his revolutionary opinions dissipate, replaced by passions for "culture," "art," and "civilization."

The Princess, thrilled by "mortification," is the only character in the novel who can resist such enticements. Embracing a nunlike dress and an austere mode of life, she appears to reject the consumerist spirit of the era. By continually emphasizing her "capriciousness," however, James also hints that the Princess's new asceticism is itself a manipulation of image for effect—a maneuver in perfect accord with a consumerist model of femininity. In a subtle way, James presents this maneuver as a model of political effectiveness: the Princess's powerless image paradoxically endows her with political power. Indeed, even her sexual "mortifications" indirectly promote her interest in destroying social hierarchies: in the context of her relationship with Paul, the Princess's masochism may be submissively feminine, but her "brutish" lover is still a chemist from Lancashire with a "vulgar nose," an alcoholic father, and a laundress mother. The Princess deploys her image and sexuality as assaults on a society she is bent on annihilating. Her pleasure in performing austerity, and in being submissive to those "below" her, threatens the foundations of power in her society, especially since she is still married to the Prince. Denied involvement in the revolutionary committee, she achieves complex subversive action in other arenas through indirect, seemingly mortifying means.

The Secret Agent follows a trajectory similar to *The Princess,* contrasting degenerate masculinity with female criminal agency, but closes less ambiguously in a sequence of violent deaths and an eruption of nauseous despair. In James's novel, the Princess models an indirect yet effective program of feminine rebellion in a climate of political paralysis; Conrad, however, aligns female criminality with forces of entropy and degeneration at work in modern civilization, the same currents that characterize the novel's depiction of modern economic and political institutions. Early in the novel, for example, Verloc goes to see Vladimir at the embassy and is ordered to commit an act of terrorism that will convince the British government to curtail civil liberty and crack down on political radicalism. This scenario is deeply ironic, not only because an official state government is waging the renegade crime of terrorism—as though civilization has turned in on itself and commenced eating its own tail—but also because the "radicals" in this text seem such unlikely representatives of individual liberty. Instead of personifying the freewheeling, reckless menace of the embassy's imagination, they resemble characters in ancient Greek tragedies, playing out a fate, moved and buffeted by forces they do not understand. In lieu of gods and divinities, modern bureaucracy and statecraft are the omnipotent yet careless and injudicious forces that control the characters' destinies. At the behest of the embassy,

Verloc essentially performs an impersonation of independent mutinous agency; this sets off a causal chain of events, involving many individuals, none of whom are aware of the complex institutional catalyst at the heart of his "act." Describing Verloc's encounter with Winnie after Stevie's death, the narrator asks: "How with his want of practice could he tell her what he himself felt but vaguely: that there are conspiracies of fatal destiny?" (216).[32]

Within this thick atmosphere of skepticism regarding individual liberty and agency, the novel is conversely haunted by the specters of female criminal agency and individual feminine betrayal, indivisible from its central concern with masculine inaction. During the scene in the embassy, for example, Vladimir reminds Verloc of his past failure as an "agent," when he succumbed to the swindle of a seductive female traitor: "The unlucky attachment—of your youth. She got hold of the money, and then sold you to the police—eh?" This memory still brings Verloc shame and humiliation: "The doleful change in Mr Verloc's physiognomy, the momentary drooping of his whole person, confessed that such was the regrettable case" (58). Verloc's career as a counterfeit "agent" has been threatened by feminine betrayal, foreshadowing the imminent sedition of his wife. The men in the novel are utterly implausible as embodiments of autonomous menace, yet female characters continually disrupt the novel's otherwise skeptical narrative of independent agency.

Moreover, masculine incapacity to act correlates directly with feminine mutiny: Verloc's betrayal at the hands of the woman traitor, for example, results in his imprisonment. James's novel made symbolic use of female imprisonment to emphasize the criminality of *The Princess*'s women, but Conrad instead depicts male incarceration, emphasizing how imprisonment debilitates and controls male subjects. Conrad's prisoners are former inmates now seemingly conditioned to social inaction and docility. Verloc, as he explains to Vladimir, received "[f]ive years' rigorous confinement in a fortress" as a result of the female traitor (57); here incarceration is a form of humiliating emasculation, since Verloc's punishment is inseparable from the woman who put him there. Near the end of the novel, after Stevie's death, Verloc actually looks forward to returning to custody: "A term of imprisonment could not be avoided. He did not wish now to avoid it. A prison was a place as safe from certain unlawful vengeances as the grave, with this advantage, that in prison there was room for hope" (214). Habituated to the emasculating protectionism of the prison, Verloc now views it as a place of safety and hope.

Conrad similarly links Michaelis's prison term to the erosion of his masculine agency: "He had come out of a highly hygienic prison round like a tub, with an enormous stomach and distended cheeks . . . as though for fifteen years the servants of an outraged society had made a point of stuffing him with fattening foods in a damp and lightless cellar. And ever since he had never managed to get his weight down as much as an ounce" (73). Michaelis ends his sentence not a "hardened" criminal, but softened, stuffed, and curvily effeminate. In Conrad's vision, the prison symbolizes an overly maternal, overly interventional society, and bears an eerie resemblance to Michaelis's vision of a utopian socialist future, spelled out in his *Autobiography of a Prisoner*. In fact, the novel explicitly links the hygienic prison of Michaelis's past with his dream of what the world would be like under socialism: the Professor says that Michaelis's book reveals "the idea of a world planned out like an immense and nice hospital, with gardens and flowers, in which the strong are to devote themselves to the nursing of the weak" (263). The Professor can barely contain his disgust at this proposition, suggesting that "extermination" is a fitter future for "the weak" (263).[33]

As the character most plainly associated with Marxist socialism, Michaelis's vision of a "hospital society" is Conrad's critique of a socialist political program that was gaining significant support in his time. *The Secret Agent* began serialization in October 1906, and the Labour Party, which coalesced out of a number of earlier socialist and labor union groups, had emerged in the January 1906 election as a serious political force, winning twenty-nine parliamentary seats. To many, the election appeared to portend the rise of thoroughgoing socialism in Britain.[34] Conrad's novel feminizes this political trend by associating it with stifling governmental maternalism. The novel's distaste for socialist governance also manifests itself in a persistent undercutting of some of the most "feminine" aspects of the socialist platform: public parks and public education, which made gardening and child-rearing the domain of the state. By 1906, "Garden Cities" and green space were all the rage in British urban planning, due to the influence of socialist thinkers such as William Morris and Raymond Unwin.[35] Parks are a regular motif in *The Secret Agent,* but Conrad emphasizes their railings and fences: Karl Yundt takes a daily walk near the "Green Park railings" (81); as Verloc walks to the embassy, he looks "through the park railings" and reflects, "all these people had to be protected" (51). Signifying the confinement of nature, parks resonate with the novel's maternalist vision of socialism. Public education was also a key cause for early socialists, and the Fabians in particular had made it their business to win seats on school boards, provide schoolchildren with a daily lunch, and otherwise ameliorate the vast educational gulf between the poor and the rich. Women socialists like Annie Besant were especially active in this area, but they ought not have bothered, Conrad's narrator insinuates, to provide literacy to the likes of Stevie: "Under our excellent system of compulsory education [Stevie] had learned to read and write, notwithstanding the unfavourable aspect of the lower lip" (49).

To suggest the imminence of such "maternalist" governance, *The Secret Agent* includes a political subplot involving imaginary socialist legislation. When the assistant commissioner visits Sir Ethelred, a prominent government official, Ethelred is busy, as his assistant Toodles says, with a "Bill for the Nationalization of Fisheries. They call it the beginning of social revolution. Of course, it is a revolutionary measure" (149). At a historical moment when a new political party was advocating the nationalization of industry and a host of new public services, Conrad's novel forecasts a dystopian socialist future: an overly controlled population, grown fat, lazy, and docile under rigid social planning and organization. Conrad employs the repellent imagery of femininity to weave this futuristic nightmare and to express the peril at the crux of his vision: interventionism, socialism, and the burgeoning welfare state, he suggests, entail the castration of the populace.

Conrad's novel orchestrates fear of the feminine in multiple ways. Male radicals have been mothered into inaction, but at the same time, women characters embody reckless impulsiveness rather than overcontrolled docility. Verloc's imprisonment is caused by a woman's betrayal, but in the case of his wife, his failed masculinity is also a *catalyst* for female criminality. Verloc's acute passivity and his incapacity as an agent bring about his violent death at the hands of Winnie. Her crime, like Florentine's "assassination" in *The Princess*, resembles the kind of seditious menace in which Verloc only pretends to engage. In the early nineteenth century, according to Knelman, a wife who murdered her husband would be charged with "petty treason"—worse than a murder charge—"because the obedience owed to a husband by his wife was similar to that owed to a king by his subject" (53). This law was obsolete by the 1880s, when the novel is set, but Conrad nonetheless invokes a flavor of regicide in the depiction of Verloc's murder by continually emphasizing Verloc's absolute authority over the family and the supremacy of his patriarchal rule. Stevie, as Winnie constantly reminds her husband, "just worships" him (178), with a "blind docility" and "blind devotion" that she has indoctrinated into her brother's mind (210). Indeed, the "submission and worship were so apparent that Mr Verloc" had developed "a great opinion of Stevie's loyalty" (211).

Verloc's relationship with his wife similarly resembles one of feudal fealty: "Mr Verloc loved his wife as a wife should be loved—that is, maritally, with the regard one has for one's chief possession" (174); Winnie, in return, "had a loyal respect for [her husband's] rights" (182). Conrad also compares Verloc to the king Odysseus and Winnie to his long-suffering wife, Penelope (176). Such continual reminders of Verloc's potent power in the home make the murder at the end of the story all the more mutinous. In the paragraph just before the stabbing, Conrad again recalls Verloc's powerful status in the marriage: "Mr Verloc was heard with an accent of marital authority. . . . 'Come here,' he said in a peculiar tone, which might have been the tone of brutality, but was intimately known to Mrs Verloc as the note of wooing. She started forward at once, as if she was still a loyal woman bound to that man by an unbroken contract" (234). The intermingling of brutality and sexuality here, alongside the "bound" language of feudalism, remind us that although the Verloc marriage is overlaid with sentimental domestic ideology, at its foundation is a rigid power differential. The novel's revolutionaries speak provocatively of their desire to bring down established hierarchies of power, but the only such "leveling" that occurs in the text is in the domestic—not political—sphere. Winnie unseats the ruler of her home, in sharp contrast to the novel's revolutionaries, who seem utterly incapable of deposing anyone, perhaps in part because they cannot identify a discrete figurehead in their society's complex distribution of power. Like James, Conrad underscores the irrelevancy and powerlessness of his political dissidents by setting them against a successful feminine act of domestic rebellion.

The murder scene itself accentuates this contrast, depicting a stark opposition between Winnie's active, murderous rage and Verloc's ineffectuality. Just as Florentine murdered Lord Frederick by stabbing him in the back, Winnie's attack is similarly nonconfrontational: "[Verloc] waited. Mrs Verloc was coming. . . . He was lying on his back and staring upwards. . . . The knife was . . . planted in his breast. It met no resistance on its way. . . . turning slightly on his side with the force of the blow, [Verloc] expired without stirring a limb, in the muttered sound of the word 'Don't' by way of protest" (234). Verloc's death registers the pathological flaccidity of his entire life: the softness of his chest, the ease with which the knife penetrates, and his lack of responsiveness suggest that his passivity is as central to the crime as Winnie's rage. Afterward, Winnie's "mental state was tinged by a sort of austere contempt for that man who had let himself be killed so easily. He had been the master of a house . . . now he was of no account in every respect" (237). Surprisingly active in its violence, Winnie's blow is "plunging" with "force" (234), though she is not depicted in the novel as a particularly strong or threatening woman. In contrast with the powerful physique of Mrs. Bowerbank, the prison warden in *The Princess,* Winnie is small with a "full, rounded form" (47). Her "full bust" and "broad hips" (46) characterize her as soft and hyperfeminine. Using gendered language to defamiliarize his depiction of crime and agency, Conrad's scenario challenges conventional understandings of individual strength, power, violence, and action.

THE NEW WOMAN CONSUMER: CAPITALISM AND CULTURAL DECLINE

That James and Conrad deploy images of degenerate masculinity and female criminality in narratives of unproductive political terror begs two key questions: Why do they find terrorism, and specifically failed terrorism, to be the battleground of masculinity, femininity, and gender? And why do they employ anticapitalist political dissidents as the figural agents of this message? I have already noted how extraordinary it is that the novels ignore Fenianism and Irish nationalism, which were so relevant to late-Victorian political crime. If relevancy was not their motive, James and Conrad might have chosen to take up a range of revolutionary ideas circulating in this period—including feminism—as the basis for their characters' political platform. Why do they both focus on anticapitalist dissidents? And how does this choice relate to the primacy of gender in each novel's depiction of politics and power?

To address these questions is to address another compelling similarity between the two novels: they depict a London dreadfully transformed according to the mandates of consumer capitalism. Conrad's novel is disparaging, to say the least, of Michaelis's vision of Marxist socialism, but like James, his novel acknowledges capitalism's failures. Both novels are set in "the depressed '80s," when poverty was rife amid a severe economic recession. James and Conrad show the government's inadequacy in addressing the grotesque inequality festering in London. As Winnie innocently asks her brother, "Don't you know what the police are for, Stevie? They are there so that them as have nothing shouldn't take anything away from them who have." "Not even if they were hungry?" "Not if they were ever so" (170). As representatives of governmental power, Winnie suggests, the police exist to enforce a brutally unequal distribution of property. Neither novel depicts socialism positively, but both acknowledge the hunger and poverty it seeks to redress.

The revolutionaries in both novels can agree on the evil of capitalism, but are nevertheless surrounded by and entrenched in a capitalist culture of consumption. A key character in *The Princess,* Millicent Henning, functions as a love interest for Hyacinth, but economically and culturally, she represents his adversary. Throughout the novel, despite his poverty, Hyacinth is continually associated with art and is said to have an innate sensitivity to aesthetic beauty. He exercises this instinct through his trade, bookbinding, in which James depicts him as something of a prodigy. A painstaking craftsman, Hyacinth symbolizes the value, authenticity, and "aura," in Benjaminian terms, of original creation, while Millicent is associated with cheap, homogenous, mass-produced goods. She is employed by one of the new department stores mushrooming in London's West End, where she works as a model for the store's premanufactured clothing: "she put on . . . articles to show them off to the customers, and on her person they appeared to such advantage that nothing she took up ever failed to go off" (96). Though Hyacinth "laughed [her] establishment to scorn, and told her there was nothing in it, from top to bottom, that a real artist would look at" (162), Millicent nonetheless brags to Hyacinth about her professional success: "You should see me work off an old jacket!" (112). Although her job evokes a traditional conception of the consumer marketplace as an arena in which feminine bodies are objectified, the novel also details her own love for "wandering through the streets of London and gazing into shop-windows" (95). Millicent, shop-commodity by day, is herself an enthusiastic consumer by night. James uses the choices she makes as a consumer, however, to exhibit an absence of discernment and taste among the segment of the market that she represents. Hyacinth calls the objects of her desire "the insipid productions of an age which had lost the sense of quality" (163). Thus James depicts the market for cheap, mass-produced goods as feminine in both its buyers and sellers.

Where does this woman-to-woman cycle of consumption leave the city's men? Hyacinth, as suggested by his diminutive appearance, is slowly being edged out of London's new consumer economy by Millicent and her ilk of modern, cheap, mass-produced, women-centered shops. From the beginning of the novel, Hyacinth is set in opposition to the consumer tide that Millicent embodies. In his childhood, Pinnie, who has a dressmaking shop of her own, was "perfectly determined he should never go into a small shop . . . giving change for a shilling across a counter" (118). Vetch, who "saw clearly that a charming handicraft was a finer thing than a vulgar 'business'" (119), instead helps him get a position with a respected bookbinding firm. Hyacinth becomes a master of his trade, but his trade itself is becoming obsolete. Rapid shifts in the publishing industry meant that most bookbinding was being done by machines, not men.[36] Hyacinth's artistry and livelihood are set to be displaced by the culture of inexpensive, mass-produced commodities favored by Millicent.

Because of her connection to this new feminized marketplace saturated with cheap goods, Millicent comes to represent a voracious, threatening, vulgar female appetite to consume. At one point in the novel, the narrator claims that her "sociability was certainly great, and so were her vanity, her grossness, her presumption, her appetite for beer, for buns, for entertainment of every kind. She represented, for Hyacinth, . . . the eternal feminine" (159). Here, "the eternal feminine" signifies not only the eternal urge to consume, but the eternal urge to consume indiscriminately. Hyacinth, the novel makes clear, will be a victim to this consumptive urge. Metaphors in which Millicent eats the protagonist abound in the novel. Pinnie regards her as a "ravening wolf" and Hyacinth as "an unspotted lamb" (95); she warns him early in the courtship, "I'm not ready to see you gobbled up before my eyes!" (155). At another point, Millicent declares, "I could swallow him at a single bite!" (99). Millicent is thus imagined as a genial yet monstrous figure. James's novel pays little attention to the economic stringencies that a London shopgirl like Millicent would have faced.[37] Instead, Hyacinth is the symbolic victim of her interminable, tasteless urge to consume.

At the end of the novel, James takes this economic allegory even further, hinting that Millicent is to blame for Hyacinth's death. Hyacinth's last action, before committing suicide, is to visit her at work. He fantasizes about escaping his oath via a romantic elopement: "a vision rose before him of a quick flight with her, for an undefined purpose, to an undefined spot . . . he might at least feel her arms around him" (584). After finding he has been beaten by his rival, however, Hyacinth leaves the shop without proposing such a flight: "She was exhibiting [an] article to the Captain, and he was lost in contemplation . . . his eyes travelling up and down the front of Millicent's person, he frowned, consideringly, and rubbed his lower lip slowly with his walking-stick. Millicent stood admirably still, and the back-view of the garment she displayed was magnificent" (585).[38] Hyacinth's unnarrated suicide takes place in the gap between this paragraph and the next; he is dead in his next appearance in the novel. James thus implies that Millicent's disloyalty drove him to suicide. Given her economic resonance in the novel, in this scene, Hyacinth is metaphorically made redundant by vulgar feminine consumerism.

Millicent's insatiable urge to consume is also an anarchic threat to civilization, as James indicates through constant references to her "primitive" revolutionary instincts. Millicent is not at all interested in socialist revolution, yet Hyacinth sees her as embodying its spirit, which he links with a kind of primitivism. He refers to "her primitive, half-childish, half-plebeian impulse of destruction, the instinct of pulling down what was above her, the reckless energy that would, precisely, make her so effective in revolutionary scenes" (268), "her primitive passions" (387), and the "primitive comfort" she affords (584).[39] To Hyacinth, she "summed up the sociable, humorous, ignorant chatter of the masses, their capacity for offensive and defensive passion, their instinctive perception of their strength on the day they should really exercise it" (160). Through such references, James links consumer culture and the feminization of public culture via consumerism to the destruction of civilization at the hands of "primitives." It is not the socialist militants who will topple history and tradition; vulgar, feminine consumerism is the barbarian at the gate. Capitalism does not represent the status quo, as the revolutionaries understand it, but turns out to be the very force that is destroying society. Millicent's association with consumption thus unalterably colors her association with revolution: "Hyacinth could easily see her (if there should ever be barricades in the streets of London), with a red cap of liberty on her head" (161). The cap would be purchased, no doubt, out of the window of the nearest shop.

Throughout *The Princess,* James depicts Millicent not as a unique or exceptional character, but a new urban "type" of femininity; she embodies a broader consumerist-feminist revolution occurring in the London streets. The narrator calls her "the genius of urban civilization" (93): "She was, to her blunt, expanded fingertips, a daughter of London, of the crowded streets and hustling traffic of the great city; she had drawn her health and strength from its dingy courts and foggy thoroughfares" (92–93). This link with the city suggests that Millicent represents the expansion of roles and opportunities that London offered women in this era. She is shamelessly comfortable in the city, believing herself to be "perfectly acquainted with the resources of the metropolis" (91), and "trot[s] about" alone, at night, on various errands (276). When Hyacinth "had said to her that the less a respectable young woman took the evening air alone the better for her respectability," she "remarked that if he would make her a present of a brougham, or even call for her three or four times a week in a cab, she would doubtless preserve more of her social purity" (276). Millicent knows that "street-walking" at night casts doubt on her "social purity," yet makes a convincing argument for rebelling against such strictures: as a working woman, she can't do errands during the day, yet can't afford the luxury of cabs in the evening.[40]

James's contemporary critics were remarkably interested in Millicent, discussing her at length in almost every review of the novel, and suggesting that she personified a recognizable shift in urban femininity. Many of the reviewers note her correspondence to a familiar new "type" of woman: the *Saturday Review* called her "a cockney *pur sang* . . . a capital study" (Hayes 183); the *Literary World* dubbed her "the most real character in the book . . . a delightful type of the blooming cockney girl" (Hayes 190); the *New York Times* identified her as "the type of the London girl. . . . Her physical structure is of the opulent kind, and her bodice hardly restrains her bouncing charms" (Hayes 179); and Annie Logan, writing in *The Nation,* commented that "the London shop-girl Millicent Henning—who, by the way, is typical—is perfect in her superabundant health and slang . . . and her hopeless, unconscious vulgarity" (Hayes 193).

The growing economic significance in London society of women like Millicent, and the shops that employed them, is signified not only by her continuous eating and drinking—as though she is ravenously gobbling up the city—but by her larger-than-life size. In contrast to Hyacinth's small bones and elfin stature, Millicent is sturdy and enormous. She has "large protrusive feet" (91), and Pinnie declares her "too tall for a woman" (92). Millicent is proud of her substantiality; she brags to Pinnie, "I enjoy beautiful 'ealth," and "spoke with a certain artless pride in her bigness and her bloom, and as if, to show her development, she would have taken off her jacket or let you feel her upper arm" (92). Her insatiable consumption puts a strain on Hyacinth's meager finances during their evenings together. On the first such outing, Hyacinth invites her to a coffeehouse, and her appetite on this occasion is characteristically voracious: she "partook profusely of tea and bread and butter, with a relish of raspberry jam, and thought the place most comfortable, though he himself, after finding himself ensconced, was visited by doubts as to its respectability, suggested, among other things, by photographs, on the walls, of young ladies in tights" (107). The coffee shop offers a public forum for female consumption, but is also feminized through its decor, which exhibits public, sexualized, and commodified images of the female body.

The Secret Agent likewise depicts a feminized modern culture of consumption, primarily through the representation of Verloc's pornography shop. Like Millicent's department store, and like the coffee shop described above, Verloc's shop trades in publicly visible commodified images of the female body: "The window contained photographs of more or less undressed dancing girls" (45). These are often sold by a woman, and the novel regularly repeats the image of Winnie Verloc behind the counter. Winnie is, in fact, Conrad's parodic version of a popular character of the day—the shopgirl—who had inundated contemporary novels and films and who signified, as with Millicent Henning, women's expanding public presence. According to Lise Shapiro Sanders, the shopgirl "embodied the very moment at which fantasy entered the process of consumer exchange: her vocation required that she mediate the desires of consumers on the other side of the counter," even "men who might desire the shopgirl herself as another type of merchandise" (1). Verloc's shop caters to male customers, and Conrad describes Winnie behind the counter in sexualized terms: "a young woman with a full bust, in a tight bodice, and with broad hips" (46); this links the pornographic images Winnie sells with the woman selling the images, as Brian Shaffer also points out. The narrator also calls attention to the "artistic arrangement of [Winnie's] glossy dark hair," implying that she herself is ready to become photographic "art," but notes "her full, rounded form" (47). Winnie is eroticized and glamorized like the "dancing girls" she sells, but Conrad emphasizes her fullness, roundness, and three-dimensionality, in contrast to the flat, two-dimensional women in the pictures.

Still, Winnie's customers are dismayed, not pleased, at encountering the flesh-and-blood version of the commodity they seek to buy: "the customer of comparatively tender years would get suddenly disconcerted at having to deal with a woman, and with rage in his heart would proffer a request for a bottle of marking ink, retail value sixpence (price in Verloc's shop one and sixpence), which, once outside, he would drop stealthily into the gutter" (46). The femininity in which the shop trades is flattened, commodified, and artificial: by contrasting the customer's reactions to two-dimensional pornographic images versus the real thing (Winnie), Conrad indicates that Verloc's customers are buying a fetishized femininity that is an invention of consumer capitalism. More-over, the passage depicts Winnie as a feminine intrusion into a form of commercial exchange—the buying and selling of pornography—that is customarily man-to-man. The unwelcome feminization of this particular area of commerce hints at the broader inroads women are making into male space.

The inflated cost of Verloc's ink accords with the novel's systematic account of consumer capitalism as an economy driven by imaginary value, disposability, and commodity fetishism. Like the young man in this scene, consumers in this novel do not so much patronize businesses as become "trapped" by them. Ossipon, for example, imagines Verloc's shop as a "police trap" (100), and an Italian restaurant visited by the assistant commissioner is similarly described as "one of those traps for the hungry . . . baited with a perspective of mirrors and white napery" (151). The reflective, blank surfaces of the restaurant suggest its insubstantiality, deceptiveness, and the false promise of its "bait." The commodity it serves is twice described as "fraudulent cookery" (151, 152), an inauthentic product, an imaginary sham.

The charade of capitalist value and the dehumanizing aspects of capitalist exchange are similarly apparent in the taxi ride the assistant commissioner takes to the Italian restaurant: "Tendering a coin through the trap door the fare slipped out and away, leaving an effect of uncanny, eccentric ghostliness upon the driver's mind" (151). Like the restaurant and like Verloc's shop, the taxi is described with the image of a "trap." The assistant commissioner metonymically becomes "the fare," and the driver barely registers the "ghostly" rider's humanity; the moment of "tendering" is anything but tender. The economic exchange in the taxi, like those in the shop and restaurant, is depicted as unreal and vaguely hostile. Walter Benjamin writes: "There are as many nuances of payment as there are nuances of lovemaking—lazy and swift, furtive or brutal. What does this signify? The shame-reddened wound on the body of society secretes money and closes up. It forms a metallic scab" (*Arcades* 492). Conrad's novel similarly reveals a society in which human exchange has become a shameful reminder that everything, and everyone, has a price affixed to it.

The underground beer hall patronized by the Future of the Proletariat is likewise described as unreal and inauthentic. It is located in the basement of the Silenus Restaurant, ironically named for a mythic lover of wine—not beer. Instead of windows, its walls have "fresco paintings," providing the illusion that one is drinking and dining "al fresco": "the fresco paintings ran flat and dull all round the walls without windows, representing scenes of the chase and of outdoor revelry in medieval costumes" (88). The music in the hall is also illusory: "An upright semi-grand piano near the door, flanked by two palms in pots, executed suddenly all by itself a valse tune with aggressive virtuosity" (88). Like the assistant commissioner's taxi ride, the player piano is associated with illusion and ghostliness: "The piano at the foot of the staircase clanged through a mazurka with brazen impetuosity, as though a vulgar and impudent ghost were showing off. The keys sank and rose mysteriously" (92).

Like the Silenus, the Italian restaurant, and the taxi ride, Verloc's shop has a flimsy and tenuous connection with material reality. The shop is described as "a square box of a place" (45), and is just one of many packages in the novel that seem to contain very little. Some of the shop's products include "a small cardboard box with apparently nothing inside" (46), "closed yellow paper envelopes, very flimsy" (45), and other empty objects "looking obviously and scandalously not worth the money which passed in the transaction" (46). Even the women in the pictures are merely a commercial manipulation of the visible: "Now and then . . . one of the faded, yellow dancing girls would get sold to an amateur, as though she had been alive and young" (46). Here, Conrad associates consumerism with elusive, imaginary value and the empty, feminine manipulations of both product and seller. Just as James dwells on the ephemeral worthlessness of the cheap goods that Millicent buys and sells, in contrast to the intrinsic or authentic value of Hyacinth's bookbinding, so Conrad emphasizes the illusory emptiness of the pornography sold by Winnie. Although critics tend to correlate mass-produced pornography with the degradation of the female body, considering it a consumerist manifestation of sexist oppression, Conrad uses it to symbolize the feminizing spirit of consumerism, gradually infecting all of public culture.[41]

James locates civilization in art, while Conrad locates it in masculine endeavor, but both see feminized consumer culture as its anarchic antithesis. In this way, James and Conrad participate in what Andreas Huyssen has described as a characteristically modernist rejection of feminized mass culture, as a means of shoring up their own literary value and timelessness: "aesthetic discourse around the turn of the century consistently and obsessively genders mass culture and the masses as feminine, while high culture . . . clearly remains the privileged realm of male activities" (47). That James's and Conrad's novels both are and are not "dynamite novels" suggests their conflicted relationship with the consumer marketplace: both authors want to sell, yet also exhibit distaste for popular fiction. The novels distinguish themselves as "literary" products by associating modern consumerism with cheap, mass-produced, worthless texts. On the second page of *The Princess,* for example, a young Hyacinth engages in the sort of window-shopping that the novel more commonly associates with women:

> the boy was often planted in front of the little sweet-shop on the other side of the street, an establishment where periodical literature, as well as tough toffy and hard lollipops, was dispensed . . . attractively exhibited in the small-paned, dirty window. He used to stand there for half an hour at a time, spelling out the first page of the romances in the *Family Herald* and the *London Journal,* and admiring the obligatory illustration in which the noble characters . . . were presented to the carnal eye. (54)

Associating popular papers with candy and carnality, James presents them as ephemeral, easily digestible, and unsophisticated: texts that appeal to a child. The stories' "obligatory" illustrations suggest they are products of formula rather than art, separating them from James's novel. *The Princess* was published serially in the *Atlantic Monthly,* but this was not the sort of journal to print illustrated fiction; hanging over the first installment of James's novel, in the September 1885 issue, is the magazine's banner: "A Magazine of Literature, Science, Art, and Politics." Conrad likewise describes mass-produced texts in terms of ephemerality and disposability: he refers to "a dismal row of newspaper sellers" who "dealt with their wares from the gutter;" to an "eruption of the damp, rubbishy sheets of paper soiled with printers' ink;" and to "posters, maculated with filth." Despite being widely consumed by passers-by, these newspapers and posters remain culturally insignificant: "the effect was of indifference, of a disregarded distribution" (101). In the first pages of the novel, he describes the radical newspapers sold in Verloc's shop as "obscure" and "badly printed" (45), the flotsam and jetsam of modern print culture.

Through these representations of ephemeral texts, James's and Conrad's argument about terrorism and individual political expression becomes even more peculiarly gendered. As two authors who self-consciously position themselves against a dominant cultural condition—characterized by proliferating, feminized, mass-produced literature and culture—James and Conrad share many of the same concerns as the novels' terrorists, who pit themselves against prevailing social orthodoxy and struggle to find a way to express divergent ideals. At the beginning of *The Secret Agent,* Vladimir tells Verloc that "bombs are your means of expression" (67), but as the botched bombing later in the story suggests, even the most radical of individual expressions are now absorbed within modern economic and social structures. Novels are also individual expressions meant to reach masses of people; in their depiction of terror, James and Conrad are not only pessimistic about political expression, but about the entire project of individual creation. The fear that they grapple with, as authors, is not all that different from the fear that haunts the Professor, Conrad's "perfect anarchist": "he felt the mass of mankind mighty in its numbers. They swarmed numerous like locusts, industrious like ants, thoughtless like a natural force, pushing on blind and orderly and absorbed, impervious to sentiment, to logic, to terror, too, perhaps. . . . he had such moments of dreadful and sane mistrust of mankind. What if nothing could move them?" (103). James's and Conrad's novels seem to ask the same question, to worry that the reading public is too accustomed to modernity's shocks to be moved anymore. The authors inflect their critiques of feminized mass culture with a version of "the anxiety of influence": an anxiety about their own capacity to influence.

The novels not only reject a feminized culture of consumption, then, but correlate that culture with threats to masculine identity, linking the enervated, ineffectual terrorists to the meretricious deceits of modern consumer capitalism. They suggest that in such a society, the traditionally feminine subject position of the prostitute becomes the ineluctable position of all citizens. Both novels feature male revolutionaries who succumb to such commodification. Conrad's anarchist Ossipon survives by a habitual exchange of romance for money, sponging off young bourgeois women whom he meets "on benches in Kensington Gardens" or "near area railings": this "put some material means into his hand. He needed it to live" (266). Yundt and Michaelis also depend on women for their idle existences. Similarly, in *The Princess,* Paul Muniment embarks on a sexual relationship with the Princess while securing from her a huge sum of money for the cause. He reaps the economic rewards of a semi-romantic friendship with Lady Aurora and a less ambiguous relationship with the Princess. In both novels, the new social order accommodates only those men willing to enact prostitutional commodification. Ending his novel with a final portrait of Ossipon, who now feels too "menaced" (266) to make his living off women, Conrad writes that his "robust form . . . was marching in the gutter as if in training for the task of an inevitable future. Already he bowed his broad shoulders, his head of ambrosial locks, as if ready to receive the leather yoke of the sandwich board" (269). Wearers of the sandwich board—a nineteenth-century invention—sell their bodies like prostitutes, as Susan Buck-Morss has described; that Ossipon will bear "the yoke of the sandwich board" suggests that his body will be emasculated and commodified under consumer capitalism. He will not demolish the system, but the system will demolish him.

Ending on this ominous note, Conrad's novel seems adamantly dismissive of the possibility for individual agency within modern social and economic conditions, though the fact that he publishes the novel at all suggests individual expression is not an *entirely* hopeless enterprise. He tosses his fictional bomb into the firmament, while maintaining the impossibility of its effect; as the Professor says, "The condemned social order has not been built up on paper and ink, and I don't fancy that a combination of paper and ink will ever put an end to it" (95). James's novel makes a similar critique, but one that is less categorical in scope. Both novels use the language and ideology of gender to conceptualize individuals' relation to power within a complex economical and political reality, and both novels suggest that individual action must be different— must be "feminine"—to produce effects in the modern world. While Conrad finds such a condition to be perverse, and presents civilization's restraints on masculinity as a tragic condition of modernity, James can't help but admire women like Princess Casamassima and Millicent Henning, who have learned to survive and even thrive through bodily manipulation and masquerade. As the Princess and Millicent illustrate, covert exercise of power through image proves to be a successful mode of action, despite its collusion with a distasteful, feminized consumer capitalism.

"AN INVITATION TO DYNAMITE"

Female Revolutionaries in Late-Victorian Dynamite Narrative

FIVE

Nineteenth-century iconography commonly represented "the spirit of revolution" with the image of a woman, but with the rise of dynamite narrative in the 1880s, female revolutionaries emerged as complex characters rather than abstract or allegorical symbols.[1] There were hardly any real female political criminals in fin de siècle Britain, until the Women's Social and Political Union (WSPU) began a militant, "guerrilla" suffrage campaign in 1903, yet years before this, fictional female political criminals were a common feature of British dynamite narrative. This chapter considers three late-Victorian dynamite narratives that focus on revolutionary female protagonists: Oscar Wilde's first play *Vera; Or, the Nihilists* (1883); Olivia and Helen Rossetti's autobiographical novel *A Girl among the Anarchists,* published under the pseudonym Isabel Meredith (1903); and *The Dynamiter* (1885), a novel by Robert Louis Stevenson and his wife Fanny Van de Grift Stevenson. These texts suggest that the emergence of modern "terrorism" calls for new conceptions of criminal agency, but also that the emergence of modern feminism and democratization calls for new conceptions of political agency; they show that in the context of first-wave feminism and women's swelling political voice, the female political criminal took on a powerful new symbolic value.

Consider, for example, Britain's widespread interest during the 1880s and 1890s in a female assassin who was neither British nor Victorian: Charlotte Corday. Corday assassinated Jean-Paul Marat, leader of the radical French Jacobins, in 1793. She supported the Girondists—moderate republicans—and viewed Marat as a threat to democracy and to France. So she dressed up, had her hair done, pretended to be Marat's comrade, and stabbed him in his bath. Authorities guillotined her shortly thereafter, but contrary to their hopes, an autopsy on her corpse proved that she was, indeed, a virgin.[2] Corday was regularly memorialized in Victorian literature, and was a visual subject for tableaux vivants and staged photography.[3] At the end of the century, there was a surge of interest in Corday, and numerous popular histories of her life appeared in print: Jeannette Van Alstine published the first full-length English biography of Corday in 1890, for example, and Mary Jeaffreson published another in 1893, marking the centenary of Corday's execution.[4] In the story of Corday, late-Victorian readers found a curious parallel to New Women and suffragists: a woman who defined herself in public, political terms rather than private ones. She functioned as both a French "other," against whom to define English identity, and a "self" who encapsulated modernity, democracy, and feminism as Britain was experiencing them.

Cesare Lombroso discussed Corday at length in his influential study *The Female Offender,* published in English in 1895, and references to Corday abound in other late-Victorian works of criminology. In his widely read study *Crime and Its Causes,* William Douglas Morrison reported to English readers that Corday was the subject of major dispute in international criminological circles. At the Paris Congress of Criminal Anthropology in 1889, when Corday's skull "was subjected to examination, Lombroso declared that it was truly a criminal type of skull; [Paul] Topinard, on the other hand, gave it as his opinion that it was a typical female skull" (181). Lombroso was Italian and Topinard was French, but the conflict over whether Corday fit the "criminal type" was not simply a national contest: it reflected a broader debate within criminology about whether specifically political crimes derived from biological or sociological bases. As a woman, Corday occupied a particularly key position in this debate, since women's status as political actors was already subject to dispute. Debates about the nature of political crime thus paralleled debates about women's political access: both revolve around a central disagreement about essential identity versus politically constructed subjectivity.

In the late-Victorian period, Britain had Europe's most tolerant policy regarding political criminals. The British government did not extend special treatment to political crimes committed on its *own* soil, but under the Extradition Act of 1870, it liberally granted exile to dissidents from other countries. This policy reflected a tacit belief that political crime constituted a special category of deviance: it implied that political criminals were not biologically or constitutionally predisposed to crime, like "regular" criminals, but rather were driven to their actions by historical and political circumstances. Britain's sanctuary for such exiles was a major source of conflict with other European powers such as Russia, as I discuss in chapter 4, but also a major source of debate and contention within Britain. The 1905 Aliens Act reflected widespread public anxiety about immigration and cosmopolitanism, not only due to xenophobia, territoriality, and job shortages, but also to paranoia about foreign radicals and terrorism.[5]

Exiled radicals actually had little to do with political crime in Britain, however.[6] Though one would never guess it from dynamite fiction, Irish nationalists committed almost all the terrorist acts of the dynamite era, as I discuss in chapter 4. In the 1880s and 1890s, Irish-American Fenians regularly targeted London's railway stations, political buildings, and national monuments. During this time, the United States' refusal to extradite Fenian dynamiters, who had the overt and covert support of many in the heavily Irish U.S. population, was met with outrage in Britain. An 1884 editorial in the *Times* sums up the general feeling: the United States "is a very paradise for the dynamiter. It supplies him with arms, it sends him out upon his mission of evil, and it gives him a refuge when his work is done. There is no other civilized country in the world where he would have these chances within his reach, or where public opinion would tolerate the stigma to which America submits by suffering them."[7] Dynamite narrative is full of sympathetic depictions of female radicals, but tends to steer clear of the "Irish question"—for example, Joseph Hatton's *By Order of the Czar,* an 1890 dynamite novel about a Russian female nihilist, supports nihilism and harshly criticizes the czarist regime, yet includes a digressive denunciation of Fenianism: "America had shamefully abused the privileges of blood and friendship in permitting a gigantic conspiracy to be hatched and kept alive on her free soil, to the detriment and danger of the mother-country" (1:222).[8] The passage serves to disconnect the apparently justifiable political crimes of Russian nihilists from the "shameful" acts of Irish nationalists. In law and in literature, a fundamental conflict existed in Britain's treatment of political criminals: lenient toward continental dissidents, appalled by Fenian dynamiters. This meant that the concept of "political crime" was inordinately divisive. To call a crime "political" was to acknowledge that it stemmed from legitimate or at least comprehensible grievances. To call someone a "political criminal" was to admit them, to some extent, into the political sphere.

Writers in the dynamite genre engage such problems by contemplating the psychology, motivations, and character of the "terrorist." At the root of such imaginary narratives are profound questions, the same questions that Lombroso and Topinard asked with respect to Charlotte Corday: are political crimes manifestations of individual deviance or the inevitable outcome of social conditions? Are these modern crimes "private" or "public"? The relatively unfamiliar threat posed in the 1880s by campaigns of political terror was at variance with British crime fiction's tendency to locate criminal agency in the lone individual. Detective stories favored a "detective versus criminal" plot structure, as I describe in the first two chapters, but this conception of criminality was ill-suited for narratives of political crime. Not only did organized political insurgency threaten to deindividualize criminal guilt, as the controversy over Corday's skull suggests, it was often aimed at collective rather than individual targets, randomizing victimization and raising unnerving questions about the complicity of private lives in crimes of the state. Dynamite narrative, as a genre, works to convey this broadening out of criminal guilt and victimization, which was inherent in collective political crimes. This was a new task for crime fiction, and women's tenuous relation to political agency made them apt subjects for it.

The female political criminals of Wilde, the Rossettis, and the Stevensons express the new, uncomfortable sense of public-private interconnectedness embedded in modern terrorism. Because of women's contested political access, a female political criminal captured the ambiguous nature of "terrorist" agency that the dynamite genre sought to represent. These authors use the female revolutionary to show that modern manifestations of "terrorism" or "political crime" demand broader, more collective notions of criminality *and* political representation. Because women's agency was already viewed as an ambiguous proposition, and because women were already understood less as autonomous actors than as channels for the will of the social body, the figure of the woman terrorist dispersed guilt and victimization in the same way that political crimes seemed to do. Moreover, depicting terrorists as women, who in legal terms were extrapolitical subjects, linked the modern problem of political crime to debates about who should have political representation.

Dynamitings and "terrorism" were new additions to the fabric of life in 1880s and 1890s Britain, providing a historical basis for the emergence of dynamite narrative as a popular genre. The literature itself, however, rarely depicted realistic insurgency; the prevalence of socialist and anarchist terrorists, such as in Henry James's and Joseph Conrad's novels, is one indication that this is the case, since these groups committed no major attacks in Britain. Female revolutionaries are a similarly fantastic aspect of the genre. Aside from the anti-Fenian would-be assassin Mrs. Dudley—who was compared to Charlotte Corday in the British press but was ultimately acquitted on the grounds of insanity—there were no women assassins, bombers, or dynamiters in late-Victorian Britain.[9] In the dynamite genre, however, with its tales of assassinations and conspiratorial plots, women terrorists appeared commonly from the 1880s onward.[10] Why was this so? I argue that the narrative figure of the female revolutionary conveys a newly modern, newly deindividualized, and newly "public" narrative of crime. Wilde, the Rossettis, and the Stevensons portray revolutionary women with incompatible personal and political commitments, emphasizing that revolutionary action conflicts with traditional divisions between public and private—a salient theme in the context of New Women and first-wave feminism. The texts do not come to the same conclusion about what the "revolutionary woman" means, but they all correlate feminism, democratization, and organized political insurgencies as modern challenges to traditional political authority, and they all use the female revolutionary to embody these modern demands for wider political representation.

VERA; OR, THE NIHILISTS

Oscar Wilde completed the first version of his first dramatic effort in 1880 and the final version in 1883, making *Vera; Or the Nihilists* an early example of a late-Victorian trend in representing female revolutionaries. The unusualness of Wilde's nihilist heroine, Vera Sabouroff, conveys the unusualness of organized political crime in modern Britain. She evokes two real-life Russian nihilists, Vera Zasulich and Vera Figner, who were involved in assassinations or assassination attempts in the years leading up to the play, but for Anglo-American audiences, the figure of the female terrorist was a novelty.[11] Moreover, while Wilde's play intersects with widespread international coverage of Vera Zasulich's case in particular, his Vera little resembles the "Vera Zassulic" described by Stepniak in *Underground Russia*. Published in 1882, after Wilde had written *Vera* but before he revised it for the stage, *Underground Russia* acquainted a great number of English-speaking readers with the principal figures of Russian nihilism. In the section on Zassulic, Stepniak claims: "In the whole range of history it would be difficult, and, perhaps, impossible to find a name which, at a bound, has risen into such universal and undisputed celebrity." Still, according to Stepniak, Zassulic herself "obstinately shunned fame" (106), and "has nothing about her of the heroine. . . . She is not beautiful. . . . She is very negligent with regard to her appearance. . . . She has not the slightest trace of the desire which almost every woman has, of displaying her beauty" (107). Wilde's Vera Sabouroff resembles this Vera in her celebrity, but little else.

Wilde wrote *Vera* at a moment in his life when he was deeply fascinated by various diva actresses, including Lillie Langtry, Sarah Bernhardt, Ellen Terry, and Helen Modjeska, and the character of Vera Sabouroff reflects his profound interest in the power and potentially dangerous glamour of the woman on stage.[12] *Vera* is the first of Wilde's dramas to render the female criminal as the perfect embodiment of the actress's fatal allure and active spectacle, but later works such as *The Duchess of Padua* and *Salomé* also employ murderous women to signify the aura and power of female glamour. Wilde imagined that such parts would be played by famous actresses, who would bring to the roles the force of their own celebrity in a modern, image-centered culture. He sent copies of *Vera* to several of his favorites, hoping they would play his nihilist heroine. When Marie Prescott ultimately starred as Vera in the New York production, Wilde specially provided vermilion silk for her costume, as was often noted in publicity surrounding the play. Prescott's personal fame was central to the play's marketing and promotion: figure 29 shows the program cover from the New York production, prominently emphasizing Prescott's name, and figure 30 shows a tribute to her talents as an actress from page 2 of the program. Reviews of the performance indicate that Prescott did not live up to the hype, but whatever the failings of Wilde's first drama, *Vera* is remarkable and important in its early representation of the figure of the female terrorist. Like other female criminals we have seen, Vera Sabouroff suggests the growing significance of women's image in a visually oriented consumer society, but more unusually, she also poses a range of fascinating questions about feminism's connection to political terror and democratic reform. Wilde's depiction of Vera thus unites seemingly disparate debates about women's public presence in the modern world, foregrounding the political resonance of debates about gender and visuality considered throughout this study.

Fig. 29. Cover of program from the New York production of *Vera; Or, the Nihilist*. (Courtesy of the William Andrews Clark Memorial Library, University of California, Los Angeles.)

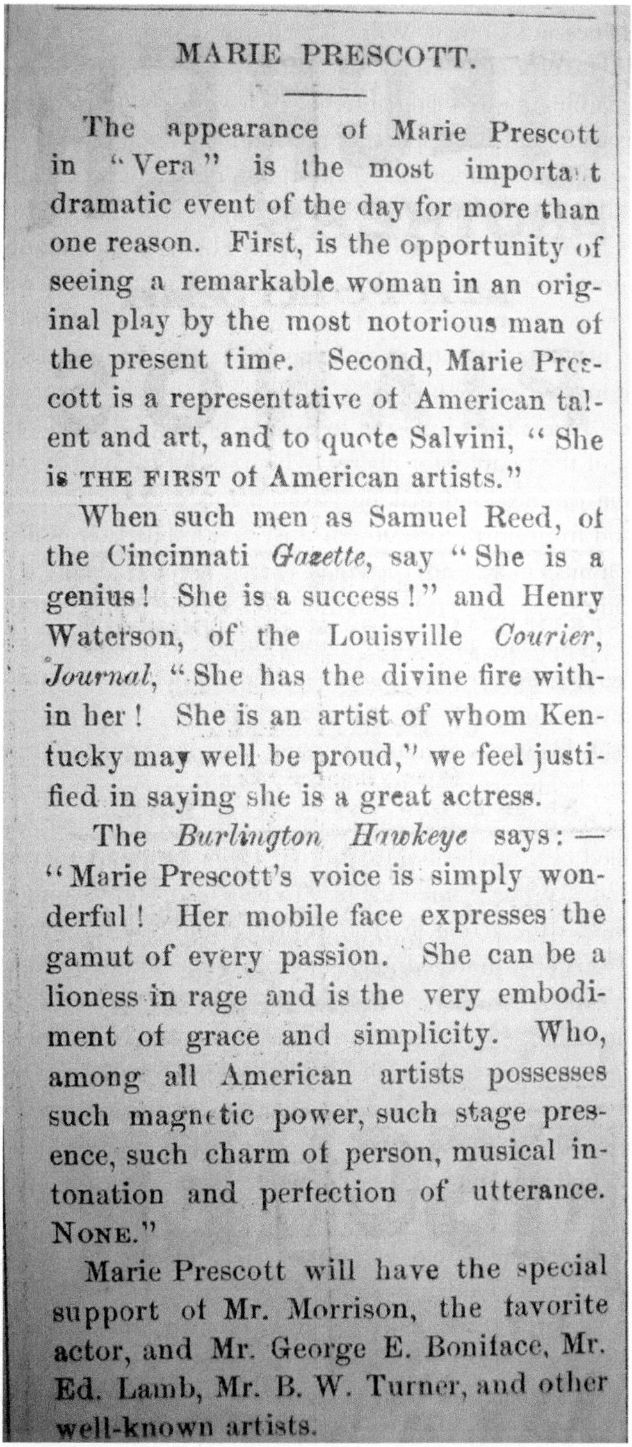

MARIE PRESCOTT.

The appearance of Marie Prescott in "Vera" is the most importa t dramatic event of the day for more than one reason. First, is the opportunity of seeing a remarkable woman in an original play by the most notorious man of the present time. Second, Marie Prescott is a representative of American talent and art, and to quote Salvini, " She is THE FIRST of American artists."

When such men as Samuel Reed, of the Cincinnati *Gazette*, say "She is a genius! She is a success!" and Henry Waterson, of the Louisville *Courier, Journal*, "She has the divine fire within her! She is an artist of whom Kentucky may well be proud," we feel justified in saying she is a great actress.

The *Burlington Hawkeye* says: — "Marie Prescott's voice is simply wonderful! Her mobile face expresses the gamut of every passion. She can be a lioness in rage and is the very embodiment of grace and simplicity. Who, among all American artists possesses such magnetic power, such stage presence, such charm of person, musical intonation and perfection of utterance. NONE."

Marie Prescott will have the special support of Mr. Morrison, the favorite actor, and Mr. George E. Boniface, Mr. Ed. Lamb, Mr. B. W. Turner, and other well-known artists.

Fig. 30. From page two of the program for the New York production of *Vera; Or, the Nihilist*. (Courtesy of the William Andrews Clark Memorial Library, University of California, Los Angeles.)

Like James and Conrad, Wilde hoped that writing a dynamite narrative would be profitable. In an 1880 letter, he describes his ambition for *Vera* in unambiguously material terms: "I have not yet finished furnishing my rooms, and have spent all my money over it already, so if no manager gives me gold for the *Nihilists* I don't know what I shall do; but then I couldn't really have anything but Chippendale and satinwood—I shouldn't have been able to write" (99).[13] His taste for luxurious furnishings notwithstanding, Wilde's motivation for writing *Vera* was political as well as pecuniary. In an 1881 letter to an Oxford friend, Wilde called the play "my first attack on Tyranny" (117), and in an 1883 letter, published in the *New York World* to advertise the New York production, he wrote: "I have tried in [*Vera*] to express within the limits of art that Titan cry of the peoples for liberty, which in the Europe of our day is threatening thrones, and making governments unstable from Spain to Russia, and from north to southern seas" (214). The later Wilde found no such "limits" in art—in *The Picture of Dorian Gray,* "There is nothing that art cannot express" (14)—but this letter reveals Wilde's early debt to Percy Bysshe Shelley and clearly communicates his political purpose for *Vera:* to render dramatically the modern tide of democratic and socialist movements in Europe.

When Wilde was writing and revising *Vera,* Russian authorities were continually being attacked by nihilist revolutionaries, so the political content of his play was disturbingly pertinent. In 1881, Czar Alexander II was killed by a nihilist bomb, causing *Vera*'s London performance to be canceled.[14] Wilde wanted the play to be staged, and in some versions of *Vera,* he set the action in 1800 to protect the play from censorship. The final version is undated, but quite obviously addresses the political conditions of contemporary Russia: the story occurs after the 1861 emancipation of the serfs (in the prologue, a Colonel says, "You peasants are getting too saucy since you ceased to be serfs" [134]), and the play's many references to extortionate taxation connect it to a major source of anti-Czarist outrage in the 1870s.[15]

Despite the timeliness of the play and its pronihilist slant, critics have not taken its politics seriously, preferring to see it as an exercise in conventional sensationalism. In a 1907 assessment of Wilde's dramatic oeuvre, Archibald Henderson called *Vera* "a mere *Schauerstück* [thriller] of the weakest type" (Beckson 272). More recently, Julie Buckler has argued that "in staging . . . melodramatic affinities as late as the 1880s, Wilde's Vera affirms essentially conservative values in politics *and* art" (66). Recent rereadings of melodrama have disputed the idea that it is a fundamentally conservative or apolitical form, however, and while Wilde's first drama is undeniably immature within his oeuvre, many of its apparent weaknesses (such as unelaborated character motivation) suit the generic context of nineteenth-century melodrama.[16] Melodrama, in fact, shares a key formal feature with dynamite narrative as it developed in the late-Victorian era: the disavowal of logical cause and effect structures of plot progression. Dynamite narrative does this through chronological disordering—both *The Princess Casamassima* and *The Secret Agent* follow a chaotic timeline, for example—but melodrama also disavows cause and effect through seemingly inadequate character motivation or abrupt shifts in plot or tone. The effect in both cases is to call into question notions of modern progress and to destabilize narrative authority. Wilde's melodramatic dynamite drama is far more politically engaged than most critics have recognized, and its melodramatic form contributes to the play's overall assault on traditional structures of authority. Through his revolutionary characterization of Vera the nihilist, Wilde depicts feminism, democracy, and nihilist political crime as anti-hierarchical, anti-patriarchal, and anti-autocratic forces in the modern world.

My argument about *Vera* taps into a broader dispute about the status of Wilde's politics; literary critics have embraced Gay Wilde and Irish Wilde, but Socialist Wilde is still a figure of contention.[17] Sos Eltis has argued that Wilde's socialist politics were a key component of his authorship, duly recognized by his contemporaries, and Jonathan Freedman considers "The Soul of Man under Socialism"—an essay that commonly sparks discussions of this topic—brilliant socialist polemic precisely because it presents socialism as "the inevitable fulfillment of the central assumptions of its seeming antagonist, bourgeois individualism" (73). The doubleness, paradox, and play in Wilde's writing, however, have led other critics to suspect his political engagement. Some maintain that Wilde is simply too individualistic for one to take his claims for socialism seriously. Simon Joyce reads Wilde's socialism as "idiosyncratic" and "consciously solipsistic" ("Sexual" 514). Amanda Anderson claims that Wilde defines self-realization in terms of social rebellion, so that "'Socialism' in Wilde's conception" is "self-consciously utopian," a "desire for a purer realm of freedom" outside social negation (154). Josephine Guy argues that to the extent that the essay makes any argument at all, "Soul of Man" advocates not socialism but Individualism, a political philosophy resembling libertarianism and *opposed* to socialism ("The Soul").[18]

Disputes about Wilde's politics partly stem from the functionally different categories at work in nineteenth-century radical politics, and attention to this context suggests that "socialism" and "individualism," for Wilde, are not mutually exclusive. At the time Wilde was writing, Marxist socialism was beginning to take root in Britain, but so were the ideas of anarchist socialists like Peter Kropotkin, whom Wilde admired. The anarchists were part of the First International coalition of socialist groups, but rather than advocating a powerful centralized state as Marxist socialists did (at least as an intermediary condition), anarchists envisioned a society of small, cooperative, communist collectives, based upon the principles of free choice and voluntary association. Far from wanting to centralize the state, they believed that the state, by exercising coercion, violates individuals' inherent right to freedom.[19] The group had some overlap with the Individualist movement with which Guy associates Wilde: anarchists opposed private property (the lodestar of Individualism), but like the Individualists emphasized autonomy and personal liberty, believing bureaucracy and statecraft to be inherently corrupt.[20]

Wilde, as Eltis has shown, was quite attracted to the anarchist vision; as he said in an 1894 interview, "I think I am rather more than a Socialist. I am something of an Anarchist" (15). His regard for Kropotkin is widely documented, and in 1889, Wilde signed a public petition protesting the hanging of anarchists in Chicago's Haymarket fiasco, a risky decision for a man who wanted an audience, given mainstream animosity toward anarchism.[21] Russian nihilism, like anarchism, was an anti-authoritarian political philosophy; Stepniak describes it as "a struggle for the emancipation of intelligence from every kind of dependence, [which] advanced side by side with that for the emancipation of the laboring classes from serfdom" (3–4). Considering Wilde's political tendencies, it is not surprising that his play is generally supportive of Russian nihilism, nor that Vera is a heroic figure. Not all of its nihilists are as admirable as Vera, but the play concurs with the nihilist position on czarist rule: it depicts the czarist regime in Russia as a stagnant, repressive despotism that devalues individual liberty. Russia's human rights abuses were notorious in nineteenth-century Europe; dissenters to the czar or his vast network of bureaucrats could be exiled to Siberia, without benefit of trial, merely for speaking out against the state. *Vera* does not offer a straightforward political program, yet is emphatically a play about the importance of individual liberties. It champions individualism as a salutary corrective to autocracy and as an avenue toward collective good. The play thus makes essentially the same individualist-socialist argument that Wilde made eight years later in "Soul of Man," suggesting that his political opinions were far less erratic than many critics have claimed. Both works argue for a socialism that is economically collectivist, does not impinge on individual expression, and is suspicious of institutional centralization. In this way, *Vera* expresses a political perspective that would persist throughout Wilde's career.

Despite widespread international awareness of czarist brutality in Russia, Wilde's sympathetic depiction of nihilist political criminals raised contemporaries' eyebrows. Russia was the first nation besieged by modern "terrorism," and as other parts of the world experienced this new form of organized political crime, Wilde's treatment of the subject jarred with the prevalent reactionary mood. Mixed reviews of the New York performance were obviously tinged by fears of political terrorism. The *New York Times* prefaced its review by editorializing on the "difference between the frank and beautiful love of freedom [in the United States] and the lurid horrors of Nihilism." The reviewer was openly repelled by Wilde's politics: "The Nihilist, as we know him to-day, is an enemy of social order. . . . We are unable to feel pity for the men who threw dynamite under the carriage of the Czar Alexander. . . . A dramatist, in consequence, who puts a gang of Nihilists upon the stage on the ground that they are interesting characters of the time and that their convictions make them dramatic, does so at his own peril" ("Amusements").[22] Wilde's drama does exploit fear of, and fascination with, political crime, making use of secret oaths and other tropes of dynamite sensationalism, but with his choice of protagonist, Wilde takes a highly innovative approach to his material: Vera's gender perfectly expresses the newness and unfamiliarity of organized political crime in the modern world. Such a character was far too alien for many of the drama's critics. Reviewers of the New York production sniffed at its depiction of women, finding Vera unbelievably unfeminine.[23] The *New York Daily Tribune* argued that the very idea of a female revolutionary doomed the play to fail: "To make a woman the leader of a national insurrection was foolish" (qtd. in Reed xxxiii). Resistance to Vera as a character was clearly not only because she was a nihilist, but because she was a nihilist woman.

Wilde's play documents a genuine feminist strain in Russian nihilism, yet relies heavily on a conflict between Vera's gender and her politics. The step toward radicalism, Wilde stresses, is a much longer stride for women, who have less training and preparation in political consciousness. Indeed, it is particularly significant that Wilde's Vera is of humble origins, unlike the female revolutionaries in *The Princess Casamassima, A Girl among the Anarchists, The Dynamiter,* and most other dynamite narratives of the day. Philip May's *Love: The Reward,* an 1885 novel also featuring a female nihilist named Vera, is typical in this regard. May's nihilist heroine is of noble birth but has been shut up in a convent for most of her girlhood, like Charlotte Corday: "She was a little Cinderella, who had come from the convent instead of from the kitchen" (1:144). Wilde's play, predating all of the aforementioned texts, takes greater political risk in providing Vera with peasant origins, alienating her further than a woman of higher birth from audience sympathies and from means of political access.

We learn early in the drama, for example, that Vera's brother Dmitri became a nihilist while being educated in the Russian metropolis of Moscow; Vera, in contrast, is left in the rural wilds, where she is expected to milk cows and marry her peasant neighbor. That she exhibits interests in politics and ethics is surprising and peculiar to those around her. As the prologue of the play opens, Vera's father, Peter Sabouroff, and her would-be suitor Michael discuss whether Vera will ever agree to marry. The root of her intransigence, they believe, is that she has "too many ideas," too much "seriousness," and "is always thinking of others" (120–22). Vera's expansive intellect and sympathy, it seems, are preventing her from settling comfortably into her domestic lot as a woman. In Vera's first appearance in the prologue, upon returning home and hearing Michael's plea for her love, she says that "there is so much else to do in the world but love" (125). Vera's resistance to love and marriage pointedly link her to a burgeoning discourse of female autonomy in 1880s Britain.[24]

By act 1, despite pressure to marry and stay home, Vera has become the most feared nihilist in Russia. Her femininity and lesser physical strength have not hindered her effectiveness in this sphere: the nihilist goal of assassinating the Czar, she says, could just as easily be accomplished by a woman as a man: "Oh, to think what stands between us and freedom in Europe! a few old men, wrinkled, feeble, tottering dotards whom a boy could strangle for a ducat, or a woman stab in a night-time" (150–51). This line articulates one of the most feared aspects of terrorism: the idea that political crime put the sort of national or public influence usually limited to the state into the hands of rogue individuals. James's and Conrad's novels refute this notion of terror by depicting utterly inept revolutionists, but in making his nihilist a woman, Wilde instead underscores the idea that political crime gives power and influence to otherwise insignificant individuals, which correlates it with democracy as a political force.

Indeed, as we have seen in other genres of crime narrative, Vera's femininity actually helps her circumvent forces of social control. The Czar has put an enormous price on her head, but she is "as hard to capture as a she-wolf is, and twice as dangerous" (141). In act 1, she attends the Grand Duke's masked ball at the palace in disguise, and as a beautiful woman in full ball dress, is never suspected. The General of the police force admits that she has terrorized the nation's leader: "I heard at the council to-day that that woman Vera Sabouroff, the head of [the nihilists], had been seen in this very city. The Emperor's face turned as white as the snow outside. I think I never saw such terror in any man before" (167). He calls Vera the most "dangerous" woman in Europe, but also claims that "she is not a woman at all; she is a sort of devil!" (168). The General's remarks stress the unsettling duality of Vera's identity, as a woman and a nihilist. Just as the play's nihilists view the existing social order as on the verge of being turned upside down, so Vera—as nihilist and woman—constantly threatens to be the "opposite" of what she seems. This "nihilist" form of characterization has the effect of destabilizing femininity and political criminality as specific *categories* of identity.[25]

Throughout the play, Wilde extends this dual critique of gender and politics to the topic of paternalism, linking nascent feminism with the democratic and antiautocratic force of nihilism. Women and nihilists are presented as "modern," while patriarchal authority on the familial and state level is revealed as outworn. In Peter Sabouroff, Vera's father, Wilde creates a satirical portrait of the respectable, heartless patriarch. Set in the aftershocks of a particularly harsh Russian winter, the play depicts Peter as utterly unmoved by the suffering of others in his community: "Let God and our little Father the Czar look to the world. It is none of my work to mend my neighbour's thatch. Why, last winter old Michael was frozen to death in his sleigh in the snowstorm, and his wife and children starved afterwards when the hard times came; but what business was it of mine?" (122). Peter goes on to enumerate a list of local tragedies, including a flood that killed a group of children trapped in a schoolhouse, none of which are any concern to him. He repeats four times, "Let God and the Czar look to it" (122–23).

Russia has its own "little Father," the Czar, and in the play's religious cosmology, God is a patriarchal authority not unlike the Czar: "heaven is a despotism," one character says (181). The inherent fault in such structures of belief, in Wilde's depiction, is that they centralize all power into one paternal figurehead, leaving no sense of agency in those below him. Fostering the little domain of his inn, Peter feels no compulsion to act for others, and he sees justification for such narrowness in the political and religious structures he has been taught to revere. With Peter, Wilde's play shows the failure of autocratic, paternalist structures of authority in religion, the home, and the state. Vera, in contrast, fully appreciates how the ideology of religious patriarchy lends justification to corrupt political patriarchy, and recites an inverted version of "Our Father" in honor of the czar: "a father whose name shall not be hallowed, whose kingdom shall change to a republic, whose trespasses shall not be forgiven him, because he has robbed us of our daily bread; with whom is neither might, nor right, nor glory, now or for ever" (149).

Peter's children thus reject their father's conception of paternalist authority. While studying law in Moscow, Dmitri becomes involved with nihilist radicals and commits his life to overturning autocratic power: "To give liberty to thirty millions of people enslaved to one man" (131). Dmitri is sent to die in the mines of Siberia, however, after he is caught printing a nihilist newspaper. Wilde pointedly makes Dmitri's crime one of political discourse rather than violence, ensuring audience outrage at his sentence. Vera also rejects her father's unquestioning acquiescence to czarist authority. Even before learning of her brother's imprisonment, which prompts her conversion to nihilism, she has already begun to question the political status quo.[26] When her father's inn is visited by a group of military police escorting a chain gang to Siberia, she asks their leader, "Who are our masters?" Questioning authority is a dangerous practice in czarist Russia, however, as the leader tells her: "these men are going to the mines for life for asking the same foolish question" (128). Vera is indignant about the treatment of the prisoners, but Peter views it merely as the making of his fortune. When he realizes that a new road will bring his inn more business from soldiers escorting prisoners, he is elated: "Men in chains! Why, we are in luck, my child!" (125).

Through his depiction of the melodramatically wicked Czar, Wilde's play skewers the paternalist notion that one is better off when taken care of under patriarchal authority. That Wilde extends his critique of paternalism to government as well as families is particularly significant in light of late-Victorian feminism and legal interventionism. In contrast to Arthur Conan Doyle's stories, which support an interventionist state at the expense of the patriarchal home, Wilde's play depicts state authority as merely an inductive manifestation of patriarchal authority in the home. This point is particularly clear in act 2, when the drama moves inside the walls of the palace. The Czar has been imprisoning his son in the palace out of fear that the Czarevitch will murder him in a fever for accession. When the Czarevitch greets his father in act 2, the Czar responds: "Don't come too near me, boy! Don't come too near me, I say! There is always something about an heir to a crown unwholesome to his father" (182–83). Later, he asks an advisor whether he shouldn't just murder his son to rid himself of the risk: "Shall I banish him? Shall I [*whispers*] . . . ? The Emperor Paul did it. The Empress Catherine there [*points to picture on the wall*] did it. Why shouldn't I?" (195; Wilde's ellipses). Wilde's characterization of the Czar reminds us that patriarchal institutions of monarchy, inheritance, and patrilineage have a long history of encouraging perverse mistreatment of others rather than security or stability.

Indeed, the Czar cares neither for his son, whom he plots to kill, nor for the people he rules as "father" of the nation. A proclamation announcing the implementation of martial law is warranted "By order of the Czar, father of his people" (149), but the act is intended to starve the populace. A ruthless advisor, Prince Paul, tells the Czar that martial law "will carry off your surplus population in six months, and save you any expense in courts of justice." The Czar finds this Malthusian argument sound: "Quite right. There are too many people in Russia, too much money spent on them, too much money on courts of justice" (194). Wilde uses the heartlessness of the Czar to put the nihilists' crimes in perspective—there are far more Russians killed by the Czar than political figures assassinated by the nihilists—and his drama asks whether violence at the hands of the state is any more justified than violence at the hands of the nihilists; Vera reflects on "how easy it is for a king to kill his people by thousands, but we cannot rid ourselves of one crowned man in Europe!" (150).

Wilde's political critique also extends to hereditary aristocracy. Russia's ruling class, in *Vera,* ruthlessly exploits the people who finance it. In one scene, the Marquis de Poivrard asks another aristocrat, "What is the use of the people except for us to get money out of?" He then demands "forty thousand roubles . . . my wife says she must have a new diamond bracelet" (242). The heavily taxed peasants who provide such men with riches are—like the prisoners to Peter Sabouroff—of no account except to generate wealth. Wilde's Russian aristocrats betray all the symptoms of a decadent, obsolete institution: one courtier says, "I am bored with life, Prince. Since the opera season ended I have been a perpetual martyr to ennui." Prince Paul responds, "The maladie du siécle! You want a new excitement, Prince. Let me see—you have been married twice already; suppose you try—falling in love for once" (179). Such epigrammatic repartee rings familiarly of Jack and Algernon, Wilde's celebrated caricatures of the English aristocracy in *The Importance of Being Earnest,* but *Vera*'s satire of decadence is decidedly more caustic: one courtier tries, for example, to arrange another's death in order to facilitate an affair with his wife.

Vera emerges as a threat to this moribund patriarchal order, not only because of her nihilism, but because of her independent femininity. She refuses the attentions of Michael, the farmer whose courtship is sanctioned by her father, and even converts him to nihilism. Upon joining the nihilists, she forsakes her father and vows never to marry at all, in accordance with the nihilist oath: "To strangle whatever nature is in me; neither to love nor to be loved; neither to pity nor to be pitied; neither to marry nor to be given in marriage, till the end is come" (135).[27] The nihilists pledge to annihilate the hierarchies of the past in favor of a new society, yet still, Wilde's version of Russian nihilism does not fully assimilate women into its fraternal ranks, a point that becomes clearer as the central conflict of the plot takes shape: Vera violates her nihilist oath by falling in love with the Czarevitch, who has revolutionary sympathies and joins the nihilists posing as a medical student named Alexis. Wilde presents this conflict as a tension between political and personal commitment as well as a tension between Vera's womanhood and radicalism. At one point, she asks herself, "why did he come amongst us with his bright young face, his heart aflame for liberty, his pure white soul? Why does he make me feel at times as if I would have him as my king, Republican though I be?" (156–57). Later, in the midst of reciting the nihilist oath, she breaks off, "Oh, I am a woman! God help me, I am a woman! . . . I am a traitor. I love" (255). Vera's femininity made her espousal of the nihilist oath more shocking for 1880s audiences, and Wilde treats her conflicting loyalties as a symptom of that femininity.[28]

Vera most explicitly addresses the conflict between her femininity and her nihilism at the end of act 3, when she agrees to assassinate Alexis because he has taken the title of czar upon his father's death: "I am no woman now . . . my heart is as cold as steel" (233). Given her choice of weapons, Vera opts for the phallic dagger rather than poison, a choice inflected with a rejection of the feminine, since murderesses were uniquely associated with poison, as discussed in chapter 2. In the same scene, Vera imagines herself committing infanticide, a virulent refutation of maternal "instinct": "if I was a mother and bore a man-child, I would poison my breast against him, lest he might grow to a traitor or to a king" (234). At the height of this dramatic scene, Wilde directly links

Vera to the historical female political criminal most familiar in the An-glo-Victorian imagination; Vera says, "Methinks the spirit of Charlotte Corday has entered my soul now. I shall carve my name on the world, and be ranked among the great heroines. Ay! the spirit of Charlotte Cor-day beats in each petty vein, and nerves my woman's hand to strike, as I have nerved my woman's heart to hate" (237). Corday was a heroic figure in the Victorian imaginary, but represented the ambiguous nature of female political agency, as I discuss at the beginning of the chapter.

Wilde's invocation of Corday parallels Thomas Carlyle's in *The French Revolution,* a history that Wilde described in "The Decay of Ly-ing" as "one of the most fascinating historical novels ever written," since "facts are either kept in their proper subordinate position, or else entirely excluded on the general ground of dullness" (980). *The French Revolution* was published in 1837 and pored over by legions of Victorian readers; it practically ensured Corday's symbolic value for the Victorians by pre-senting her as the epitome of Manichaean, angel/demon femininity:

> She is of stately Norman figure; in her twenty-fifth year; of beautiful still countenance: her name is Charlotte Corday. . . . What if she, this fair young Charlotte, had emerged from her secluded stillness, sud-denly like a Star; cruel-lovely, with half-angelic, half-daemonic splen-dour; to gleam for a moment, and in a moment be extinguished: to be held in memory, so bright complete was she, through long centuries! (645)

Noting her youth, beauty, seclusion, and high birth, Carlyle aligns Cor-day with idealized femininity, yet she is also "cruel-lovely" and "half-daemonic," compound descriptors that signify the profound bifurcation at the root of her identity as a woman *and* a political assassin. The passage presents Corday's political deed as at odds with her sex; she "emerge[s] from her secluded stillness," into the realm of political combat, only "for a moment." Carlyle reconciles her violent deed with her feminine body by describing her political agency in mystical terms, as though it came from somewhere outside herself.

When Vera calls upon Corday's spirit, Wilde similarly mystifies her decision to assassinate the Czar: her body remains feminine in this pas-sage—"my woman's heart" and "my woman's hand"—but is possessed by another spirit, allowing her to agree to the assassination despite her love for Alexis. Vera's mystical communion with Corday presents her as a channel for social and historical forces rather than an independent political agent, but Wilde pointedly rejects this characterization in the final scene of his play, when Vera abandons her mission and decides *not* to assassinate the young czar. Hovering above Alexis's body, brandishing her dagger, she has a change of heart. After hearing his intentions for reform, she determines that it will be better for the people of Russia to have him alive than dead: "you must live for liberty, for Russia, for me!" (260). Knowing that the nihilists below are waiting for the dagger to signal her completion of the deed, she decides to stab herself and toss the bloody knife to the conspirators, thwarting them from entering the palace and killing Alexis. Her words in this scene show she is not motivated by love; she reneges on her nihilist oath, but public commitment still trumps personal attachment. Her last words, after she stabs herself, are also the last words of the play: "I have saved Russia! [*Dies*]" (261).

This ending valorizes the effectiveness of women's political agency, albeit in the problematic form of self-immolation. Vera's act of individual heroism can be read as feminist, but also entails her rejection of a collective revolutionary movement in favor of an individual or liberal model of political agency. The feminism of *Vera*'s conclusion is undeveloped, yet throughout the play, Vera's support for democracy and her rebellion against patriarchal authority are inseparable from her feminist autonomy. A letter written by Constance Lloyd, who would marry Wilde soon after *Vera*'s staging, gives us a window into his ideas about the ending: "Oscar says he wrote it to show that an abstract idea such as liberty could have quite as much power and be made quite as fine as the passion of love" (Wilde, *Complete Letters* 222). In keeping with melodramatic tradition, *Vera* privileges individual heroism and advocates a democratic sensibility, yet the play also breaks from melodrama in valuing "liberty" above heterosexual love. Vera's final gesture could be said, indeed, to exemplify the most fundamental individual liberty of all: the right to die.

The political consequences of Vera's suicide are unclear, since the play ends with her death, and does not resolve whether the new czar follows through on his promises of reform. In the last act, Alexis's private meditations on the seductive power of the crown and scepter suggest that Vera may have misjudged his incorruptibility, yet the play's ending seems to promote a reformist rather than a revolutionary solution for political disputes that were constantly erupting into violence at the end of the nineteenth century. Earlier in the play, one of the aristocrats states, "Reforms in Russia are very tragic, but they always end in a farce" (244); it is significant, however, that only unappealing characters express such cynicism about reform. Ultimately, the play does not advocate a coherent plan for democratic change, but it does position Vera squarely in the realm of political action, even though she is a woman and even though she is a nihilist. In linking together the modern political phenomena of democracy, first-wave feminism, and political terror, *Vera* calls for a serious reconfiguration of public and political representation at the end of the nineteenth century.

Wilde's first drama should give critics pause in underestimating the political thrust of his later satirical comedies, for it reminds us that Wilde's public debut as a dramatist occurred via a play sympathetic to Russian nihilist terrorism. Under the circumstances, Lady Bracknell's humorous lines in *The Importance of Being Earnest,* for example, are decidedly more menacing: "Fortunately, in England, at any rate, education produces no effect whatsoever. If it did, it would prove a serious danger to the upper classes, and probably lead to acts of violence in Grosvenor Square" (17). *Earnest* was Wilde's biggest hit, and its most crucial prop is the handbag that held the baby Jack, which Miss Prism left in the cloakroom at Victoria Station. Remarkably, the 1884 Fenian dynamiting of Victoria Station was also achieved via a "heavy small bag" left in the station's cloakroom ("Dynamite Outrage" 10). This may appear coincidental, but consider Lady Bracknell's response when Jack tells her that he was found in "an ordinary hand-bag" left in the cloakroom of Victoria Station: "To be born, or at any rate bred, in a hand-bag, whether it had handles or not, seems to me to display a contempt for the ordinary decencies of family life that reminds one of the worst excesses of the French Revolution. And I presume you know what that unfortunate movement led to?" (19). These lines might appear to exemplify the Wildean non sequitur, but Lady Bracknell's association of "terror"—via the Reign of Terror—with a bag left in the cloakroom at Victoria Station actually followed logically in late-Victorian England. Moreover, when Lady Bracknell goes on to remark that "a cloak-room at a railway station . . . could hardly be regarded as an assured basis for a recognized position in good society" (19), Wilde explicitly correlates antidemocratic ideology with explosive truths emerging from bags left in railway station cloakrooms.

If *The Importance of Being Earnest* is indeed associating Fenian dynamitings with aristocratic exceptionalism, it is not politically afar from the overtly democratic *Vera*. Indeed, given Wilde's Irish background and his support for Irish nationalism, it is impossible to read his description of the corrupt Russian empire in *Vera* without being reminded of England's own empire, or to encounter his nihilist political criminals without thinking of Irish republicans. Wilde does not directly name Ireland in the play, but his nihilists describe Russia's brutal sway over neighboring Poland—"unhappy Poland! . . . we must not forget our brothers there" (534)—and his Russian peasants work their land for mere survival, while others profit, like Irish tenant farmers working for English landlords. In a manuscript draft of *Vera,* held at the Clark Library, Wilde spelled out this connection more explicitly in an act 2 speech by the Czarevitch: "The land which is theirs we have taken from them." Whether or not Wilde's audience saw such parallels, Fenian dynamite must have played a role in the critical hesitation surrounding *Vera*'s treatment of terrorism. For in the context of the czar's assassination and the first Irish nationalist dynamiting in London—both of which occurred in 1881—*Vera* put forth a surprisingly radical investigation into the nature of political crime in the modern world.

A GIRL AMONG THE ANARCHISTS

Vera was loosely inspired by a real female revolutionary, but *A Girl among the Anarchists* represents a far more direct redaction of biography into dynamite narrative. The lives of its authors, Helen and Olivia Rossetti, intersected with a staggeringly wide range of nineteenth- and twentieth-century literature, politics, and art, yet the women have remained relatively obscure to scholars of British culture. Their parents were William Michael Rossetti and Lucy Madox Brown; thus Christina Rossetti was their aunt, Dante Gabriel Rossetti their uncle, John Polidori their great-uncle, Ford Madox Brown their grandfather, and Ford Madox Ford their cousin. The sisters grew up amid bohemian intellectualism and republican, secularist political ideals, but as teenagers, they rejected their family's respectable radicalism for thoroughgoing anarchism. At the ages of sixteen and twelve, they began to publish an anarchist newspaper called the *Torch* from the basement of their parents' home.[29] William Michael Rossetti was "an ardent lover of Shelley and freedom," according to Olivia, and "was rather amused and rather proud of" his daughters' anarchist activities (Tryphonopoulos and Surette xv). He was also a civil servant in the British government, however, and eventually the *Torch* had to relocate elsewhere.[30] The Rossettis' involvement in the paper lasted until 1896, at which time Olivia moved to Italy with her Italian anarchist lover and Helen left England for a long sea voyage meant to cure her consumptive lungs. Soon, both sisters abandoned anarchism for internationalism, and Olivia worked many years for David Lubin, one of the League of Nations' progenitors. Ultimately, however, the two women became supporters of hypernationalist Italian Fascism.[31]

In 1903, long before converting to Fascism, the Rossettis published *A Girl among the Anarchists,* narrating with fictional license their experiences as teenagers in the late-nineteenth-century London anarchist movement. The novel is heavily inflected by the genre and tropes of dynamite fiction. Written under the pseudonym Isabel Meredith, which is also the name of the main character, *Girl* depicts an unusually independent revolutionary female protagonist. Like Wilde's Vera, however, the protagonist eventually abandons her radicalism, and the novel concludes with an abortive courtship and an unresolved political quest. The novel's ambivalent ending indicates the impossibility of women's full development as political subjects under existing social conditions, and the Rossettis' semiautobiographical dynamite narrative thus correlates feminist discontent at women's lack of political representation with the frustrations that prompt radical campaigns for political change.

I suggest in chapter 4 that *A Girl among the Anarchists* was a key source for Conrad's *The Secret Agent,* published four years later. Conrad revisits a central event of the Rossettis' narrative, Martial Bourdin's botched Greenwich Park bombing of 1894, and appears to have been heavily influenced by its account, though he never acknowledged it (see chapter 4, note 10). If my claim is correct, it suggests the Rossettis' importance in defining the anarchist movement for contemporaneous dynamite literature, which is unsurprising given their prominent social position in London's literary and cultural elite. Interestingly, however, the Rossettis' amalgamated autobiographical "self," Isabel Meredith, does not benefit from a prominent social position. In fictionalizing their story, the Rossettis drastically alter their life and situation, and the changes they make help convey the novel's feminist contentions. They depict Meredith as a woman on her own, lacking the protective net of patriarchal domesticity. This situation is not presented as frightening or debilitating, as in George Gissing's *The Odd Women,* where the Madden sisters are left "adrift" by the sudden loss of their father, nor as sterile and empty, like Vivie Warren's life at the end of *Mrs. Warren's Profession,* but rather as rich in freedom and possibility.

As the story begins, Meredith's parents have died, leaving her with an unusual degree of autonomy. She lives virtually alone in bohemian London; her brother also resides in the house, but spends most days and nights at a hospital training to be a doctor. Meredith says, "I was used to looking after myself and depending on my own resources for amusement and occupation" (1). The novel thus begins like a New Woman novel; Meredith's search for fulfillment and occupation, in a setting inhospitable to women, is what brings her to radicalism. Given women's limited opportunities outside the home, she grows weary and bored: "Time used often to hang rather heavily on my hands in the big house where I was generally alone. I was the housekeeper, but such cares did not take up much of my time. . . . I became restless and dissatisfied" (11). In the tradition of 1890s New Woman novels, housekeeping and domesticity do not fill Meredith's interests and ambitions, and she instead seeks a role in public life.

Like the late-Victorian New Woman, Meredith is independent and self-sufficient; she wanders around the city at night, sometimes returning from political meetings at one in the morning or later (54), and regularly makes late-night visits to disreputable pawnshops: "since my connection with the Anarchist movement . . . I had become quite familiar with the ins and outs [of pawnshops]" (224). She also has detailed knowledge of London public transportation, which she negotiates on her own (178), and becomes just as comfortable in the political sphere as in public space: "my name had become well known in the International Anarchist Party" (120). In revolutionary politics, Meredith finds an outlet for her energy and autonomy. Initially, she is attracted to state socialism, but she finds a more satisfyingly revolutionary platform in anarchist communism. She is enthusiastic about the anarchist plan to abolish poverty—a central theme of the book—and philosophical anarchism appeals to her belief in "the right to complete liberty of action" (18), since it is less dogmatic than Marxism or state socialism. In this narrative context, Meredith's intense attraction to the ideal of "liberty" seems as much a feminist as an anarchist impulse.

Outside of paternal authority, Meredith finds a surrogate community and an alternative form of home with her anarchist comrades. Sometimes, after working late, she sleeps in the newspaper's office with other members of the staff, many of whom are male. The staff is often likened to a large egalitarian family, a microcosm of the form of social organization that the anarchists want to bring about: voluntary and communitarian rather than hierarchical. Meredith rejects the "housekeeper" domesticity she is born into, defined by property ownership and a gendered division of labor, and embraces an alternative kinship with anarchist comrades. Their revolutionary agenda, the novel suggests, involves finding new models of social organization suited for an egalitarian and communitarian society, unlike patriarchal domesticity.

Exploring forms of community beyond the hierarchical and patriarchal family, Meredith also explores—from the outside—sexual alternatives to bourgeois marriage. Her sympathetic account of anarchists who advocate free-love principles suggests that such arrangements accord with feminist objectives: jealousy and possessiveness in love enforce women's social role as sexual property; free-love advocates, who move beyond such parsimoniousness, show greater respect for women's personal liberty. One such advocate, Giannoli, explains his free-love doctrine to Meredith: "It was a woman . . . who completely altered my views of life, and made me see how perverted and unnatural are our ideas of sex and love and morals" (196). He reclaims the rhetoric of "perversion," applying it to normative bourgeois sexuality rather than free love: "All my previous ideas and prejudices appeared to me monstrous and iniquitous. I saw the falseness of all our ideas of morality, the absurdity of placing conventions before nature and the detestable character of our dealings with women" (200). The novel thus offers a feminist argument for free love, and indeed women initiate all the free-love unions discussed in its pages, including one that a young woman "insisted" upon (205). The fin de siècle saw a widespread effort, in radical circles, to theorize a model of sexuality better suited for the future democratic and egalitarian society.[32] Meredith participates in this discourse by imagining a kind of love rooted in communitarian social principles.

Meredith herself does not engage in free love, nor in the "propaganda by deed" advocated by her more extreme revolutionary comrades, but she is nevertheless a revolutionary heroine and a political criminal, who takes part in activities that could land her in jail.[33] She endures detective and police harassment for her work on the anarchist newspaper, and describes in the course of the novel various efforts to spirit wanted dynamiters out of the country, to harbor men being searched for by the police, and to provide money and counsel for men who have been arrested. Meredith characterizes her interactions with the police in these instances in terms of resistance to governmental paternalism. As an anarchist, she is not persuaded by the idea that legal interventionism is a sound means of ensuring liberty, and in this way she differs from many contemporary feminists. Late-Victorian women's groups championed the campaign for interventionist legal reform, as I discuss in chapter 1, but Meredith views police intervention as coercive enforcement of normative behavior in the private sphere. In one scene, she takes a male anarchist from Scotland in for the night, much to the disgust of the neighborhood constable: "As I was getting out my latch-key the local policeman chanced to pass: 'That fellow has been hanging about for the last hours, miss,' he said to me. 'Shall I remove him for you?' 'Certainly not,' I replied firmly, and opening the door, I requested my unknown comrade to enter. I can still see in my mind's eye that constable's face. It looked unutterable things" (58).

Tackling paternalism, interventionism, and free love, the Rossettis' novel addresses the newly redistricted public and private spheres of modern Britain; it conjoins the New Woman novel with dynamite narrative to describe a society in which traditional structures of authority are crumbling amid feminist and democratic appeals for liberty. Like Vera, Isabel Meredith finds a prototype for her anomalous position as a revolutionary woman in the story of Charlotte Corday. She recalls an old friend of her father's who would goad her, as a child, about her fascination for the French Revolution:

> He had nicknamed me Charlotte Corday, for . . . I had plunged into the French Revolution, glorying in its heroisms and audacity, and it had become a favourite amusement . . . to enact scenes drawn from its history. . . . The old professor loved to tease me by abusing my favourite heroes; and when he had at last roused me to a vigorous assertion of revolutionary sentiments, he would turn to my father and say, "There's a little spitfire for you; you will have to keep a look-out or she will be making bombs soon and blowing us all up." (7–8)

As in Wilde's play, Meredith's radicalization is bolstered by identification with Corday, but while Meredith and Vera both reflect the ambiguity of Corday's angel/demon image in British culture, Vera's summoning of Corday's spirit is far more ominous than Meredith's youthful emulation of the French assassin.[34]

Still, the novel does not neutralize the threat its protagonist poses as an anarchist revolutionary. In a discussion of "propaganda by deed," Meredith takes on a crucial issue of dynamite narrative: she attempts to make sense of the modern crime of terrorism, typically represented in dynamite fiction as so utterly random and purposeless that it is nearly impossible to understand as a "crime" at all. Meredith positions herself as an interpreter, a figure on the periphery between anarchism and "normal" society. A "normal man," she says, is "morally incapable of judging" fanatical anarchists because he "cannot grasp their motive, their point of view" (187). She attempts to explain that point of view, arguing that there is something "terribly, if pervertedly, logical" in a dynamiter's reasoning: "Earnest thought and reflection told him that if any section of society suffered, then society at large was guilty: all the thoughtless, all the indifferent members of society were equally responsible for its abuses" (189). The dynamiter, in other words, believes that "society at large" is responsible for poverty and oppression; it is from here that the dynamiter comes to advocate random violence: "Society at large is guilty; society at large must suffer. Society is fairly well represented by the mixed crowd in a café. I will attack this crowd indiscriminately" (189–90). Meredith rejects such logic and stresses that the vast majority of anarchists also reject it, but insists that a dynamiter believes he is "performing his duty according to his own lights just as much as a soldier when he obeys orders and fires on the enemy" (189). In comparing a dynamiter to a soldier, she reminds her audience that state-sanctioned violence also occasions civilian casualties, "collateral damage," and the death of innocent bystanders.

Much of the outrage about dynamite terrorism in late-Victorian London, of course, had to do with its seemingly indiscriminate victimization. On 24 January 1885, Fenian dynamiters set off near-simultaneous explosions in the Tower of London, the Houses of Parliament, and Westminster Hall, as I discuss in chapter 4. No one was killed, but several tourists and sightseers were severely injured. An article on the attack in the *Times* reported: "To inspire terror is with the Irish-American enemies of England . . . both an end in itself and a means to other ends. It gratifies a malignity of temper which has been festered till it has become a ruling passion." The author can only understand such random violence by imagining the Fenians as independent actors with independent failings, a "malignity of temper." He cannot view them as acting within a more generalized colonial conflict. A Fenian, the article states, "chuckles at the infliction of pain and fear upon men, women, and children absolutely disconnected with and many of them literally ignorant of, the so-called 'wrongs of Ireland.'" He "sweeps them at random into the meshes of his murderous plot" ("London"). The fact that "women and children," in particular, could be victims of dynamite bombs seemed a violation of the rules of civil engagement; thus "innocent women and children" are evoked ad nauseam in mainstream newspaper accounts of dynamite terror.[35]

Meredith's attempt to make sense of propaganda by deed, though she acknowledges that the dynamiter's philosophy is misguided and even mad, is thus especially striking in that it comes from a woman. The rhetoric surrounding dynamite attacks often appealed to the victimization of women to establish terrorism's disregard for public and private social divisions. To harm women and children, these articles suggest, represents a failure to distinguish between the politically conscious and the politically ignorant, between those who have the vote and those who do not. In the *Times,* assassins were considered worse than other kinds of murderers, but were not wholly incomprehensible since they targeted public figures: "To compass the assassination of a Sovereign or a Minister, or even the destruction *en masse* of a legislative body, must be, without doubt, condemned and pursued to punishment as crimes inconsistent with the elementary forms of civilization. But such designs are at least intelligible; they go straight to their mark" ("London"). Dynamiters, by contrast, are random; rather than targeting official representatives, they consider every member of a society its "representative." Meredith asserts that in the mind of the dynamiter, "society at large is guilty," which shockingly erodes the distinction between "innocent women and children" and valid political agents. Because the novel is largely about Meredith's efforts, as a woman, to find an outlet for her political agency, the democratic violence of dynamite stands out against legitimate British politics, which do not count women as representatives.

The novel thus correlates revolutionary democratic politics, feminism, and political crime, in that all three modern phenomena call into question traditional notions of who "represents" the nation.[36] Despite this bold assertion of what a New Woman revolutionary signifies, however, the novel's conclusion is decidedly pessimistic. The title indicates where the story will end up: the heroine is merely a "girl," not an independent woman, and is merely "among" the anarchists, not of them. She eventually gives up on her effort to assert political agency via anarchism, and correlates her rejection of anarchism with the onset of maturity, as do other characters in the story. A letter from her sister, who has long been out of the country, says: "I expect by now Isabel has had time to grow out of her enthusiasm for revolutions and economics, and will feel less drawn toward baggy-trousered democrats and unwashed philosophers" (281). The letter angers Meredith, but by the last page of the novel, she too calls the anarchist print-shop "the place which had witnessed so much enthusiasm, so many generous hopes and aspirations, and where so many illusions lay buried" (302). In the last line of the story, she leaves the anarchists for good: "I walked forth into the London street a sadder if a wiser woman" (302). This ending is deeply ambivalent. The references to Meredith's newfound maturity position the tale as a novel of development or *bildung,* but at the conclusion, she has nothing to replace the purpose and meaning that anarchism gave to her life. Instead, she is stuck at her new stage of maturity. She is no longer an anarchist, but still lacks a place in mainstream public life.

The novel depicts this dilemma as a specifically bodily one, indicating that Meredith's female body is the root of the problem, for it is not the dynamiters or free-love advocates who drive Meredith outside the movement through extremism, but the purity advocates. Toward the novel's end, Meredith becomes fixated on what she considers the folly of hygienic strains in revolutionary politics, such as the temperance movement and vegetarianism. Her frustration with those who deny their bodies emerges just as she suffers from sexual rejection; Meredith's virulent reaction against ascetic strains of anarchism thus appears to be displaced anger regarding her own inability to reconcile body and politics. The object of her desire is Ivan Kosinski, a Russian anarchist famous for "his absolute unswerving devotion to his ideas" (26). Kosinski is known to hate women, making consummation of their relationship seem unlikely: "From the first moment Kosinski interested me. His manners were not engaging; towards women especially he was decidedly hostile. . . . perhaps his evident aversion to my sex . . . had for me a certain fascination. I felt attracted towards the man" (29–30). Kosinski's misogyny stems from suspicion about women's political commitment: "Women are rarely of much use in a movement like ours. They so rarely seem able to forget *themselves,* to detach themselves from the narrow interests of their own lives. They are still the slaves of their past, of their passions, and of all manner of prejudices" (233). Meredith's inability to square her political beliefs and bodily desires is, to Kosinski, a specifically female failing, but his analysis neglects to account for the fact that it is precisely women's *bodies* that impede their full political participation.

Hence, at the end of the novel, Meredith is stuck between a radical asceticism that cannot satisfy her body, and a mainstream society that cannot occupy her mind. After suppressing her feelings for Kosinski for much of the narrative, she finally speaks: "We Anarchists are always talking of the rights of the individual, why are you deliberately sacrificing your personal happiness, and mine? . . . I love you, and I *know* that you love me" (267–68). Kosinski's response exercises a privilege that is revealed in the novel to be specifically male—the privilege of denying the body: "An Anarchist's life is not his own. Friendship, comradeship may be helpful, but family ties are fatal" (268). The novel ends with no resolution to the fundamental problem of the text: the conflict between Meredith's female body and her desire for political agency.

THE DYNAMITER

The Rossettis' novel is one of many late-Victorian narratives about anarchism; indeed, anarchists frequently appear in dynamite fiction, which as I have noted is a historically incongruous aspect of the genre, as is the absence of Ireland and Fenian dynamite. The corrupt Russian empire in *Vera* may be an implied condemnation of British imperialism, but neither Wilde nor the Rossettis directly address the "Irish question." Irish nationalism is, however, one of the causes motivating the revolutionaries in Robert Louis and Fanny Van de Grift Stevenson's 1885 novel *The Dynamiter*. Ireland is rarely mentioned in the text; still, among all the dynamite narratives in this study, it is the only one that openly correlates with the acts of political violence that the British reading public confronted in daily life. In the years surrounding the novel's publication, Irish nationalist groups mounted many attacks, dynamiting numerous buildings and railway stations, stabbing Lord Frederick Cavendish and his undersecretary in Dublin's Phoenix Park, and assassinating dozens of Anglo-Irish landlords and officials.[37] Despite *The Dynamiter*'s more intimate proximity to the reality of late-Victorian terror, however, it is a pointedly antirealist text, an assiduously antimimetic and humorous satire.

The target of the novel's satire is reflexive rather than overtly political: narrative conventions, literary realism, and genre fiction are all blasted to bits. As is often the case, the Stevensons helped solidify "dynamite narrative" as a genre by parodying it. Their novel employs hyperbolic excess, unreliable narrators, and structural irony to mock the conventions of detective, dynamite, and sensation fiction, as well as realism, colonial adventure stories, and other popular forms of Victorian narrative. While this seems like a decidedly risky literary enterprise for such grave subject matter, the novel was a commercial and critical hit. In her preface to *The Dynamiter,* Fanny states that it was "as well received as we could have hoped" (xv), and that their hopes for the novel were exclusively pecuniary: "On one of these occasions when money was absolutely necessary, we cast about for something that could be done quickly and without too much strain" (xiv).[38] Despite its inauspicious beginnings, the novel went through three editions in four months upon its publication in April 1885. The London *Times* gave it a very flattering review; Victorian tastemaker Henry James also wrote admiringly of it, as I note in chapter 4; and G. K. Chesterton likewise praised it in print. The critic E. Purcell, who often disparaged Stevenson's work, published a glowing review in the journal *Academy:* "the art is phenomenal . . . it charms by its very audacity. . . . no modern English book contains such a profusion and superfluity of talent as this little 'Dynamiter.' It is a masterpiece . . . no novelist can read it without gnawing envy" (Maixner 196).

Why was the novel so eminently uncontroversial, in spite of the levity with which it treats the perilous subject of Irish dynamite? The depiction of its female revolutionary, Clara Luxmore, is largely responsible for the novel's appeal. In Clara's first appearance in the text, she is fleeing from the scene of a dynamite bomb, but is "charming both in face and figure, elegantly dressed and gloved: a lady undeniable" (12). Like other female criminals of the era, she is likable, attractive, and appealing. Throughout the narrative, she manipulates the novel's unsuspecting male protagonists into aiding insurgent conspiracy. The novel begins when these three young men, fresh out of university, decide to become detectives to escape financial straits. Anticipating Conan Doyle, who had not yet invented Sherlock Holmes, they imagine the detective as the consummate gentleman: "our manners, habit of the world, powers of conversation, vast stores of unconnected knowledge, all that we are and have builds up the character of the complete detective. It is, in short, the only profession for a gentleman" (6).

The men prove to be no good at detecting, however, and are continually hoodwinked by Clara, who is a key predecessor for characters such as Conan Doyle's Irene Adler. Clara's ability to con is partially due to her image. One of the men describes her in terms that evoke cinema's glamorous female criminals, discussed in chapter 3: "Her face was warm and rich in colour; in shape, it was that piquant triangle, so innocently sly, so saucily attractive . . . ; her eyes were large, starry, and visited by changing lights; . . . her arms, bare to the shoulder, gleamed white; her figure, full and soft in all the womanly contours, was yet alive and active, light with excess of life" (139). References to "starry" eyes with "changing lights," "gleaming" white arms, and a body "light with excess of life" liken Clara to the flickering, fleeting figure of the *passante*—Baudelaire's dazzling yet vanishing woman of the modern city. Her very name, Clara Luxmore, literally evokes "clear light." "Innocently sly" and "saucily attractive," Clara is desirable yet ungraspable, aligning her with a peculiarly modern and consumerist conception of glamour and desire, in which distance intensifies visual enticement. Walter Benjamin's well-known Marxian reading of the *passante* has described this figure as a phantasmagoric abstraction of consumer capitalism, emblematic of nineteenth-century consumerism's manipulations of desire via vision and distance (exemplified, in the latter half of the century, by plate-glass windows and department store display).

Recent feminist work by critics such as Deborah Parsons, however, has also linked the figure of the *passante* with the rise of modern, autonomous femininity, and the Stevensons' novel resonates with such readings; for Clara is not only characterized by her intangible allure, but by her independence and autonomy, which connect her with the figure of the New Woman. Her mother explains at one point in the novel that Clara left her family to participate in revolutionary politics:

> she ran away from home. . . . Some whim about oppressed nationalities—Ireland, Poland, and the like—has turned her brain; and if you should anywhere encounter a young lady (I must say, of remarkable attractions) answering to the name of Luxmore, Lake, or Fonblanque (for I am told she uses these indifferently, as well as many others), tell her, from me, that I forgive her cruelty, and though I will never more behold her face, I am at any time prepared to make her a liberal allowance. (79)

Like Vera, Clara conjoins the late-Victorian figure of the New Woman with the rise of democratic social movements, but also with modern, consumerist forms of feminine glamour of less interest to the era's major New Woman novelists such as Sarah Grand or Thomas Hardy. The Stevensons depict their female revolutionary as an extra-domestic, autonomous woman, but while Vera and Isabel Meredith are shocking political criminals largely because they are women, Clara's desirable, attractive femininity functions to preclude umbrage at the buoyancy with which the authors handle their subject.

Clara is nevertheless an extremely volatile narrative presence, associated with all kinds of modern threats to the social order. Perhaps the most fundamental of these threats is her disruption of novelistic form. Occasionally, she takes over the story from its third-person narrator and tells tales in first-person narrative voice. Like Scheherazade, she deploys narration as a form of subversive power, spinning sensational yarns about Mormon Utah and colonial Cuba to bend the novel's male protagonists to her ends. Part of the genius of the novel, much appreciated by its contemporaries, is that it is not always clear which parts are "real" and which are Clara's lies, reflexively reminding readers that all fiction is a lie. The book is thus surprisingly ungrounded and "anarchic" in form, and its chaotic point of view gives it a whiff of amorality or modern relativism that emerges largely from Clara's role in the text. That both Robert and Fanny Stevenson claimed authorship of the novel, as indicated on its title page, reinforced this idea of modern women undermining traditional structures of narrative authority, by violating the convention of a unified authorial voice.

The form and effect of Clara's narration, in fact, echoes dynamite terror itself, as represented in the late-Victorian press. Newspapers of this era often depict terrorism as a confusingly disorienting excess of technological modernity; after the January 1885 bombing involving three explosions, the *Times* wrote: "the worst acts of mediæval tyrants and of savage tribes have now been surpassed by . . . men domiciled as citizens in the most progressive country of the modern world" ("London"). Progress and modernity mingle with primitive medievalism and "savagery" in this account. The writer presumes that modernity should correspond with progressive improvement, but a "savage" revolutionary movement rooted in the United States—the "most progressive country of the modern world"—has disrupted this faith in modernity and progress. Clara's narration similarly associates the modern with disorientation rather than progress. Her sections of the novel disregard progressive narration in a self-consciously modern way; they initially seem to advance the novel's overarching plot, but ultimately prove to be pointless digressions.

Her first "lie," moreover, likewise deals with the curious intermingling of the "modern" and the "primitive" in the United States: it is a tale of "harems" and forced marriage on the Mormon frontier of Utah. The story is told as true, but it so violates the tenets of realism that it leaves Clara's listener, one of the gentleman detectives, utterly bewildered and confused:

> It was an excellent story; and it might be true, but he believed it was not. Miss Fonblanque was a lady, and it was doubtless possible for a lady to wander from the truth; but how was a gentleman to tell her so? His spirits for some time had been sinking, but they now fell to zero; and long after her voice had died away he still sat with a troubled and averted countenance, and could find no form of words to thank her for her narrative. (49)

Reviews of the novel regarded such "lies" as modern literary experimentation, but like dynamite, Clara's unreliable narration represents modernity's disorientation, its denial of traditional assumptions that function as a stable ground for perspective. Indeed, the novel's chief dynamiter, Zero, later makes an explicit comparison between women and dynamite: "chemicals are proverbially as fickle as woman, and clockwork as capricious as the very devil" (117).

With its chaotic point of view and its seemingly indiscriminate vacillations between the "real" narrator and Clara's erratic tales, the novel echoes another key attribute of late-Victorian dynamite: arbitrariness. Just as the novel jumbles perspective by haphazardly intermingling reliable and unreliable voices, dynamiters were said to disregard the perspective of their victims, to bomb indiscriminately the politically savvy and the politically ignorant. As I discuss with respect to the Rossettis' novel, it was considered particularly ignominious that extrapolitical subjects such as women and children could be victims of political terror. Clara's illicit, ungrounded narration thus evokes the egalitarian arbitrariness of dynamite. At one point, Zero exclaims: "behold this field of city, rich, crowded, laughing with the spoil of continents; but soon, how soon, to be laid low! . . . Then shall the pallid constable flee side by side with the detected thief" (134). In dynamite's randomness and capacity for creating unexpected juxtapositions—the pairing of a constable and a thief, for example—Zero finds a democratic appeal.

Despite the inclusion of Clara's volatile, mutinous narration, however, *The Dynamiter* does dispense moral principle at key points in the text. The novel's explosive satire is framed, at the beginning and end, in the earnest, hyper-conventional language of bourgeois domestic sentiment—a complete shift in tone from the vast midsection of the novel.[39] In its conclusion, Clara falls in love with one of the male detectives and renounces her past, and the exiled Prince of Bohemia, a character who also appeared in Stevenson's *The New Arabian Nights* (1882), chastises the repentant Clara for her dalliance with dynamite:

> "I speak with some severity, and yet I pick my terms. I tell myself continually that you are a woman; and a voice continually reminds me of the children whose lives and limbs you have endangered. A woman," he repeated solemnly—"and children. Possibly, madam, when you are yourself a mother, you will feel the bite of that antithesis: possibly when you kneel at night beside a cradle, a fear will fall upon you, heavier than any shame. . . ." (203)

When it comes to revolution, the prince is hardly a neutral arbiter—readers of *New Arabian Nights* will remember that "a recent revolution [had] hurled him from the throne of Bohemia" (226)—but here he dwells not on Clara's revolutionary instincts but on her unwomanliness and on the supposed unnaturalness of her disregard for children. The pathology of the specifically *female* revolutionary thus takes narrative precedence at the novel's resolution, staving off a coherent discussion of political violence.

After all the satirical excess of the novel—a full third of which is made up of Clara's melodramatic fibs—the tone shifts to moral realism with Clara's eleventh-hour conversion: "Oh! Harry . . . I am a dangerous and wicked girl. . . . From first to last I have cheated and played with you. And what I am I dare not even name to you in words. Indeed, until to-day . . . I never grasped the depth and foulness of my guilt" (188). On its surface, this conclusion is far more conventional than most contemporaneous narratives about female criminals, yet in many ways it is less conventional than it seems. Having already been established as an inveterate liar, Clara cannot fully reclaim credibility when renouncing her past; even more significantly, at the story's end, she is the only one of the novel's dynamiters to survive, and she is the only one who is female. Her ability to segue from radical revolutionary to bourgeois wife in the final pages of the book is a testament to the malleability of her identity, and establishes the extent to which her beauty and image transcend all other aspects of her character.

Still, at the novel's conclusion, the Prince steps forward as a representative of male authority, and his final lecture depicts marriage and domesticity as a fund of moral value in the service of English nationalism:

> Is it not one of your English poets, that looked abroad upon the earth and saw . . . innumerable troops manoeuvring, war-ships at sea and a great dust of battles on shore; and casting anxiously about for what should be the cause of so many and painful preparations, spied at last, in the centre of all, a mother and her babe? These, madam, are my politics; and the verses, which are by Mr. Coventry Patmore, I have caused to be translated into the Bohemian tongue. Yes, these are my politics: to change what we can; to better what we can; but still to bear in mind . . . for no word however nobly sounding, and no cause however just and pious, to relax the stricture of these bonds. (204)

Alluding to Coventry Patmore, the prince here suggests that no matter what political grievances dissenters may have, the nation is always ethically superior by virtue of the domestic relations at its core. Clara takes issue with the Prince's conception of politics, but assures him, "I love my husband," which the prince deems "a good answer" (204).

The novel opens in the same key as it ends: upholding the natural, inherent worth of Englishness by referencing the "innocent women and children" threatened by Irish dynamite. Its dedication is to Constable William Cole and Sergeant Thomas Cox, two police officers who were injured while disposing of dynamite planted in the January 1885 bombing: "Whoever be in the right in this great and confused war of politics . . . your side, your part, is at least pure of doubt. Yours is the side of the child, of the breeding woman" (vi). The "child" and "breeding woman" function here as in the prince's speech: whatever England's political dealings, its domestic nucleus proves its decency. Past critics of the novel have viewed the dedication as disingenuous, but Stevenson's letters uphold its point of view, and contemporaries saw it as sincere.[40] It is not surprising that critics have seen *The Dynamiter*'s dedication as insincere, since it is so at odds with the rest of the book. At one point in the novel, Zero expresses comic outrage at the implication that one of his bombings was a "fiasco": "'You will pardon me again,' returned Zero with positive asperity; 'a child was injured'" (186). That the Stevensons could joke about the dynamiting of children and still have a blockbuster on their hands indicates that their use of gender ideology in the novel's frame to diffuse its volatility was an incredibly powerful symbolic deployment.[41] In this context, *The Dynamiter*'s dedication and conclusion serve to recast the sides of political conflict the Stevensons depict: the essential conflict at the heart of modern political crime, we are to believe, is not between bourgeoisie and proletariat, the represented and the disenfranchised, men and women, or, in the case of the Irish question, colonizers and colonized.[42] Instead, it is between home and the streets, babies and bombs. This accords with a broader cultural tendency, evident in this novel, to depict radicalism as anathema to the bonds of the nuclear family. In *The Dynamiter,* the supposedly self-evident value of normative domesticity effectively shuts down political debate.

Despite this ending, the vast bulk of *The Dynamiter*, like *Vera* and *A Girl among the Anarchists,* employs the female revolutionary as an attractive representation of modern challenges to established authorities; she unites democracy, first-wave feminism, and political terror as modern challenges to the configuration of national and public representation. Perhaps it was not finally in the best interest of feminism to have the New Woman coupled with dynamite, nor, certainly, with an overweening emphasis on women's capacity to exercise power via visual spectacle, but it remains true that the rise of British dynamite narratives about female political criminals was followed, shortly thereafter, by an outburst of *real* female political criminals. As Wilde surely would have appreciated, art did not imitate life, but life imitated art. In 1903, the Women's Social and Political Union founded the first militant suffrage organization in Britain, which broke from the feminist movement's tradition of lawful agitation. Such radicalism may have been inspired, if we are to believe F. Henrietta Müller's 1884 pro-suffrage letter to the *Times,* by suffrage advocates' close attention to militant dynamite. Defending her decision to refuse taxation since she is denied representation, she writes: "The power, whether active or latent, to make oneself troublesome is the power which obtains justice; ultimately this is a premium on turbulence and disaffection. It is an invitation to dynamite" (Müller).

As this letter portends, the dispute over suffragette political crime engaged many of the same questions at issue in the three works I have discussed. From 1903 to the start of World War I, the militant wing of the British campaign for women's suffrage committed numerous "terrorist" acts, including bombings, arson, and sabotage. A suffragette named Mary Richardson famously slashed Velázquez's painting *The Toilet of Venus* in the National Gallery, an act of iconoclasm against the image of a female nude very much at odds with the image-centered brand of mainstream feminism we see in popular dynamite narrative.[43] The British government, known for affording "special" status to political crime, denied that such acts were "political" at all, viewing them instead as a kind of pointless, hysterical vandalism. Criminologists approved of this view; though Havelock Ellis supported women's suffrage, he argued, "To rank such crimes among political offenses would be disastrous, for . . . it would soon become impossible to claim any special privilege even for legitimate political offenders" ("Letter" 234). Ellis's comment reveals a painful tautology: the suffrage campaign was all about giving women a "legitimate" political voice, but women cannot commit political crimes if they are not recognized as political agents.

Wilde, the Rossettis, and the Stevensons address this same circularity: the question of whether or not women can be political actors intertwines, in their works, with the question of whether or not political "crimes" can be legitimately political "acts." All three of these dynamite narratives end in variously unsatisfying ways—*Vera* and *A Girl* totally ambiguously, *The Dynamiter* with a nod to the conventional marriage plot—which perhaps speaks to their uncertainty regarding the project with which they are engaged. None of these authors knew how feminism would change the political sphere, nor did they know what the effects of terrorism or democracy would be, but they all foreground a central problem of representation and inclusion at the heart of these distinct political movements. In their depictions of female terrorists and in their focus on questions of gender, body, appearance, and image, the three works suggest that ultimately the political effects of feminism, democracy, and terror will be judged not according to ostensibly empirical or objective measures, but in terms of the images and representations through which they are seen. These narratives of female revolutionaries thus connect "representation" in its literary and visual sense with "representation" in its political sense, portraying a political modernity in which the image-centered culture of consumerism is inextricably tied to the possibility of a newly inclusive, newly feminist public sphere.

AFTERWORD

S*abotage,* Alfred Hitchcock's 1936 film adaptation of *The Secret Agent,* brought the visual aspects of dynamite narrative to the forefront of the story, making film itself a salient feature of the plot. In Joseph Conrad's novel, Verloc and Winnie keep a shop that sells pornography and radical propaganda; in Hitchcock's film, they operate a movie theater. In Conrad's novel, Stevie's bomb explodes in the middle of Greenwich Park; Hitchcock's Stevie unwittingly blows up a bus with a bomb disguised as film equipment. Stevie also carries two reels of a sensational film entitled *Bartholomew the Strangler,* and in a wonderful moment of suspense and dramatic irony, the bus driver nearly refuses to let him board since early film stock was so dangerously flammable. Hitchcock also retains consumerism as a central term in Conrad's narrative: Stevie blows up the bus instead of Piccadilly Station, as Verloc intended, in part because a toothpaste entrepreneur delays him by coercing him into becoming a live model for his product. Hitchcock's adaptation of Conrad's novel thus captures a key link among the three genres I have been considering: Detective series, early crime film, and dynamite narrative all rely on a particular conception of modern life in which shock, spectacle, images, and consumerism are almost inextricably related. Preserving the novel's vision of an explosive, visual, consumerist modernity, the film reminds us that the character and the value of modernity itself are at stake in the new genres of crime narrative that emerge at the fin de siècle.

Sabotage does not gender visuality and consumer culture as relentlessly as *The Secret Agent,* however, and this is just one example of how the film alters the significance of women, and especially criminal women, in its source. Many of Hitchcock's changes to the plot of *Secret Agent* work to create a more conventional narrative of gender. Winnie Verloc becomes a sympathetic victim—a *Woman Alone,* according to the film's alternate title for its U.S. release—who doesn't so much stab her husband as hold the knife while he runs into it. *Sabotage* also introduces a new character, Sergeant Ted Spencer of Scotland Yard, who is an amalgamation of Alexander Ossipon and the assistant commissioner, but unlike either of them is dashing and gallant. At the end of the film, he becomes Winnie's rescuing hero and romantic love interest. *Sabotage* thus relies on a highly conventional narrative of gender; its ending promises what we might call the "excelsior domesticity" of the Victorian marriage plot, a steady escalation toward a future domestic perfection.[1]

Of all the works discussed in this study, very few end in the manner of Hitchcock's movie. *The Dynamiter,* with which the last chapter concludes, does offer an end-of-the-novel marriage as resolution for its complex terrorist plot, but for the most part, New Woman Criminal narratives resist such forms of closure. Female criminals elude capture in the Sherlock Holmes stories; *The Exploits of Three-Fingered Kate* ends with another successful heist by Kate, but no indication that there won't be another film in the series; *A Girl among the Anarchists* echoes New Woman novels in the ambiguity of its ending; and in *The Sorceress of the Strand* and *Vera,* the female criminals die, but their deaths are pointedly not at the hands of the authorities. Such ambiguous conclusions accord with the vision of modernity that these narratives propose, for within fin de siècle crime narrative, competing definitions of the "modern" are insistently gendered: male criminals are regulated via modern, hegemonic, and scientific discipline, while fictional female criminals, as we have seen, represent a modernity that is unmanageable, unfixed, visual rather than fully articulated, and chaotically democratic.[2] W. J. T. Mitchell has argued that "spectacle and surveillance epitomize the basic dialectic between illusionism and realism in contemporary visual culture: they might be thought of as the 'soft' and 'hard' technologies for the formation of subjects in our time" (327). Crimes genres of the fin de siècle foment the late-twentieth-century visual dialectic that Mitchell describes, but forcefully remind us that the process of forming subjects in our time may sometimes be "hard," may sometimes be "soft," but is invariably gendered. With New Woman Criminals, vision itself seems to function in a completely different way than we see with male criminals of the era: rather than rendering the gaze in terms of a powerful seeing eye examining a vulnerable subject, New Woman Criminal narratives conceive of the gaze as a reciprocal practice or even an image-centered practice, in which subject and object are both implicated and both active.

Recognizing the gendering of various versions of modernity, criminality, and the gaze reveals, most obviously, the extent to which these are historical constructions rather than part of a natural order. Visuality is inextricably tied to consumerism in the genres we have considered, for example, and both are linked to women's increasing significance in public life. Indeed, the female criminal in fin de siècle crime genres reveals the formation or solidification of a conception of modern life wherein women's public presence seems indivisible from a consumerist, image-centered, and chaotically freewheeling democratic modernity that is always changing but not always progressing. Many scholars have considered crime fiction and film as central to the formation of visual modernity, but we have not always been attuned to the distinct role of gender within this formation, nor to the way in which such narratives directly intersect with debates about democracy, historical progress, and the boundaries of the political sphere.

Narratives of female criminality, I have attempted to show throughout this study, often link image-centered notions of the gaze not only with consumerism, but with the rise of an ostensibly democratic consumer sphere. The association that we see between women, consumption, and democracy in narratives of female criminality speaks not, I believe, to the "natural" desires of newly empowered women and working classes, or to a "natural" connection between democracy and consumer culture, but to an opportunistic cultural development in which consumerist concepts and rhetoric came to align with progressive movements for feminism and democracy. Some feminist authors, such as L. T. Meade, respond by appropriating consumerist discourse for feminist ends; others, such as the Rossetti sisters, attempt a wholesale rejection of mainstream economic and political outlets for individual expression. Most of the authors in this study are not engaged in explicitly feminist or antifeminist projects, yet their work is no less invested in the female criminal's relation to an imagistic, consumerist, and democratic modernity. The previous chapters have tended, perhaps, to portray the opportunistic alignment among these terms as detrimental or corrosive to genuine gender or class equality. What the female criminal of fin de siècle crime narrative most obviously indicates, however, is not that imagistic consumerism works in the service of "good" or "bad," democratic or antidemocratic, feminist or antifeminist ends, but that it is an incredibly adaptive, mutable, and unanchored force. Like the New Woman Criminal, its relative morality is the least visible thing about it.

NOTES

INTRODUCTION

1. A year later, in 1902, the U.S. film company Biograph produced a near-exact copy of *The Countryman,* entitled *Uncle Josh at the Moving Pictures Show.* Both films are held at the British Film Institute (London) and the UCLA Film and Television Archive. Surviving copies of *Countryman* are unfortunately incomplete, so the film's climactic ending is no longer extant.

2. For other examples, see Max Nordau's *Degeneration,* a best-selling 1895 book that blames "a severe mental epidemic . . . [a] black death of degeneration and hysteria" (537), in part, on modern literature. Likewise, the 1897 *Westminster Review* article "Crime in Current Literature" bemoans literature's apparent turn to the criminal: "What is chiefly to be deplored is the extraordinary rapid increase of that class of fictional literature whose specialty is the detective story," which is "certain, sooner or later, to be disastrous to the community" (A.C. 435–36).

3. Felski, Jameson, and Rothstein, among others, have described the difficulty of finding a satisfying definition for "modernity," but Singer offers a valuable summary of the term's complex meanings in the late-nineteenth-century epistemological moment *(Melodrama).* The definition of "modern life" that I use here—a society understood to be faster, more dangerous, more nerve-racking, more image-centric, and more consumerist than that which preceded it—does not pinpoint "modernity" as a thing in itself, but captures how the late-Victorians use the term to describe their circumstances.

4. See Knelman or Zedner for more on historical female criminals of the period.

5. See D. A. Miller's pioneering study *The Novel and the Police* (1988), or books by Greenslade, Jann, Leps, Rothfield, Thomas, and Thoms. More recent work by Grass and Joyce, and in Haslam and Wright's collection, has attempted to move beyond this model.

6. I do not mean to suggest that these are mutually exclusive. Goodlad argues, for example, that John Stuart Mill (ahead of his time in "Civilization") theorized consumerism as a new form of discipline: "Mill's 'postmodernist' move was not only to foresee the reign of representation in a commodity culture, but also to articulate its impact on the individual as a 'mass of influences'" (30). What I *am* suggesting is that narratives of female criminality *present* consumption as a means of independent agency opposed to forms of discipline.

7. In my discussions of both fiction and film, I will distinguish between narrative *series* and *serial* narratives. A series is a multipart narrative with recurring characters and formulas wherein each episode has a self-contained plot and the episodes need not be read in order. Serials, by contrast, are multipart narratives that trace one long plot through multiple episodes over a length of time. Serial novels were popular in the early and mid-Victorian period, but Hughes and Lund argue that late-nineteenth-century fiction "jarred with the fundamental dynamics of serial literature," contributing to its decline (230). As the serial waned, the series became increasingly popular following the emergence of Conan Doyle's Sherlock Holmes stories in 1891. The series format as employed by Conan Doyle had a profound influence on film and other twentieth-century narrative forms.

8. An 1890 article from *Blackwood's*, "Crime in Fiction," argued that crime fiction "steadily demoralises the palate for anything milder and more delicately flavoured: the habitual dram-drinker will have his stimulants stronger and stronger" (173). See Wiltse for more on detective series as addicting.

9. See, for example, "The Cinema and Hypnotic Suggestion." Chapter 3 expands on this topic.

10. The first politically motivated dynamite attack in Britain occurred in 1881, and before the end of the century there would be nearly one hundred more. According to the *Oxford English Dictionary,* the first English use of *terrorist* in its modern sense (i.e., "a member of a clandestine or expatriate organization aiming to coerce an established government by acts of violence against it or its subjects") was in 1866, and this new meaning came into general use as Russian radicals began aggressively using terrorist tactics against the oppressive czarist regime in the 1870s and 1880s. See chapter 5 for more on Russian nihilism. See Houen (*Terrorism*) for more on definitions of terrorism (7).

11. My understanding of New Women is particularly indebted to work by Ledger (*New*), Mangum, Nelson, Nord, Parsons, Showalter, Vicinus, and Walkowitz (*City*). See also articles in Richardson and Willis's collection.

12. It is debatable whether the proliferation of shopgirl positions represents an expansion of opportunity for women in the consumer sphere or women's heightened oppression in the consumer sphere. The figure of the shopgirl was often represented as an icon of modern female freedom in public, as I discuss with respect to James's novel in chapter 4, but real shopgirls suffered from exploitative working conditions, long hours, and low pay. Sanders provides a useful discussion of this contradictory figure. For more on women and consumerism in this era, see Bowlby, Felski, Andrew Miller, Parsons, Rappaport, Showalter, Walkowitz (*City*), or Whitlock (*Crime*). For more on consumer culture, see Birken or Richards.

13. The 1882 Married Women's Property Act was especially landmark. See Rappaport for a detailed discussion of this act.

14. Recent feminist critics such as Bartsky and Bordo have theorized how, in image-saturated cultures, the outward representation of traits deemed "feminine" becomes a more important designator of gender-role fidelity than behaviors or activities. Feminists since Sandra Gilbert and Susan Gubar have recognized the danger of this focus on image: anorexia nervosa is perhaps the most trenchant example of how "femininity" can become a disease. For anorexics, perceived control over body and image provides a sense of near-magical power, just as we see with fictional female criminals.

15. This quotation famously echoes a passage from Chapter 47 of Dickens's 1848 novel *Dombey and Son*—"Oh for a good spirit who would take the house-tops off . . . and show a Christian people what dark shapes issue from amidst their homes"—but while Dickens uses this image to advocate self-knowledge and self-awareness, Conan Doyle transforms it into an argument for external authority over and intervention into the home. Dickens's narrator wants to remove roofs to let in light, "rousing some who never have looked out upon the world of human life around them," such as Mr. Dombey, "to a knowledge of their own relation to it" (702). Holmes wants to remove roofs to enhance his own vision and knowledge, not that of the people inside them.

16. Aslami has described a split between historians who locate "the emergence of a new idea of the state in the late nineteenth century, foreshadowing the welfare state that took form during the 1940s," and those who argue that the "late-nineteenth-century state merely continued the interventionist work of Benthamite and mid-century centralizing reforms" (59). Both groups, however, identify a range of late-century developments as key to the history of the interventionist state, and Aslami also identifies a growing discursive tendency at this time to "infuse" the abstraction of the state "with thoughts, feelings, and capacities on the order of a liberal individual" (60).

17. According to the Matrimonial Causes Act of 1857, "cruelty" alone was not sufficient grounds for a wife to leave her husband. This changed with the 1878 act. See Surridge for more on Victorian wife battery.

18. It wasn't only liberals, in the traditional sense, who objected to legal interventionism: the prominent socialist Ernest Belfort Bax opposed legislation protecting wives and children from violent husbands (Boos and Boos 5). Most socialists disagreed with Bax, however.

19. Lombroso authored the first major work of criminology, *L'Uomo delinquente*, in Italy in 1876; it was not translated into English until 1911, but Ellis's 1890 study *The Criminal* brought Lombroso's ideas into English discourse. Lombroso also wrote with William Ferrero the first major study of female criminality, *La Donna delinquente* (1893), published in England as *The Female Offender* in 1895. Charles Goring's *The English Convict,* released in 1913, put to rest this early, anthropological strain of criminology.

20. See Leps or Thomas for more on the simultaneous rise of criminology and crime fiction.

21. Hargrave Adam likewise elaborated a biological-determinist position on prostitution, claiming many prostitutes are drawn by "sexual mania" or the love of "fine raiment" (36). Real late-Victorian prostitutes, of course, had very few economic options; many were orphans and virtually all were working class (Walkowitz, *Prostitution*).

1. Joyce, for example, notes, "From Holmes's perspective . . . all of London is potentially knowable" and "*totalizable*" (*Capital* 151). Also see Accardo, Arata (*Fictions*), Jann, Kestner, Rothfield, or Thomas.

2. Belsey and Jann both argue that Conan Doyle's women characters present an obstacle to Holmes's logic and rationality, since they do not always behave in predictable ways. My argument pertains to women's visibility and image, but since scientific rationality depends on objective observation, my claims are in some ways congruent with theirs.

3. See, for example, Christ and Jordan, Armstrong (*Fiction*), or Meisel.

4. My analysis focuses on the short stories that appeared in the first three collections, *The Adventures of Sherlock Holmes, The Memoirs of Sherlock Holmes,* and *The Return of Sherlock Holmes,* all of which were published in the *Strand* from 1891 to 1904. (Some of the stories from *The Return* also appeared in the U.S. magazine *Collier's.*) I occasionally make reference to the earlier Sherlock Holmes novels, *A Study in Scarlet* (1887) and *The Sign of Four* (1890).

5. The two early novels, *A Study in Scarlet* and *The Sign of Four,* were initially published with few illustrations, and did not sell well. After the huge success of the *Strand* stories, the novels were reissued with rich illustration.

6. Other such publications included *Ludgate Monthly* (1891–1901), *Pearson's Magazine* (1896–1939), *Harmsworth's Magazine* (1898–1933), and the *Royal Magazine* (1898–1939).

7. For more on Victorian magazine culture and publishing, see Brake, Law, or Fraser, Green, and Johnston.

8. The *Illustrated London News* and *Punch* employed heavily illustrated layouts from midcentury, but not in the context of telling stories.

9. As Wakeman describes, in the mid-1880s, wood block printing was effectively made obsolete by a range of new photomechanical technologies in visual reproduction.

10. According to Orel, "a Holmes story by itself could raise . . . circulation by more than 100,000 copies" (5).

11. See Popple for more on the x-ray as a form of popular amusement in Britain. See Crary's *Suspensions* and *Techniques* for more on nineteenth- and early-twentieth-century visual innovation.

12. Benjamin claims photography "is no less significant for criminology than the invention of the printing press is for literature," and notes detective fiction's debt to it: "The detective story came into being when this most decisive of all conquests of a person's incognito had been accomplished" (*Charles* 48). Gunning writes that photography "provides the ultimate means of tying identity to a specific and unique body. In this way the process of criminal identification represents a new aspect of the disciplining of the body which typifies modernity" ("Tracing" 20).

13. "Golden Pince-Nez" also has a female killer, but the murder turns out to have been accidental.

14. See Leps for more on this topic: "If the theoretical ambitions of [Holmes's system] are vast, its actual state of elaboration leads to the identification of individuals as representative types—results homologous to those of criminology" (194).

15. For more on turn-of-the-century degeneration theory, see Chamberlin

and Gilman, Greenslade, Hurley, Ledger ("In Darkest"), or Pick. Nordau's *Degeneration* was a popular crossover work in this field.

16. Conan Doyle was an anti-immigration activist, and his political opinions appear to inform his depiction of Beppo. Glover notes that Conan Doyle was a supporter and member of the British Brothers' League, "a locally based successor to the APIDA [Association for Preventing the Immigration of Destitute Aliens]" which "held its first major public meeting in Mile End in January 1902" (25).

17. Arata argues in *Fictions of Loss* that the genre of detective fiction is inherently unsuited to addressing crime as a systemic problem, and that it always individualizes deviance. The character of the elite master criminal, according to Joyce, serves to deny crime's rootedness in socioeconomic conditions ("Sexual" 503).

18. Conan Doyle borrows this phrasing from Stevenson's *The New Arabian Nights,* which describes a character's face as "a sort of danger signal" (244). *New Arabian Nights* also has a character named Beppo, again illustrating Conan Doyle's debt to Stevenson (see chapter 5).

19. Longhurst (58) and Thomas (*Detective* 227) discuss the significance of an Irish name, Moriarty, for the character that most completely embodies the "criminal type." Conan Doyle had an ambivalent relationship with his own Irish background. Born and raised in Scotland, he rejected Catholicism, and his political views on Ireland were not progressive. He was opposed to Home Rule until 1912, when it became a foregone conclusion (Stashower 322). He also lobbied to curtail immigration, including Irish immigration.

20. With respect to anthropological theory and African colonization, Stocking claims that when "the juggernaut of European expansion began its final push into the darker regions of the world," in "the last quarter of the nineteenth century," "evolutionary anthropology provided a portion of the ideological motive power" (273). See Otis for more on Conan Doyle and imperialism. With respect to turn-of-the-century racial anthropology's role in the Holocaust, see Kuklick (78), Greenslade (11, 255), or Stocking (292).

21. Holmes and Watson's domestic arrangements at Baker Street house a man-to-man bond that could be viewed as loving and homoerotic, connecting them to the "homosexual panic" of the 1890s. This cultural controversy surrounding New Hellenism and male homosexual desire reached its apex in Oscar Wilde's 1895 trial. Conan Doyle often invokes Wildean rhetoric in characterizing Holmes's aestheticist qualities, and Holmes's masculinity is less orthodox and more queer than most critics acknowledge. For more on this topic, see Arata (*Fictions*), Barolsky, Rothfield, or Wiltse.

22. See Surridge for a discussion of domestic abuse in this story.

23. English social scientists believed Celtic races were more "primitive" than Anglo-Saxons, and consequently less able to restrict their emotions. See Urry or Stocking.

24. According to Pound's history of the *Strand,* Paget was chosen by the art editor rather than the author. Conan Doyle's letters indicate that the two had no communication about the illustrations, at least in the first series that included "Scandal in Bohemia," though he was pleased when he saw them (42).

25. Flora Millar, in "Noble Bachelor," is in some ways parallel to Adler: she is a chorus girl with an aristocratic lover, who is accused but found to be innocent of doing away with her lover's new wife.

26. In "The Naval Treaty," Holmes states "out of my last fifty-three cases my name has only appeared in four, and the police have had all the credit in forty-nine" (231).

27. See, for example, "Second Stain," "Abbey Grange," or "Charles August Milverton." Morris also explores this topic, but comes to a rather different conclusion than mine: "in explaining the women's motives and in making the women [killers] sympathetic, there is a latent advocacy of violence and law-breaking" in the texts (5).

28. Conan Doyle was a member of England's Divorce Law Reform Union, serving as its president for ten years. Some critics have viewed his activism in this area as an outgrowth of his own unhappy marriage to an ill wife, but Stashower argues: "His concern over this issue . . . rested with obtaining equal divorce rights for women, since the current system gave an unfair bias toward the husband. Conan Doyle's convictions on this issue probably owed more to his mother's unhappy circumstances than to his own" (210).

29. Surridge offers a fuller discussion of the Holmes series in the context of Victorian debates about domestic abuse. As a child, Conan Doyle himself had been the victim of arbitrary and painful paternal invective, and critics such as Accardo read the prevalence of abusive and otherwise failed fathers in the Holmes stories as an imprint of his psychological trauma from his alcoholic father (58).

30. These three stories might profitably be considered in the context of the "Revolting Daughters Controversy," a debate in the 1890s periodical press about how much freedom young, unmarried daughters living at home should be allowed to exercise. See Nelson for selections from this debate.

31. Articles by Hall and Hennessy and Mohan also attribute Conan Doyle's persistent focus on this plot to the cultural reverberations of the Married Women's Property Acts of 1870–82. Their readings of how the stories portray women and property are at odds, however. Hall argues, "Holmes seems to be battling an older order's reactionary and regressive attempt to return to an era in which male control of property could not be questioned" (296), while Hennessy and Mohan maintain that "Holmes is in collusion with a 'band' of patriarchs implicated in suppressing that which poses an economic and sexual threat to patriarchal gender relations" (333). I view Holmes as supportive of antipatriarchal interventionist reform, while simultaneously balking at the prospect of women's enhanced public power.

32. See Andrew Miller for an interesting discussion of this parallel in *The Eustace Diamonds*.

33. As Stocking describes, there was a widespread nineteenth-century belief that high degrees of degeneracy were to be found among European settlers of the West Indies, since living in a hot climate could supposedly produce a degenerative racial effect over generations. See Favor for a close examination of Conan Doyle's depiction of foreign women.

34. It was quite rare for Victorian murderesses to use guns (Knelman 8), so Conan Doyle depicts the avenger as particularly outré, even among murderesses.

CHAPTER TWO

1. While these two theories of vision are opposite, they are not mutually exclusive. Sontag argues that cameras "define reality in the two ways essential to the

workings of an advanced industrial society: as a spectacle (for masses) and as an object of surveillance (for rulers)" (178).

2. Elizabeth Thomasina Meade was born in Ireland, but after moving to London wrote approximately 280 books and countless magazine stories under the name L. T. Meade. In a reading of one of her slum novels for girls, *The Princess of the Gutter* (1896), Koven claims Meade "denounced" sensational fiction (217), but she herself published scores of sensational stories in addition to girls' fiction. Like other of Meade's crime series, *The Sorceress* is co-credited to "Robert Eustace," a name that Slung identifies as the pseudonym for Dr. Eustace Robert Barton, who "served as a medical/scientific collaborator to a varied group of authors" (70). According to Greene, "It is generally concluded that Meade did the actual writing, while Eustace supplied the scientific gimmicks and gadgets" (ix).

3. Meade was the editor of *Atalanta* magazine for girls from 1887–93, and a member of the Pioneer Club. Rappaport considers the Pioneer Club the most feminist, progressive, and politically active of the late-Victorian clubs for women (91). Koven notes that Meade "actively supported" the Society for the Prevention of Cruelty to Children, founded in 1884, which positions her squarely within the interventionist strain of feminism discussed in chapter 1. This is apparent in books such as *A Girl of the People,* a slum novel that depicts a young heroine who challenges an abusive and alcoholic father. Besides girls' stories and crime fiction, Meade authored many light feminist works, such as "A Young Blue-Stocking" (*Ludgate Monthly,* 1892), about a woman torn between attending Girton College and marrying her sweetheart. Meade's novel *A Sweet Girl Graduate* (1891) left its mark on popular feminism: newspaper accounts of early-twentieth-century suffrage demonstrations often refer to suffragists in academic gowns as "sweet girl graduates" (Tickner 166).

4. Sources from the period refer to Madame Rachel by various names, including Madame Sarah Rachel ("Central Criminal Court, Sept. 21"), but most court reports call her Sarah Rachel Leverson. According to Wyndham, she was born Sarah Russell, married a man named Levison, and added the "Rachel" on her own (241–42). Some official sources spell her last name *Levison,* some *Leverson.* The correct spelling of her last name is unknown, since she herself could not read or write. Willis claims that the name of Madame Sara in Meade's series is "perhaps a deliberate reference to New Woman writer Sarah Grand, who used the title Madame" ("Female" 64). Such a resonance may be in play here, but in light of her occupation, shop, and so on, Madame Sara's name and title allude most directly to Madame Rachel.

5. In 1862, Rachel appealed to the Court of the Exchequer to obtain payment from a client, Mrs. Carnegie, who had neglected to pay her bill after engaging Rachel to remove a scar from her bosom so she could wear a low-cut dress. Then, in 1878, Rachel was sued by a Mrs. Pearce for fraud; Mrs. Pearce was a young Italian newlywed, twenty-three years old, who had sought skin treatment from Rachel. Readers of "The Blood-Red Cross," the second story in *The Sorceress,* would have recognized Sara's victim, Antonia Ripley, as an amalgam of Carnegie and Pearce. Ripley is a young Italian bride, like Pearce, who wants a mole removed from her bosom so she can wear a low-cut dress, like Carnegie. On the Carnegie case, see "Court of Exchequer, June 19." On the Pearce case, see "A Curious Tale."

6. Rachel died October 1880 in Knap-hill Prison, Woking. The *Times* obituary lists her age as sixty ("The Late Madame Rachel"), though she had often declared herself much older than this as a means of promoting her age-defying products (Boase 324).

7. Willis discusses *The Sorceress* and *The Brotherhood* in "The Female Moriarty," and Halloran compares *The Sorceress* and the Holmes series in a 2002 article. Neither piece discusses Madame Rachel.

8. Rachel was again convicted of fraud in 1878, in the case instigated by Mrs. Pearce that I discuss in note 5, but the 1868 case garnered far more publicity since it occurred in the heyday of Rachel's commercial success and advertising saturation. Only five articles about Rachel's 1878 trial ran in the *Times,* for example, compared to fifty for the 1868 trial. Because the 1868 case was most influential in determining her cultural legacy, it is the focus of my analysis.

9. The street ballad is printed in *Curiosities of Street Literature* (1871). For allusions, see Braddon's *Lady Audley's Secret* (1862), Serjeant Ballantine's *Some Experiences of a Barrister's Life* (1882), Montague Williams's *Leaves of a Life* (1890), and *London in the Sixties (with a Few Digressions)* by "One of the Old Brigade" (1908). Collins based Mother Oldershaw of *Armadale* (1866) on Madame Rachel, and according to Whitlock, Charlotte Yonge's *Love and Life* (1880) also has a character based on her. Rachel's story was dramatized in Hay's *Beautiful For Ever: A Farce in One Act* (1868), and Jones's *Beautiful For Ever: A Play for Women* (1978). In 1870, Arthur Lloyd published a popular song about Rachel and Borrodaile, "Mrs. Mary Tucker Sparrowtail; Or, Beautiful For Ever."

10. Unless otherwise noted, quotations from the 1868 trial and from surrounding press coverage are taken from *The Extraordinary Life and Trial of Madame Rachel* (1868), a compilation of trial transcripts, editorials, letters to editors, and coverage of the case from various newspapers and periodicals. I read this book at the British Library, but it is available elsewhere in the United States and Britain.

11. The British Library has a copy of this manual.

12. In Srebnick's discussion of the infamous U.S. case of Madame Restell, she notes, "French-sounding pseudonyms were common for abortionists" (100). Note, too, ubiquitous ads for "Madame Frain's Famous Female Mixture" in late-Victorian periodicals, such as *Ludgate Monthly* in 1893. During the nineteenth century, an extensive market developed for abortifacients disguised as patent medicines, which depended upon the expansion of forums for broad advertising in the periodical press. Knelman writes that following investigative reports by the *Pall Mall Gazette* and the *British Medical Journal* in the late 1860s, advertisements for abortifacients were banned from the London dailies, but "were still accepted in the popular weeklies" (168). In the 1890s, the medical journal *The Lancet* claimed that in a week's worth of British periodicals, one hundred publications contained advertisements for abortifacients (Riddle 235). Intriguing as this evidence is, it does not verify Rachel's involvement in extracosmetic activities; it is certainly possible that such gossip arose as a reaction against her legitimate success as a businesswoman. Reports that Rachel practiced mesmerism and witchery sometimes accompany rumors about procuration and abortion, casting doubt on all such accusations. The resonance of the abortion rumors lingers in Meade's portrayal of Rachel, but it is not clear whether this is because of Collins's influence or because of reports existing independently of his novel.

13. For more on these developments, see Bowlby, Ledger (*New*), Parsons, Rappaport, Showalter, or Walkowitz (*City*).

14. See, for example, Bartsky or Bordo. Similarly, the work of feminist film critics Mulvey and Doane suggests how modernity—characterized by the emergence of cinema as well as consumerism—furthers women's habituation to spectacularity as a specifically gendered form of discipline.

15. Consider Conan Doyle's depiction of Moriarty: "the man had hereditary tendencies of the most diabolical kind. A criminal strain ran in his blood" ("Final Problem" 252). This echoes the theories of criminologists such as Ellis, who wrote: "Both crime and drink are the morbid manifestations of organic defects which for the most part precede birth" (*Criminal* 144).

16. Here Lombroso, Ellis, and Nordau foreshadow the concerns of eugenicists like Karl Pearson. From a eugenic point of view, an organism that hides a "defect," "disorder," degeneracy, or old age to increase its chance of reproducing is hurting the race. Cosmetics are thus antieugenic, since they have the potential to dissemble "natural" instincts that eugenicists like Pearson believed were present in the sex selection process.

17. Meade was not alone among fin de siècle feminists in associating feminism with imperial capitalism; Sarah Grand, as Jusová has recently argued, undertook a similar task. The New Woman, for some writers, became an embodiment of imperial dominance, a strategy that countered the argument that the New Woman posed a degenerative threat to the strength of the nation.

18. Undoubtedly, Rachel's decorative choices were intended to bolster customers' belief in the authentically exotic origins of her products. In an advertisement in the *Times,* for example, Rachel writes: "All articles bearing the above name are spurious and dangerous unless they have the Royal Arabian Signet attached" (5 February 1866, 15).

19. See Madame Rachel's inventory list in *Beautiful For Ever!* (vi–viii).

20. The *Chambers's Journal* joked about Rachel's products' origins, asking, "why should there not be a Putney Bloom, a Turham Green Preservative Balm, or even a Camden Town Preparation for the Chin?" (Corson 339).

21. After her 1868 conviction, Rachel was forced to sell her belongings, and advertisements for the sale indicate that she furnished her home in a manner that emphasized Britain's imperial power, like her products' names. A notice for "Madame Rachel's Sale" in the *Times* refers to "the splendid contents" of her residence, including rare Indian, Japanese, and Chinese furniture, and "a very valuable and magnificent pair of incense burners, on costly carved ebony stands, formerly the property of the King of Delhi" (10 March 1869, 16).

22. See Ellis on the lack of female genius in mathematical or scientific spheres (*Man* 366).

23. Morrison claimed, for example: "The care and nurture of children has been [women's] lot in life for untold centuries; the duties of maternity have perpetually kept alive a certain number of unselfish instincts; these instincts have become part and parcel of women's natural inheritance . . . [and] acquired the power of a hereditary characteristic" (152).

24. Knelman notes that about 48 percent of Victorian women accused of murder used poison (8). See Ruddick for an account of the 1876 poisoning of Charles Bravo, for which his wife, Florence, was tried but not convicted.

25. Maybrick claimed not only that she used arsenic as a complexion aid, but that her husband James used it "as a tonic—it was considered a sexual stimulant," which accounted for the presence of the poison in his body. She testified that he had asked her to give him arsenic (Knelman 118).

26. The Forster Act of 1870 established universal public education in Britain.

CHAPTER THREE

1. For exemplary work in the field of early film studies, see Elsaesser and Barker's volume, which focuses on formal analysis of early film, or Charney and Schwartz's volume, which focuses on cultural and historical analysis.

2. Daly and Sanders have recently interwoven analysis of turn-of-the-century British literature and film, Daly focusing on Boer War films and Kipling's "Mrs Bathurst" and Sanders focusing on the figure of the shopgirl.

3. Hansen considers early U.S. cinema in relation to Habermas's theories of the public sphere and Negt and Kluge's theories of the "proletarian public sphere." Hiley, establishing that the early British film audience was demonstrably working class at least until World War I, follows Hansen in arguing that "the British cinema auditorium was indeed a proletarian public sphere, in which the context of performance was determined by the interplay between its working class audience and the screened image. Much of the meaning of a film was indeed created within the auditorium, not simply by the accompanying music and sound effects, but more importantly by the reaction of the audience" ("British Cinema" 164). This audience "encouraged a communal style of performance. There was a great deal of talking" (162), contradicting "middle class virtues of individual spectatorship and concentrated attention" that many filmmakers would soon work to inculcate (166).

4. For British filmmakers' response to this state of affairs, see Furniss ("Where Are the English Films?" or "English—By the Americans"), or a 1909 interview with George Howard Cricks, who opined: "At the present time the English output of film pictures is certainly not more than one tenth of the world's production. Well, British industry is not going to take that sitting down. . . . the English people in the long run prefer British sentiment and feeling in the pictures they pay to see in our theatres" ("The Future" 12).

5. See *The Bioscope,* 16 June 1910, 11, and *The Film Censor,* 26 June 1912, 2.

6. Due to the relative paucity of its output, critics have paid less attention to the early British industry than, for example, the U.S. film industry. Most work in this area has aimed to uncover a national cinematic tradition: see the first two volumes of Low's venerable history of British film as well as Barnes, Murphy, and Burton and Porter. Chanan takes a different approach in his fascinating Marxian-materialist study.

7. This film is held in the National Film Archive (NFA) at the British Film Institute (BFI) on the "Biograph Compilation #5" reel. The NFA catalog identifies the film as a scene from a longer film, no longer extant, called *Women and Wine. Duel to the Death* is listed in the third edition of Gifford's catalog of British film (an index of every film ever known to have been made in Britain). Most films discussed in this chapter, unless otherwise indicated, were viewed at the British Film Institute, but some exist in multiple locations. The International

Film Archive Database (FIAF) is an excellent resource for locating archival holdings of early film.

8. *Duel to the Death* was directed by William Dickson, an associate of Thomas Edison and a key figure in early film. While working in the United States, he produced what was perhaps the first censored film: his 1894 Kinetoscope film *Carmenchita* was banned in New Jersey for revealing a dancer's ankles in an erotic "butterfly dance." (Kinetoscope films preceded cinema by a few years; they are viewed through an individual "peepshow" device rather than projected on screen.) After returning to his homeland Britain in 1897, Dickson became the chief cameraman for British Mutoscope and Biograph.

9. This film is available at the BFI.

10. Rabinovitz and Stamp have argued that in the United States, prefilm consumer culture primed female spectators for cinema: "the visual spectacle offered by the array of products on display in department stores and shop windows provided woman-oriented 'domains for looking' that formed an important precursor to film viewing at the turn of the century" (Stamp 18).

11. See especially "In Your Face" and "Tracing."

12. The film is available at the Library of Congress as well as the BFI.

13. My chapter will focus on films that have survived and can be viewed, but all too many films from this period are no longer extant. Contemporary film periodicals give us a sense of what these missing films were like, so I will occasionally use such journals to provide contextual detail.

14. This quotation is from *Film House Record,* 15 October 1910, 243. For another contemporary review, see *Bioscope,* 17 November 1910, 32.

15. *Film House Record,* 29 October 1910, 252.

16. *The Cinema,* 12 March 1913, 75.

17. *The Cinema,* 22 January 1913, 73.

18. This film is held in the BFI. Its canister indicates that it is "incomplete," though it is not apparent in comparing the film to contemporary descriptions that a section is missing.

19. While unnamed in the film, Dora's sweetheart is identified as "Dick Charteris" in *Bioscope*'s description of the film (9 May 1912, xix).

20. C. L. Pirkis's Detective Loveday Brooke similarly exploits her invisibility by dressing, for example, as a female servant (see my article "Trouble with She-Dicks"). Other relevant female detectives for comparison include L. T. Meade's "The Bloodhound" (part of *Brotherhood of the Seven Kings,* 1898) and *The Detections of Miss Cusack* (1899–1901); Emma Orczy's *Lady Molly of Scotland Yard* (1910); Clarence Rook's Miss Van Snoop (1898); and George Sims's Dorcas Dene (1897–98).

21. It was not until 1913 or so that middle-class audiences regularly attended the British cinema, in contrast to early film's broader appeal elsewhere. Middle-class cinema attendance increased with the establishment of permanent, dedicated movie palaces, which attracted a different clientele than the penny storefronts that dominated film exhibition prior to World War I. See Burrows, Chanan, or Field for more on this topic.

22. See, for example, *Daring Daylight Burglary* (Sheffield Photograph Co., 1903) or *Stop Thief* (Williamson, 1901).

23. *The Cinema,* 19 February 1913, 70.

24. The film is held at the BFI.

25. The film is held at the BFI.

26. Film catalogs identify the tenants as Irish; perhaps this information was given through other means than the film itself (see note 53). The film was made by British Gaumont, and is now held in the UCLA Film and Television Archive.

27. B & C was the British film company most "deeply rooted" in magazine mass-culture, according to Turvey, and was most likely to make films of "non-standard morality" (69, 73). Its *Exploits of Three-Fingered Kate* was highly influential. Its series format is obviously a descendant of magazine crime series, but became extremely popular in filmmaking too. Singer's work on U.S. "serial queen" films convincingly describes the feminist significance of this popular genre, but note that Kate predates it: the first Kate film debuted in 1909, whereas American serial-queen melodrama flourished between 1912 and 1920 ("Female Power" 90). A popular French series called *The Queen of Criminals,* which began in 1911, also followed *Three-Fingered Kate.*

28. Nollen mentions a 1901 stage parody of Holmes called *Sheerluck Jones* (57); this may have inspired the filmmakers.

29. *Bioscope,* 7 October 1909, 93.

30. *Film House Record,* 14 May 1910, 98.

31. *Film House Record,* 29 October 1910, 250.

32. *The Pictures,* 30 August 1912, 18.

33. *The Cinema,* October 1912, 19.

34. *The Cinema,* April 1912, 18.

35. For advertisements, see 20 April, 8 June, 20 July, and 9 November 1912 issues. For "Our Postbag," see 17 August 1912, 32.

36. *The Pictures,* 5 October 1912, 10.

37. *The Pictures,* 6 July 1912, 21.

38. Ivy Martinek, the actress playing Kate, is not really three-fingered, but is quite obviously just holding down two fingers of her right hand.

39. Indeed, in Holmes's first appearance on film—a 1900 U.S. film called *Sherlock Holmes Baffled*—he is outwitted by a vanishing burglar (Nollen 61). For the next ten years, "straight" adaptations of Holmes were made in the United States, France, and Denmark, but not the United Kingdom. In 1913, when middle-class audiences began to attend the British cinema in greater numbers, the French company Éclair released a set of straight Sherlock Holmes adaptations that had been filmed in Britain, and aggressively promoted the series in British trade journals. Advertisements reclaimed Holmes for Britain: "Taken in England and acted by British Artistes under the supervision of Sir Arthur Conan Doyle," or *"All British* films, acted by *English* actors in *England,* and produced under sole rights of the well-known *English* writer, Sir Arthur Conan Doyle" (see *Bioscope,* 28 August 1913, 680, and 22 May 1913, 558). Appealing to English authenticity and to national pride in Conan Doyle (who was actually born in Scotland), such rhetoric contrasts sharply with *Three-Fingered Kate,* which ended a year earlier in 1912. Nevertheless, by the end of the series, Éclair had moved production from Britain to the United States; perhaps the series hadn't performed well in Britain after all.

40. This film is held in the BFI as well as the Library of Congress.

41. Though irrelevant to my analysis of the film, I don't want to omit men-

tioning this film's nonstandard chronology. As in Edwin Porter's famous 1902 film *Life of an American Fireman,* this film utilizes back-to-back scenes that show the same period of time from two different points of view. The innovation of cross-cutting did not yet signify simultaneity of action, hence the gap in continuity. I discuss a similar chronological strategy later in the chapter with regard to *Women's Rights.*

42. A description of the film in *Bioscope* (13 January 1910, 57) indicates that the butler's name is James, while the maid is never given a name. The reviewer calls the film, "One of the finest plays we have witnessed for a long time."

43. A more positive version of the same scenario occurred in the 1911 Hepworth film *Rachel's Sin.* Here, a man takes the blame for murder when the woman he loves accidentally kills her vicious, drunken husband. In this case, however, she remains faithful to him while he is in jail. As in *A Woman's Treachery,* the film privileges fidelity in love above fidelity to the law. For a description of this film, which no longer survives, see *Bioscope,* 9 November 1911, 445.

44. An exception is the 1905 Hepworth film *Den of Thieves,* which features a housemaid who serves as informant and accomplice to a gang of robbers. She is eventually caught, and agrees to lead the police to the criminals.

45. The film was later retitled *The Anarchist's Doom;* it is held in the BFI.

46. See *Bioscope,* 10 July 1913, 145.

47. Militant suffrage agitators were called "suffragettes," while women using legal means to campaign for the vote were "suffragists." The Women's Social and Political Union (WSPU) was the home of the militant suffragettes, while the National Union of Women's Suffrage Societies (NUWSS) was the mainstream organization. See Nelson for a collection of contemporary pro- and antisuffrage writings. See Hamer, Tickner, and Stanley for more on the British suffrage campaign. See Haslam for discussion of a prison narrative by Lady Constance Lytton, a member of the WSPU, and for more on suffragettes' experience in the penal system.

48. Gifford titles this film *The Lady Barber.*

49. An advertisement for the film depicts picketing women whose posters proclaim, "We will *not* tell our age" as well as "Votes for Women" (*Film House Record,* 4 March 1911, 387). The film is held at the BFI.

50. See "Insanity or Crime?" for contemporary film periodicals' response.

51. Stott notes that antisuffrage posters were also informed by degeneration theory (*Fabrication* 202).

52. Chaplin's film is also known as *The Busy Day.* I viewed it at the BFI and the Library of Congress, but it is available in many film archives.

53. The film is also called *Ladies' Skirts Nailed to Fence,* but its correct title (*Women's Rights*) clarifies how audiences understood the subject of the film. In its current state, the film does not make the women's politics explicit, but catalog accounts refer to the women as "suffragettes" and assert that they are discussing enfranchisement. Surviving copies of early films don't relay all of the information that audiences would have received: "exhibition aids" such as lecturers, narrators, printed programs, sound effects, or "even actors speaking dialogue behind the screen" were common (Sopocy 123). Intertitles were rare before 1905, but catalog accounts of *Women's Rights* indicate that audiences learned through some means that the women are suffragettes.

54. *Film House Record,* 24 December 1910, 308.

55. See description and review in *Bioscope,* 17 April 1913, 167, and 15 May 1913, 519.

56. *Bioscope,* 30 November 1911, 613. Pathé was a French company, but its "animated newspaper" *Pathé Animated Gazette* was the major producer of British newsreels in this period.

57. Stamp's work on U.S. suffrage films suggests that there was transatlantic cooperation between the British and U.S. campaigns in their use of film. Emmeline Pankhurst, a fixture in the British movement, "guest starred" in a U.S. pro-suffrage film called *Eighty Million Women Want–?* Stamp notes that suffrage groups were "among the earliest advocacy bodies to exploit moving pictures at a time when the cinema's powers of social commentary were not always appreciated" (154).

58. Davison's death was long presumed to have been suicidal martyrdom, but after reassembling the evidence, Stanley and Morley conclude that "no proof of Emily Davison's motives is possible. She made no written statement about her intentions concerning the Derby act" (165).

59. In 1912, the London City Council put forward a motion to prohibit all "pictorial representation in cinematograph theatres" because of its "demoralizing influence" (Field 29). The move didn't pass, but many such threats emerged in precensorship Britain and many municipalities moved to ban cinemas. Contemporary film periodicals offer much information on this issue: see "Crime on the Pictures," "Criminal Scenes Censored," "Cinematograph and Crime," Geear, "Is Sensational Taste Too Pronounced?," "Our Opinion," or Townshend.

60. In the earliest years of film, pictures were often shown in pitch-black rooms except for the light given off by the film itself, unlike theaters today with floor and exit lights. Many exhibitors attempted to overcome this moral limitation of the medium: early trade magazines are full of advertisements for the "Eye-Rest System of Illumination," the "Angel Cinema," "Daylight Cinema," and other lighting systems (see *Bioscope,* 10 April 1913, 145, and 5 September 1912, 707).

61. Several scholars have considered female spectators of early film in U.S. culture. See Stamp, Rabinovitz, or Cooper, who argues that advocates of film censorship "tacitly agreed to personify the public as a feminine consumer" (121).

62. Benjamin's influential theories of film parallel such arguments: "There came a day when a new and urgent need for stimuli was met by the film. In film, perception in the form of shocks was established as a formal principle" (*Charles* 132). For more on this topic see Singer ("Modernity") or Daly.

63. This kind of suspicion of film was particularly virulent in Britain. Perry writes: "the British allowed cinema to develop in a hole-in-the-corner manner with magistrates, in the constant quest for scapegoats for social evils, eagerly attaching blame for petty crime . . . to the darkened movie halls" (9–10). See "Pictures and Juvenile Crime" for a contemporary contribution to this debate.

64. Hiley and Burrows discuss this topic at length.

CHAPTER FOUR

1. See Melchiori for an extensive discussion of the genre. Arata (*"Secret"*) discusses Conrad's novel in the context of dynamite narrative. For examples of dy-

namite stories, see Tom Greer's *A Modern Daedalus* (1885), E. Douglas Fawcett's *Hartmann the Anarchist: or, The Doom of the Great City* (1893), or the texts I discuss in chapter 5.

2. Thomas Hardy's 1881 novel *A Laodicean* also interweaves modern womanhood with a dynamite plot, correlating these two themes. Its heroine, Paula Power, is "ultra-modern" (17) and has her own telegraph machine and her own gymnasium, "in imitation of those at the new colleges for women" (170). Her uncle, Abner Power, is the novel's dynamiter, as a minor subplot reveals. In his youth Abner associated with a group "whose object was the extermination of tyrants and despots, and the overthrow of established religions" (369). He invented for them a new kind of explosive machine, but soon had "a fit of revulsion" and adopted "a conservative taste in politics" (370). In attempting to destroy his invention, he disfigures his own face. By relating these characters via the surname "Power," Hardy links late-nineteenth-century feminism with the threat of dynamite technology.

3. Though published in 1907, Conrad's novel looks back to the 1880s and 1890s: it is based on an 1894 event, set in 1886, and in the dedication Conrad dubs it a "simple tale of the nineteenth century."

4. The Fenians' first organized political offensive in Britain was the Clerkenwell Prison bombing in 1867, but this was a gunpowder bombing, and dynamite soon emerged as a far more destructive technology, thus the major cultural reverberations of the first Fenian dynamiting in 1881.

5. Albert Parsons, a U.S. anarchist tried in the Haymarket affair, called dynamite "the equilibrium . . . the disseminator of power . . . the abolition of authority" (qtd. in Sandison, "A World" 158).

6. In an 1888 article in *Century Magazine,* James described a "kind of highflown serenity" in *The Dynamiter*'s manner and style (Maixner 307). See Sandison (*Robert*) for a discussion of how *Secret Agent* draws on the novel. One of the subplots in *The Dynamiter* is introduced as "a simple tale," which is the subtitle of Conrad's novel.

7. While writing *The Princess,* James wrote to his brother William that he hoped it would be popular; on James's unmet expectations concerning its popularity, see Trilling, Jacobson (44), or Tilley (4). While revising *The Secret Agent,* Conrad similarly wrote that he hoped it had "an element of popularity in it" (*Letters* 3:439) and that he "should like it to appear somewhere where it would be read" (*Letters* 3.326). He was disappointed by its reception, as indicated by a 1908 letter: "Otherwise things are not well with me. The S[ecret] A[gent] may be pronounced by now an honourable failure. . . . I own that I am cast down. I suppose I am a fool to have expected anything else. I suppose there is something in me that is unsympathetic to the general public" (*Letters* 4:9).

8. See Sypher, Tilley, or Melchiori.

9. Though not explicitly stated, the embassy is obviously Russian, since its representative is named "Vladimir," speaks in "guttural Central Asian tones" (69), has "somewhat Oriental phraseology" (208), and "look[s] at Europe from its other end" (209). The embassy is in "Chesham Square," and the real Russian embassy was in Chesham Place (Guimond and Maynard 4). Trench-Bonett and Guimond and Maynard discuss Conrad's well-known anti-Russian sentiment.

10. Contemporary anarchists believed Bourdin's brother-in-law, H. B.

Samuels, was in the pay of state authorities, which may well have been the case (see Nicoll, Oliver, Quail, or W. C. H. for more on this). Conrad's source for this idea, along with the *Commonweal* article discussed in note 11, may have been Helen and Olivia Rossetti's 1903 autobiographical novel *A Girl among the Anarchists,* which I discuss in the next chapter. *A Girl* recounts Bourdin's botched bombing from the perspective of London anarchists: "the Anarchists talked of a very different order of 'conspiracy.' . . . Among the chief mourners was the deceased man's brother. . . . It was this brother whose conduct had given rise to suspicion among his companions, and 'spies' and 'police plots' were in every one's mouth" (40–41). The Rossettis are certain that Samuels was behind the bombing, in league with the police, to provoke public outrage against anarchism: "That the whole conspiracy was a got-up affair between [Samuels] and the police was evident" (71). This aspect of the case was not widely reported in the press at the time, so it is reasonable to assume that Conrad was inspired by the Rossettis. Ford Madox Ford, Conrad's close friend, introduced him to Helen and Olivia (see Arata's *"Secret,"* Mulry, or Newton), and the female protagonist in Conrad's short story "The Informer" is obviously modeled on one or both of them. Internal evidence likewise indicates Conrad's indebtedness. The first page of *Secret Agent* refers to the Rossettis' anarchist newspaper, the *Torch,* sold at Verloc's shop, and the description of Bourdin's exploded body in *A Girl* (39) is similar to Conrad's account (196).

11. In its inaugural February 1885 issue, the *Commonweal* (the official paper of the Socialist League, edited by William Morris) suggested that Russia—not the Fenians—was behind the January 1885 bombing of the Houses of Parliament, the Tower of London, and Westminster Hall, or at least that Russia goaded the Fenians into it. The newspaper's theory, applied to the 1894 bombing of the Greenwich Observatory, may have prompted Conrad's idea for *Secret Agent*. The Fenians, according to *Commonweal,* seem to have "someone behind them, who follows up a deliberate aim in these otherwise aimless explosions." Russia wanted Britain to extradite Peter Kropotkin and other political exiles, thus had reason to act the agent provocateur. I have not seen this allegation regarding the 1885 bombing in other contemporary sources.

12. James does use the terms interchangeably, but Tilley has shown that James received his information about these groups from the London *Times,* which had its own trouble keeping the groups straight, and which did not explain their motivating ideology (Tilley 23–24). That James's characters don't have a clearly defined revolutionary philosophy could signify a broader cultural ignorance also exemplified by the *Times,* or could be a way of indicating their confusion and ineptitude.

13. Following World War I, research pertaining to shell-shocked veterans essentially invalidated turn-of-the-century theories of degenerate masculinity (Greenslade 225).

14. See Showalter or Arata (*Fictions*) for more on the male romance, characterized by all-male or nearly all-male casts of characters and adventurous plots involving male-centered activities like sea voyages and colonial expeditions. LeeAnne Richardson has recently put this genre in dialogue with New Woman fiction, countering a more general critical tendency to view the two late-century genres as oppositional.

15. In this novel, masculine degeneracy is not confined to poor men like Hyacinth. The aristocratic Captain Sholto is "one of those strange beings produced

by old societies that have run to seed, corrupt, exhausted civilizations" (352). The Prince Casamassima has "the aspect which, in late-coming members of long-descended races, we qualify to-day as effete" (234).

16. On the basis of this inconsistency, critics such as Greenslade, Stott, and Thomas have claimed that *The Secret Agent* is disparaging of criminal anthropology and degenerative theory. Conrad does distance himself from the crude understanding of criminality championed by Lombroso, as many of his contemporaries had also done by 1907, but theories of degeneration retained currency long after criminal typology had been debunked, and they remain at work in *The Secret Agent*'s epistemology. Various critics have read the novel in light of the late-Victorian discovery of entropy (Whitworth 43–45), which may be a corollary of this concern. For more on this topic, see Greenslade, Hampson, Houen, Jacobs, Ray, Saveson, Stott ("The Woman"), or Thomas.

17. Conrad's narrator refers to Verloc's "dislike of all kinds of recognized labour" as a "defect which he shared with a large proportion of revolutionary reformers." "The majority of revolutionists are the enemies of discipline and fatigue mostly" (82). In *Heart of Darkness,* Conrad expressed his distaste for colonialism by portraying the imperialists as trying to get something for nothing; here, he imagines political radicalism in similar terms, even comparing Ossipon to a marauding Norwegian sailor "bored with the world after a thundering spree" (81).

18. Hyacinth regrets this vow for the rest of the book, ultimately killing himself to escape it; in this way he can be read as a political variation on the conventional nineteenth-century protagonist who repents an early, imprudent marriage or engagement (see Jane Austen's *Sense and Sensibility* or Conan Doyle's "Boscombe Valley Mystery").

19. Freud was following scientific orthodoxy when in 1905, just before the publication of this novel, he defined a "perversion" as a sexual act not potentially procreative. Krafft-Ebing had made the same claim almost twenty years earlier in his groundbreaking *Psychopathia Sexualis,* originally published in 1886 (the same year as *The Princess*). According to Freud in "The Sexual Aberrations," the first essay from *Three Essays on Sexuality:* "Perversions are sexual activities which either (a) extend, in an anatomical sense, beyond the regions of the body that are designed for sexual union, or (b) linger over the intermediate relations to the sexual object which should normally be traversed rapidly on the path towards the final sexual aim" (16). The "final sexual aim" was male orgasm inside a female body (enabling procreation).

20. Shaffer argues that *Secret Agent* "appropriates" the discourse of late-Victorian anti-onanism campaigns "as a means of commenting on the perils of anarchism" (453).

21. Most of *The Princess*'s critics take for granted that Lord Frederick was Hyacinth's father (e.g., Graham, McGurl, Scanlan, Sypher, and Tingle), as did contemporary reviewers, but Hyacinth's aristocratic parentage is less certain in the novel. Hyacinth and Pinnie make an active decision to believe that Lord Frederick was his father (167–68), while Vetch is skeptical (75, 77). The book is full of illegitimate children and unfaithful or illegal marriages, casting every character's origins into doubt. Readers of *Roderick Hudson* know the Princess is illegitimate, though it is not brought up here, and Millicent's paternity is questionable, given her mother's liaisons with the local stove-polisher (94).

22. James's travel memoir *A Little Tour in France,* published in 1884 (right before *The Princess*), describes pervasive revolutionary activity in France, which James disapprovingly calls "the red radicalism of France, the revolutions, the barricades, the sinister theories" (168).

23. According to Zedner, there were no female wardens in British prisons until 1883, which means that Bowerbank could not have existed during the period in which this scene is set. She may have existed in 1885, when serial publication of *The Princess* began, but still would have been quite new. See Onslow for more on Victorian debates about prison "careers" for women.

24. These descriptions tap into late-Victorian theories of antisocial behavior in women, which scientists believed was consistent with a preponderance of masculine traits. That James was attempting social-scientific naturalism in this scene is clear from a December 1884 letter; describing his visit to Millbank to research the scene, he says, "you see I am quite the Naturalist" (*Letters* 61).

25. Ouida's Princess Napraxine, like the Princess Casamassima, has "cosmopolitan" origins and a marriage of convenience to a wealthy prince (4). She is not active in revolutionary politics, but is associated with nihilism. One character reflects that Princess Napraxine is "indifferent to all political movement," but "If she be anything, she is that horrible thing a Nihilist, only because Nihilism embodies an endless and irreconcilable discontent, which finds in her some secret corner of vague sympathy" (152). Early in the novel, her husband describes her defusing a nihilist bomb meant to blow up their house: "She took the whole affair up and dropped it into the fountain. She forgot to mention it till the next morning" (13). Later, the princess reflects: "I could have been a revolutionist, I think. . . . Some day, Russia will be in revolt from one end to another, but the day is not yet, and I doubt much that any good will be done when it comes. The evil lies too deep" (258–59).

26. It is debatable whether Paul's opinions actually shift in the course of the novel or just become more apparent. By the end, we know that he is not trusted at the upper levels of the revolutionary organization, that he has a troublingly Malthusian disregard for individuals, and that he favors more prisons and more capital punishment (views at odds with the revolutionary organization). He also aspires to own a bourgeois home in the suburbs (440).

27. Here, I depart from standard critical skepticism regarding the Princess's radical commitment. See Howe (142) and Morris (156). It is commonplace to attribute the Princess's socialism to nymphomania or romantic ignorance, though she has experienced firsthand the nightmare of naturalized, economically determined institutions of gender oppression. In *Roderick Hudson,* we learn that it was directly after her marriage that she "launched her mysterious menace" against the world of the prince (443).

28. In the 1909 edition, this is changed to the more telling, "I don't trust women—I don't trust clever women!" (470).

29. The Princess's difficulty in drumming up interest in women's oppression among male socialists reflects the experience of radical late-Victorian women. Many prominent British socialists believed the campaign for women's rights was too "individualist" for socialism (see Pearson's "The Woman Question" and "Woman and Labour," for example). See Walkowitz (*City*) for an analysis of such debates within Pearson's Men and Women's Club. E. Belfort Bax, a pioneering

socialist who was close with Engels, attacked feminism as a distraction from class politics in works such as *The Fraud of Feminism* (1913) and *The Legal Subjection of Men* (1909). See Boos and Boos for more on feminism and antifeminism within British socialism. The friction among British socialists with regard to gender was typical of international socialism, too. According to de la Motte, "although the Second International at its foundation congress in 1889 had adopted a paragraph in its programme stressing that the equality of women was to be a leading principle for all member parties, the conjunction of socialism and feminism was in practice not without its problems. On the one hand, women's issues were often underestimated because of a mechanistic understanding of Marxism resulting in reductionist attitudes about class as well as patriarchal views on gender among labour leaders; and, on the other hand, some women overestimated the immediate importance of their own problems in relation to the class struggle" (34).

30. In an analysis of upper-class Victorian women's charity work in the slums, Koven argues, "Same-sex love . . . was an important though elusive dimension of [elite women's] gospel of social housekeeping in late Victorian London" (222), which is a relevant context here.

31. Howe is the only other critic who has picked up on this masochistic dynamic (142), but he reads it as "comic" (149). I view it as a serious investigation of class, gender, and power. The Princess's desires were also masochistic in *Roderick Hudson*. She tells Roderick that the kind of man she wants is a "conqueror" (234), which he is not, and claims she would say to a man who "wished to do me a favour," "I beg of you with tears in my eyes to interest me. Be a brute, if necessary, to do it; only be something positive and strong—something that in looking at I can forget my detestable self" (187–88). Her wish is granted in *The Princess,* where she can finally exclaim to her lover Paul, "you are such a brute!" (579).

32. James's preface to *The Princess* reveals a similar interest in depicting Hyacinth as, to some extent, an unwitting plaything of the gods (37–39).

33. Conrad seems to have believed that Michaelis's and the Professor's views were not, in the end, all that distinct: in an 1885 letter, he wrote, "Socialism must inevitably end in Caesarism" (*Letters* 1:16).

34. From the launch of the Social Democratic Federation in the early 1880s, socialism steadily expanded its membership and influence in Britain. By 1906, British anarchism was virtually dead (though it would revive again prior to World War I), while socialism had gone mainstream with the Independent Labour Party and then the Labour Party. See Quail for more on anarchism in 1906. See Glasier or Taylor for more on the rise of the ILP. Some early socialists (such as William Morris) had their doubts about the ILP's "socialism," but the party did absorb many prominent socialists who had previously been revolutionary or antiparliamentarian or both, such as Bruce Glasier and Fred Henderson.

35. See Boos for a discussion of Morris's influence on the garden cities movement.

36. Scanlan notes that "by 1885 bookbinding was itself an anachronism" (385), "a trade on the verge of becoming obsolete" (399). Meissner reads the declining nature of Hyacinth's profession as James's "attack" on William Morris (58), but I would argue that James's critique of consumerism is not incompatible with Morris's.

37. Rather than stressing the drudgery, long hours, and poor pay experienced

by shopgirls, James depicts Millicent as reveling in "the wantonness of her full-blown freedom" (95). See Sanders for more on shopgirls. For more on women and department stores, see Birken, Rabinovitz, or Rappaport.

38. This department store rendezvous between Millicent and Captain Sholto echoes a widespread belief of the era that shop labor provided "an environment in which working women might have the opportunity, whether real or imagined, to meet and be courted by men above them in wealth and social station" (Sanders 55).

39. Following Herbert Spencer's work on repression in 1876, Victorian anthropologists theorized that "the repression of immediate impulsive response was the essential mechanism of evolutionary progress" (Stocking 227). The supposed lack of full civility in women, primitives, criminals, and children was accounted for by the belief that they were "governed more by impulse" (229).

40. James is engaging with a contested issue of his day. See Walkowitz (*City*) on the Miss Cass case.

41. See Lindner for more on Conrad and consumerism.

CHAPTER FIVE

1. W. J. T. Mitchell argues, for example: "The use of the female image of revolution was . . . a commonplace in nineteenth-century iconography, Delacroix's bare-breasted *Liberty Leading the People* being the most familiar example. This was an image that could be conjured with by both radicals and conservatives: Burke caricatured the revolutionaries . . . as a mob of transvestites and abandoned women" (174).

2. See Trowbridge or Van Alstine.

3. Nineteenth-century literature about Corday includes dramas by C. A. Somerset (1853), William Bayle Bernard (1855), and James Mortimer (1876), fiction by Rose Ellen Hendriks Temple (*Charlotte Corday: An Historical Tale,* 1846), and poetry by Emma Marie Caillard (*Charlotte Corday and Other Poems,* 1884). Her popularity as a literary subject makes it particularly surprising that she is never mentioned in *A Tale of Two Cities,* Dickens's novel of the French Revolution, which was based upon Carlyle's *The French Revolution* but disregards the section on Corday that I discuss later in the chapter. Weiss describes Corday's appearance in Victorian tableau vivant and staged photography (94).

4. See also Austin Dobson's *Four Frenchwomen* (1890), *Lessons from Women's Lives* (1877), Wirt Sikes's *Studies of Assassination* (1881), and Trowbridge's *Daughters of Eve* (1912).

5. See Glover for more on the Aliens Act.

6. While large populations of socialists, anarchists, and nihilists lived in London, and many international radical newspapers were based there, these groups were responsible for no major political crimes in late-Victorian Britain. (The exception is the botched 1894 bombing of the Greenwich Observatory, discussed in the last chapter; it was thought to be the work of anarchists, but may well have been caused by an agent provocateur. See note 10, Chapter 4.) The many bombings and assassinations in this period stemmed from other groups, such as the Fenians in the 1880s and 1890s and the suffragettes in the first two decades of the twentieth century. Nevertheless, as Melchiori also discusses, most writers of dyna-

mite narrative evoke the climate surrounding Irish nationalist terror but apply it to a distinct political context (i.e., socialism, anarchism, and other democratic or anticapitalist movements gaining force in Britain).

7. For the whole editorial, see 12 April 1884, 9. For more such examples in the *Times,* see 14 April 1884, 9; 15 December 1884, 9; or the inflammatory and inaccurate "Parnellism and Crime" series that began on 7 March 1887. The most relevant piece in the series is 10 March 1887, 8.

8. *By Order of the Czar,* which Hatton would later adapt into a drama published in 1904, features a female revolutionary named Anna Klosstock, a strikingly beautiful Russian Jew who becomes a nihilist after being raped and publicly whipped by a general in the czarist government. Years later, she avenges herself by luring the general to his death, but the novel always depicts her nihilism in terms of personal vengeance rather than political commitment, unlike the other members of the nihilist "Brotherhood" to which she belongs: "Ferrari's devotion to the Brotherhood . . . had nobler springs than Anna's, who had but one dominant passion, that of revenge" (3:9).

9. Britain's only female assassin in this period was a twenty-five-year-old widowed English nurse named Lucilla Yseult Dudley, who shot Fenian leader O'Donovan Rossa in New York, February 1885. The shooting, which was not fatal, was in retaliation for Fenian dynamite attacks in London, but Dudley was acquitted on the grounds of insanity. In its extensive coverage of the case, the London *Times* compared Dudley to Charlotte Corday, noting, "It is a case of that very rare order among the crimes committed by women, a crime done on purely public grounds" (4 February 1885, 9).

10. Other late-Victorian stories featuring female revolutionaries include Stepniak's "A Female Nihilist," originally published in *Cornhill Magazine* (November 1884) and added to the second edition of *Underground Russia* (1885); Charles Eden's *George Donnington* (1885); Philip May's *Love, The Reward* (1885), discussed later in the chapter; and L. T. Meade's *The Siren* (1898). Houen (*Terrorism*) and Melchiori discuss some of these texts. See note 8 for a discussion of Hatton's 1890 novel *By Order of the Czar.* Vernon Lee's *Miss Brown* (1884) depicts a femme fatale named Sacha Elaguine who pretends to be a repentant nihilist conspirator as a means of generating sympathy and attention; the novel is harshly critical of aestheticism in general and Wilde's circle in particular, and one might argue that Brown intends Madame Elaguine as a satire of Wilde's nihilist heroine, Vera.

11. See Tilley or Eltis for more on these women. Other famous Russian female nihilists were Maria Kaljushnia, Olga Liubatovich, and Sofia Perovskaya, who plotted to assassinate Czar Alexander II and whom Stepniak profiled, like Vera Zasulich, in *Underground Russia.*

12. See Ellmann or Powell for more on Wilde's relationships with these actresses, some of whom inspired early poems such as "Madonna Mia" and "The New Helen."

13. All references to Wilde's letters are from *Complete Letters.* Wilde did eventually make money on the play; as a "Memorandum of Agreement" held at the Clark Library attests, Marie Prescott offered Wilde "1000 dollars for the exclusive right to produce the play, plus 50 dollars for each performance of the play thereafter." Prescott mounted a brief New York production and U.S. tour.

14. Rowell argues that lack of funding was the real reason, but Reed claims

Wilde would have *made* money from the performance, and most critics trust contemporaneous sources attributing the cancelation to political sensitivity. Wilde had good reason to believe his sympathetic account of nihilist regicide would alienate British audiences: in 1881, the British government sentenced Johann Most to eighteen months in prison for cheering the czar's assassination in print. See Ellmann or Eltis for more on *Vera*'s cancellation. See Joll, Phillips, or Quail for more on Most.

15. The serfs were not granted ownership of their land when they were granted emancipation, so were heavily in debt to the aristocrats and subject to excessive taxation. Quotations from *Vera* refer to the Methuen edition, unless otherwise noted. Note that in the stage production of *Vera*, Wilde did not want the mise-en-scène to be undated: in a letter discussing stage design, he emphasized that "the conspirators are to be *modern* . . . It is to be realistic not operatic conspiracy" (151).

16. Singer, for example, reads melodrama as a working-class genre of protest (*Melodrama*). Daly describes melodrama as "essentially modern" with "roots in the French Revolution and the industrial revolution" (14).

17. Gagnier offers a careful summary of this debate as it stood in 1986 (*Idylls* 29–31). It has not ceased since then.

18. Guy and Small's *Oscar Wilde's Profession* argues that because Wilde wrote to make money, his work conforms to the status quo: "the late nineteenth-century literary market was ruthlessly competitive and commercial . . . professional writers who needed to earn a living with their pen were in no place to resist or even contest those values. . . . the idea that Wilde was a writer who 'exploited' or 'subverted' consumer culture, as some recent critics have wanted to argue, makes little sense" (10). I find this unconvincing, and am more inclined to agree with Freedman that the logic of consumer capitalism accounts for its own critique, so that to subvert it does not imply a lack of commercial success: Wilde understood, Freedman argues, that "capitalism is not merely a form of economic organization, but rather a cultural one, an ensemble of attitudes toward and assumptions about the world that often controvert or undercut its own official system of values" (74).

19. See Oliver, Phillips, or W. C. H. for more on late-Victorian anarchism. Marx viewed the anarchists with contempt (*Selected Writings* 333–38).

20. Contemporary journals provide an excellent overview of the landscape of fin de siècle radicalism in Britain. On anarchism, see *Anarchist, Alarm, Liberty, Freedom,* or *Torch*. On state socialism and revolutionary socialism, see *Commonweal, Our Corner, Progress,* or *Social Democrat*. On Individualism, see *Free Life: Organ of Voluntary Taxation and the Voluntary State, Jus,* or *New Freewoman: An Individualist Review*.

21. Wilde had inherited his mother's tendency toward radical views, and while a student at Oxford, was deeply influenced by John Ruskin's ideas of social reform. Under Ruskin's direction, he even helped build a road in an impoverished district (Ellmann 49). He also participated in emergency relief labor after the flooding of the Thames (Bentley 35), and in 1889, demonstrated in solidarity with the dockworkers' strike (Ellmann 284). See Ellmann for more on Wilde's socialist activities (especially 290–91), and his friendship with the exiled nihilist Stepniak (122).

22. Not all reviews of *Vera* were poor: the *New York Mirror* called it "a work that takes rank among the highest order of plays" (Beckson 6).

23. See, for example, selections from the *New York Herald*'s or *Spirit of the Times*'s reviews, reprinted in Reed.

24. Wilde's final, unpublished version of the play—staged in 1883—added a few additional lines to this exchange. Michael tells Vera, "I don't love anyone but you," and she replies, "That is very wrong of you, Michael, very wrong indeed. You should love everybody" (Reed 6). These lines make Vera a "softer," more "feminine" heroine, as Marie Prescott requested after reading the original script, but they also stress Vera's sympathy beyond the personal to encompass the public at large.

25. Wilde's use of the epigram, in *Vera* as in other plays, linguistically enacts a similar move, emptying clichés and received wisdom of their value through unexpected reversals. See Amanda Anderson for more on Wilde's use of the epigram.

26. Vera is in some ways a precursor for Nathalie Haldin, from Conrad's *Under Western Eyes* (1911): both are beautiful, romanticized heroines with nihilist sympathies, whose brothers are arrested and killed by the czarist regime. Nathalie, however, does not participate in revolutionary violence; instead, at the novel's end, she divides her "compassionate labours between the horrors of overcrowded jails, and the heartrending misery of bereaved homes" (277).

27. Ellmann notes that Wilde adapts this oath from *The Catechism of a Revolutionary* by Sergey Nechayev and Mikhail Bakunin (122).

28. Stepniak's story "A Female Nihilist" also depicts a Russian female nihilist who "ardently preached against love and advocated celibacy" until she herself fell in love (293).

29. In the early days of the *Torch*, Olivia and her brother Arthur took most responsibility for the paper, but sources indicate that Arthur was a rather unreliable collaborator (see Soskice 23–24, 27; Garnett 134, 147). Soon "O. and H. Rossetti" were the paper's only acknowledged editors.

30. It is unclear who, exactly, initiated the *Torch*'s removal. Ford Madox Ford, a notoriously unreliable chronicler, says the paper moved out of the house upon Lucy Rossetti's death because she was its stronger parental advocate (Hueffer 121). William Michael Rossetti's *Reminiscences* supports this view:

> my wife and I had thought and talked seriously . . . about the rather overstrained ideas which dominated our children. . . . My wife had highly independent opinions of her own, tending towards socialism. . . . She considered that on the whole it would be a pity to chill our youngsters in their generous enthusiasms. . . . I was somewhat less inclined than she to allow the children to go to the end of their tether: still, I entered into her general view, and kept my interferences within very narrow limits. (452–53)

Other sources indicate, however, that Lucy opposed the newspaper's domestic presence while William supported it (see Garnett 154–55 and 200; or Soskice 9). Olivia corroborates this view of her father in an unpublished 1958 memoir: "for all his placid demeanor and domestic virtues, William Michael Rossetti was a daring and revolutionary thinker . . . [which] made him sympathise with the French rebels of the Commune, with the Irish Fenians, with the Boers, with the militant suffragettes, with the Russian nihilists, and tolerate our juvenile enthusiasm for the 'Chicago Martyrs' of 1886" (Agresti, *Anecdotage* 28). Thirlwell's biography also espouses such a depiction (198). Regardless, William's professional situation was likely a factor in the paper's departure. While both parents contributed creative writings to early issues of the *Torch,* for example, only William's specifies that he is "not a comrade but an outside contributor" (15 Oct. 1891). His *Reminiscences* reveal that he was careful to avoid creating the appearance of a conflict between his government job and his radical sympathies. He declined, for example, to edit an edition of poems by Francis Adams, an anarchist poet whose work he admired: "At first I assented: but, when it came to the point, I considered that some things in the volume ought not to pass muster through my hands (for after all I was a Government official, whatever else I might be)" (505).

31. See Surette and Tryphonopoulos for more on Olivia Rossetti Agresti's career in fascism and her long friendship and correspondence with Ezra Pound. For examples of tracts she wrote in support of Mussolini and Fascism, see *After Mussolini What?* (1937) or *The Organisation of the Arts and Professions in the Fascist Guild State* (with Mario Missiroli). Her sister Helen Rossetti Angeli translated Tomasso Silani's *What Is Fascism and Why?* into English in 1931. None of these works discuss Jews. See note 36 for more on the Rossettis and Jewishness. For other work by the Rossettis, see Angeli's biographies *Pre-Raphaelite Twilight, Dante Gabriel Rossetti,* or *Shelley and His Friends in Italy,* or see Agresti's biographies *David Lubin* or *Giovanni Costa.*

32. A journal called *The Adult,* for example, put forth the case for free love from the 1890s radical perspective; it began publication in 1897 and was edited by George Bedborough and Henry Seymour.

33. In real life, Olivia "united herself" to Antonio Agresti well before their secular Italian wedding ceremony (Oliver 124), providing a context for the favorable depiction of free love.

34. Olivia had extensively researched the French Revolution, and gave a series of lectures on it during her anarchist years. For more on her life and career, see her unpublished memoir *Anecdotage of an Interpreter* (Agresti) or her obituary ("Signora"). For more on both sisters, see Garnett, Hueffer, Lasner, William Michael Rossetti, Soskice, Thirlwell, or Tryphonopoulos.

35. The *Commonweal*'s account of the January 1885 bombing differs sharply from the *Times;* see note 11, chapter 4.

36. When the question of who represents the nation arose in late-Victorian discourse, immigration and race were often part of the calculus, and the Rossettis often correlate the threat of anarchism with Jewish immigration into London. In the popular mind-set of the time, anarchist and Jewish immigrants had much in common: both came from the Continent, often after expulsion, and tended to associate with like-minded communities in London. Moreover, Jews were nationless, and anarchists wanted to be nationless. At the time of *A Girl*'s publication, there was widespread public criticism of Britain's lenient immigration policy, which offered refuge not only to political criminals, but to Jews fleeing discrimination and pogroms. The Rossettis interweave these two strains of public anxiety in their anti-Semitic depiction of Jewish anarchist Jacob Myers (45). In so doing, they defy anarchist principle, since anarchism was an internationalist movement that renounced "race" and "nationality" as categories of identity. The Rossettis

themselves, in fact, call for the abolishment of "all petty race-hatred and race-pride" in their newspaper the *Torch* (15 June 1893). *A Girl*'s racist depiction of Jewish anarchists thus emulates popular crime fiction rather than anarchist discourse.

37. See Robert Anderson for discussion of these events, as understood from a contemporary Unionist perspective. Conrad relied heavily on Anderson in writing *Secret Agent,* but wrote Ireland out of the plot.

38. Page references to the Preface refer to the 1971 edition, while all other references to the text refer to the 1885 edition (which did not include a Preface). It is a matter of debate which author composed the bulk of *The Dynamiter.* Critics have tended to view the work as Robert's alone, often neglecting to mention Fanny at all. In her preface, however, Fanny stresses her own contribution, claiming that the initial idea was hers (xiv) and that the writing duties were distributed evenly between them. Robert's letters about the novel, meanwhile, take the perspective of sole authorship. Sandison has recently argued that "Apart from 'The Destroying Angel' and 'The Story of the Fair Cuban,' which are clearly Fanny's work in that they operate in a patently different 'key,' Stevenson sustains a narrative discourse of brilliant artificiality that advertises the presence of the author in every graceful line of the ensnaring arabesque" ("A World" 149). This suggests that Fanny wrote the parts narrated by Clara, while Robert wrote the "real" narrator's sections.

39. Sandison claims that *The Dynamiter* subverts "traditional narrative strategies where certain assumptions about gender are the bed-rock of novelistic practice" (*Robert* 98), but I believe his argument neglects the extent to which the novel's dedication and conclusion attempt to contain its gender subversion.

40. Sandison argues that the dedication is meant to stave off readers' pique, that it is "anxious" and "disingenuous" (*Robert* 114). Melchiori proffers a similar interpretation (60). This interpretation would be convenient for my argument, but it is also true that following the January 1885 bombing, Stevenson wrote to his father: "now, to have a dynamiter lynched, and all would be for the best in the best of possible worlds" (*Letters* 73). In February 1885, he wrote to John Addington Symonds: "Police Officer Cole is the only man that I see to admire. I dedicate [*Dynamiter*] to him and Cox, in default of other great public characters" (*Letters* 81). The novelist Grant Allen publicly objected to the dedication in the pages of the *Pall Mall Gazette:* "I do not at all admire the violent condemnation which Mr. Stevenson deals to a body of misguided Irish patriots, goaded by English injustice and landlord misrule into a mode of retaliation in some respects unworthy of their laudable object. My own fiery indignation would rather have been directed . . . against the wicked and cruel system which drives brave and resolute men to such desperate means of righting their ill-used country" (Stevenson, *Letters* 439).

41. It was not only Clara who performed this service; *The Dynamiter*'s satire also targets the gender-bending aesthetic movement. The opening pages of the novel burlesque popular aestheticism's fascination with "the Orient," and the three central male characters (impoverished aristocrats who frequent the Bohemian Cigar Divan) are caricatures of aesthetes. This parody aligns the narrative with the normative authority of bourgeois domesticity, since in the 1880s aestheticism was often ridiculed for its unorthodox expressions of gender and sexuality, as in Gilbert and Sullivan's *Patience* (1881).

42. By contrast, Stevenson's South Seas story "The Beach of Falesá" (1892) employs dynamite as an *anticolonial* literary device. Its narrator discovers—seven years before Kurtz—that a white trader named Case has been using a temple outfitted with ghoulish statues, luminous paint, and aeolian harps to convince the natives of his quasi-divine powers. At the end of the story, the narrator destroys the temple with dynamite fishing bombs, which could be viewed as an attack on imperial tyranny.

43. Nead reads this event as cementing a certain stereotype of feminism and the suffragette movement; while this is no doubt true, my book suggests that there was another stereotype of the feminist at work in mainstream late-Victorian crime narrative, to which Richardson's action was opposed: a popular, image-conscious feminism perfectly compatible with consumerism's emphasis on women's body and appearance.

AFTERWORD

1. *Sabotage* isn't the only 1930s film adaptation of a turn-of-the-century crime story to introduce a heterosexual romance where none existed before: Hitchcock's 1935 film version of John Buchan's 1915 novel *The 39 Steps* and Rouben Mamoulian's 1931 film version of Robert Louis Stevenson's 1886 novella *Dr. Jekyll and Mr. Hyde* both insert attractive female temptresses into plots that are almost exclusively male. The films thus curb the unconventional homoerotic sexuality of Buchan's and Stevenson's narratives.

2. See Felski for more on gendered conceptions of modernity (4–5), though she describes a somewhat different configuration than I've identified in the course of this study.

FILMS CITED

The Anarchist's Doom. Originally released as *The Tube of Death*. Dir. Alexander Butler. Barker, 1913.

The Countryman and the Cinematograph. Alt. title *The Countryman's First Sight of Animated Pictures*. Paul's Animatograph Works, 1901.

Dr. Jekyll and Mr. Hyde. Dir. Rouben Malmoulian, 1931.

Duel to the Death. Perf. Edith Blanche and Beatrice Homer. British Mutoscope & Biograph, 1898.

Everybody against the Policeman. Clarendon, 1908.

The Eviction. Dir. Alfred Collins. Gaumont, 1904.

Foiled By a Girl. Dir. Percy Stow. Perf. Dorothy Bellew. Clarendon, 1912.

An Interrupted Honeymoon. Dir. Lewin Fitzhamon. Hepworth, 1905.

The Militant Suffragette. Alt. title *A Busy Day*. Dir. Charlie Chaplin. Keystone, 1914.

Our New Policeman. Dir. Lewin Fitzhamon. Hepworth, 1907.

Sabotage. Dir. Alfred Hitchcock. Gaumont British, 1936.

Salome Mad. Dir. A. E. Coleby. Cricks and Martin, 1909.

St. Leonard's Outrage. Pathé, 1913.

A Subject for the Rogues' Gallery. American Mutoscope and Biograph, 1904.

The Suffragette Derby of 1913. Gaumont, 1913.

Suffragette Riots at Westminster. Pathé, 1910.

The Suffragettes' Downfall; Or, Who Said "Rats"? Dir. Fred Rains. Acme Films, 1911.

Thirty-Nine Steps. Dir. Alfred Hitchcock. Gaumont British, 1935.

Three-Fingered Kate: Kate Purloins the Wedding Presents. Dir. H. O. Martinek. Perf. Ivy Martinek, Alice Moseley, Charles Calvert, and Fred Paul. B&C, 1912.

Trafalgar Square Riot. Pathé, 1913.

Uncle Josh at the Moving Picture Show. Edison, 1902.

A Wife's Revenge; Or, the Gambler's End. Cricks and Sharp, 1904.

A Woman's Treachery. Dir. Theo Bouwmeester. Hepworth, 1910.

Women's Rights. Riley Brothers, 1899.

WORKS CITED

A. C. "Crime in Current Literature." *Westminster Review* 147.4 (April 1897): 429–38.

Accardo, Pasquale. *Diagnosis and Detection: The Medical Iconography of Sherlock Holmes*. London: Associated University Presses, 1987.

Adam, Hargrave L. *Woman and Crime*. London: T. Werner Laurie, 1912.

Agresti, Olivia Rossetti. *After Mussolini What?* Original title: *The Guild State and Sanctions*. New York: Italian Historical Society, 1937.

Agresti, Olivia Rossetti. *The Anecdotage of an Interpreter*. The Reminiscences of Olivia Rossetti Agresti (1958) in the Oral History Collection of Columbia University.

Agresti, Olivia Rossetti. *David Lubin: A Study in Practical Idealism*. Boston: Little, Brown, 1922.

Agresti, Olivia Rossetti. *Giovanni Costa: His Life, Work, and Times*. London: Grant Richards, 1904.

Allen, Grant. "The Dynamiter's Sweetheart." *Strand Magazine* (August 1894): 137–47.

Altick, Richard D. *The Presence of the Present: Topics of the Day in the Victorian Novel*. Columbus: Ohio State UP, 1991.

"Amusements: Mr. Oscar Wilde's Play." *New York Times*, 21 August 1883, 4.

Anderson, Alder. "Detectives at School: M. Bertillon's New Method of Descriptive Portraits." *Strand Magazine* 27 (1904): 443–47.

Anderson, Amanda. *The Powers of Distance: Cosmopolitanism and the Cultivation of Detachment*. Princeton: Princeton UP, 2001.

Anderson, Robert. *Sidelights on the Home Rule Movement*. London: John Murray, 1907.

Angeli, Helen Rossetti. *Dante Gabriel Rossetti: His Friends and Enemies*. London: Hamish Hamilton, 1949.

Angeli, Helen Rossetti. *Pre-Raphaelite Twilight: The Story of Charles Augustus How-ell*. London: Richards, 1954.

Angeli, Helen Rossetti. *Shelley and His Friends in Italy*. London: Methuen, 1911.

Arata, Stephen. *Fictions of Loss in the Victorian Fin de Siecle*. Cambridge: Cambridge UP, 1996.

Arata, Stephen. "*The Secret Agent* (1907)." *The Joseph Conrad Companion*. Ed. Leonard Orr and Ted Billy. Westport, CT: Greenwood, 1999. 165–94.

Armstrong, Nancy. *Desire and Domestic Fiction: A Political History of the Novel*. Oxford: Oxford UP, 1987.

Armstrong, Nancy. *Fiction in the Age of Photography: The Legacy of British Realism*. Cambridge: Harvard UP, 1999.

Aslami, Zarena. "The Space of Optimism: State Fantasy and the Case of *The Odd Women*." *Victorian Studies* 47.1 (Autumn 2004): 55–85.

Athill, Diana. Introduction. Rhys vii–xiv.

Auerbach, Jonathan. "Chasing Film Narrative: Repetition, Recursion, and the Body in Early Cinema." *Critical Inquiry* 26 (2000): 798–820.

Bailey, Peter. "Parasexuality and Glamour: The Victorian Barmaid as Cultural Prototype." *Gender and History* 2.2 (1990): 148–72.

Balides, Constance. "Scenarios of Exposure in the Practice of Everyday Life: Women in the Cinema of Attractions." *Screen* 34.1 (1993): 19–37.

Barnes, John. *The Beginnings of the Cinema in England 1894–1901*. 5 vols. 1974–97. Rev. ed. Exeter: U of Exeter P, 1996–98.

Barolsky, Paul. "The Case of the Domesticated Aesthete." Orel 92–102.

Barr, Charles. "Before Blackmail: Silent British Cinema." Murphy 12–19.

Barthes, Roland. *Image, Music, Text*. Trans. Stephen Heath. New York: Hill and Wang, 1977.

Bartsky, Sandra Lee. "Foucault, Femininity, and the Modernization of Patriarchal Power." *Feminism and Foucault: Reflections on Resistance*. Ed. Irene Diamond and Lee Quinby. Boston: Northeastern UP, 1988.

Bax, E. Belfort. *The Fraud of Feminism*. London: Grant Richards, 1913.

Bax, E. Belfort. *The Legal Subjection of Men*. London: New Age, 1908.

Bazin, André. "The Ontology of the Photographic Image." 1945. *What is Cinema?* Trans. Hugh Gray. Berkeley: U of California P, 1967.

Beckson, Karl, ed. *Oscar Wilde: The Critical Heritage*. London: Routledge, 1970.

Beerbohm, Max. "A Defence of Cosmetics." *Yellow Book* 1 (April 1894): 65–82.

Belsey, Catherine. *Critical Practice*. London: Methuen, 1980.

Benjamin, Walter. *The Arcades Project*. Trans. Howard Eiland and Kevin McLaughlin. Cambridge, MA: Belknap, 1999.

Benjamin, Walter. *Charles Baudelaire: A Lyric Poet in the Era of High Capitalism*. Trans. Harry Zohn. London: Verso, 1983.

Benjamin, Walter. "The Work of Art in the Age of Mechanical Reproduction." *Illuminations*. Trans. Harry Zohn. Ed. Hannah Arendt. New York: Schocken, 1968. 217–51.

Bentley, Joyce. *The Importance of Being Constance*. London: R. Hale, 1983.

Birken, Lawrence. *Consuming Desire: Sexual Science and the Emergence of a Culture of Abundance, 1871–1914*. Ithaca, NY: Cornell UP, 1988.

Black, Paula. *The Beauty Industry: Gender, Culture, Pleasure*. London: Routledge, 2004.

Boase, George C. "Madame Rachel." *Notes and Queries* (27 October 1894): 322–24.

Boos, Florence S. "An Aesthetic Ecocommunist: Morris the Red and Morris the Green." *William Morris: Centenary Essays.* Ed. Peter Faulkner and Peter Preston. Exeter: U of Exeter P, 1999. 21–46.

Boos, Florence S., and William Boos. "*News from Nowhere* and Victorian Socialist-Feminism." *Nineteenth-Century Contexts* 14.1 (1990): 3–32.

Bordo, Susan. *Unbearable Weight: Feminism, Western Culture, and the Body.* Berkeley: U of California P, 1993.

Bowlby, Rachel. *Just Looking: Consumer Culture in Dreiser, Gissing, and Zola.* New York: Methuen, 1985.

Braddon, Mary Elizabeth. *Lady Audley's Secret.* 1862. Oxford: Oxford UP, 1987.

Brake, Laurel. *Subjugated Knowledges: Journalism, Gender, and Literature in the Nineteenth Century.* London: Macmillan, 1994.

Bristow, Joseph, ed. *Wilde Writings: Contextual Conditions.* Toronto: U of Toronto P, 2003.

Buchan, John. *The Thirty-Nine Steps.* 1915. Oxford: Oxford UP, 1993.

Buck-Morss, Susan. "The Flaneur, the Sandwichman and the Whore: The Politics of Loitering." *New German Critique* 39 (1986): 99–140.

Buckler, Julie A. "Melodramatizing Russia: Nineteenth-Century Views from the West." *Imitations of Life: Two Centuries of Melodrama in Russia.* Eds. Louise McReynolds and Joan Neuberger. Durham: Duke UP, 2002. 55–78.

Burrows, Jon. "Penny Pleasures: Film Exhibition in London during the Nickelodeon Era, 1906–1914." *Film History* 16.1 (2004): 60–91.

Burrows, Jon. "Penny Pleasures II: Indecency, Anarchy and Junk Film in London's 'Nickelodeons', 1906–1914." *Film History* 16.2 (2004): 172–97.

Burton, Alan, and Laraine Porter, eds. *Pimple, Pranks and Pratfalls: British Film Comedy before 1930.* Trowbridge, Wiltshire, UK: Flicks Books, 2000.

Carlyle, Thomas. *The French Revolution: A History.* 1837. New York: Modern Library, 2002.

"Central Criminal Court, Sept. 21." *Times,* 22 September 1868, 9.

"Central Criminal Court, Sept. 24." *Times,* 25 September 1868, 10.

Chamberlin, J. Edward, and Sander L. Gilman, eds. *Degeneration: The Dark Side of Progress.* New York: Columbia UP, 1985.

Chanan, Michael. *The Dream That Kicks: The Prehistory and Early Years of Cinema in Britain.* 2nd ed. London: Routledge, 1996.

Charney, Leo, and Vanessa R. Schwartz, eds. *Cinema and the Invention of Modern Life.* Berkeley: U of California P, 1995.

Christ, Carol T., and John O. Jordan, eds. *Victorian Literature and the Victorian Visual Imagination.* Berkeley: U of California P, 1995.

"The Cinema and Hypnotic Suggestion—Italian Doctors Investigate." *Film Censor,* 26 July 1912, 3.

"Cinematograph and Crime: The Question Raised in Parliament." *Cinema,* May 1912, 21.

Cobbe, Frances Power. "Why Women Desire the Franchise." *Women's Writing of the Victorian Period.* Ed. Harriet Devine Jump. New York: St. Martin's, 217–21.

Cobbe, Frances Power. "Wife-torture in England." *Criminals, Idiots, Women, and*

Minors: Victorian Writing By Women On Women. Ed. Susan Hamilton. Peter-borough, ON: Broadview, 1996. 132–70.

Collins, Wilkie. *Armadale*. 1866. London: Penguin, 1995.

Collins, Wilkie. *The Law and the Lady*. 1875. London: Penguin, 1998.

Collins, Wilkie. *The Moonstone*. 1868. Oxford: Oxford UP, 1999.

Collins, Wilkie. *The Woman in White*. 1860. Peterborough, ON: Broadview, 2006.

Conrad, Joseph. *Collected Letters of Joseph Conrad*. Ed. Frederick Karl and Laurence Davies. 5 vols. Cambridge: Cambridge UP, 1990.

Conrad, Joseph. *Heart of Darkness*. 1899. Case Studies in Contemporary Criticism. 2nd ed. Boston: Bedford, 1996.

Conrad, Joseph. "The Informer." *Collected Stories of Joseph Conrad*. Ed. Samuel Hynes. Hopewell, NJ: Ecco, 1991.

Conrad, Joseph. *The Secret Agent*. 1907. London: Penguin, 1990.

Conrad, Joseph. *Under Western Eyes*. 1911. Oxford: Oxford UP, 2003.

Cooper, Mark Garrett. *Love Rules: Silent Hollywood and the Rise of the Managerial Class*. Minneapolis: U of Minnesota P, 2003.

Corson, Richard. *Fashions in Makeup from Ancient to Modern Times*. New York: Universe, 1972.

"Court of Exchequer, June 19." *Times*, 20 June 1862, 11.

"Court Of Queen's Bench, Westminster, Nov. 8." *Times*, 9 November 1858, 8.

Crary, Jonathan. *Suspensions of Perception: Attention, Spectacle, and Modern Culture*. Cambridge: MIT P, 1999.

Crary, Jonathan. *Techniques of the Observer: On Vision and Modernity in the Nine-teenth Century*. Cambridge: MIT P, 1992.

"The Craze for Sensation." *Bioscope*, 2 October 1913, 1.

"Crime in Fiction." *Blackwood's Edinburgh Magazine* (August 1890): 172–89.

"Crime on the Pictures." *Bioscope*, 20 June 1912, 853.

"Criminal Scenes Censored." *Film Censor*, 26 February 1913, 3.

Curiosities of Street Literature. London: Reeves and Turner, 1871.

"A curious tale of simplicity." Editorial. *Times*, 12 April 1878, 9.

Cvetkovich, Ann. *Mixed Feelings: Feminism, Mass Culture, and Victorian Sensation-alism*. New Brunswick, NJ: Rutgers UP, 1996.

Daly, Nicholas. *Literature, Technology, and Modernity, 1860–2000*. Cambridge: Cam-bridge UP, 2004.

Dickens, Charles. *Dombey and Son*. 1848. London: Penguin, 2002.

Doane, Mary Ann. "Film and the Masquerade: Theorizing the Female Spectator." *Screen* 23 (1982): 78–87.

Doyle, Arthur Conan. *The Adventures of Sherlock Holmes*. Ed. Richard Lancelyn Green. Oxford: Oxford UP, 1993.

Doyle, Arthur Conan. "The Abbey Grange." 1904. *Return* 266–90.

Doyle, Arthur Conan. "The Beryl Coronet." 1892. *Adventures* 244–69.

Doyle, Arthur Conan. "Black Peter." 1904. *Return* 134–56.

Doyle, Arthur Conan. "Boscombe Valley Mystery." 1891. *Adventures* 75–101.

Doyle, Arthur Conan. "A Case of Identity." 1891. *Adventures* 30–48.

Doyle, Arthur Conan. "Charles Augustus Milverton." 1904. *Return* 157–75.

Doyle, Arthur Conan. "The Copper Beeches." 1892. *Adventures* 270–96.

Doyle, Arthur Conan. "The Crooked Man." 1893. *Memoirs* 155–73.

Doyle, Arthur Conan. "The Dancing Men." 1903. *Return* 73–99.

Doyle, Arthur Conan. "The Empty House." 1903. *Return* 3–25.

Doyle, Arthur Conan. "The Engineer's Thumb." 1892. *Adventures* 198–220.

Doyle, Arthur Conan. "The Final Problem." 1893. *Memoirs* 249–68.

Doyle, Arthur Conan. "The 'Gloria Scott.'" 1893. *Memoirs* 92–112.

Doyle, Arthur Conan. "The Golden Pince-Nez." 1904. *Return* 218–42.

Doyle, Arthur Conan. "The Greek Interpreter." 1893. *Memoirs* 193–212.

Doyle, Arthur Conan. "The Man with the Twisted Lip." 1891. *Adventures* 123–48.

Doyle, Arthur Conan. *The Memoirs of Sherlock Holmes.* Ed. Christopher Roden. Oxford: Oxford UP, 1993.

Doyle, Arthur Conan. "The Musgrave Ritual." 1893. *Memoirs* 113–33.

Doyle, Arthur Conan. "The Naval Treaty." 1893. *Memoirs* 213–48.

Doyle, Arthur Conan. "The Noble Bachelor." 1892. *Adventures* 221–43.

Doyle, Arthur Conan. "The Norwood Builder." 1903. *Return* 26–51.

Doyle, Arthur Conan. *The Return of Sherlock Holmes.* Ed. Richard Lancelyn Green. Oxford: Oxford UP, 1993.

Doyle, Arthur Conan. "A Scandal in Bohemia." 1891. *Adventures* 5–29.

Doyle, Arthur Conan. "The Second Stain." 1904. *Return* 291–318.

Doyle, Arthur Conan. *The Sign of Four.* 1890. London: Penguin, 2001.

Doyle, Arthur Conan. "The Six Napoleons." 1904. *Return* 176–98.

Doyle, Arthur Conan. "The Speckled Band." 1892. *Adventures* 171–97.

Doyle, Arthur Conan. *A Study in Scarlet.* 1887. *Sherlock Holmes: The Complete Novels and Stories.* Vol. 1. New York: Bantam, 1986. 1–103.

"Dynamite and Dynamiters." First article in series "Crime and Criminals." *Strand Magazine* (February 1894): 119–32.

"Dynamite Outrage at Victoria Station." *Times,* 27 February 1884, 10.

Eisenstein, Sergei. *Film Form: Essays in Film Theory.* Ed. and trans. Jay Leyda. San Diego: Harvest, 1977.

Ellis, Havelock. *The Criminal.* London: Walter Scott, 1890.

Ellis, Havelock. "Letter to a Suffragette." Addressed to Miss Mary Gawthorpe (18 September 1912). *Views and Reviews: A Selection of Uncollected Articles, 1884–1932.* First Series: 1884–1919. London: Desmond Harmsworth, 1932. 233–34.

Ellis, Havelock. *Man and Woman.* London: Walter Scott, 1894.

Ellmann, Richard. *Oscar Wilde.* New York: Knopf, 1987.

Elsaesser, Thomas, ed., with Adam Barker. *Early Cinema: Space, Frame, Narrative.* London: British Film Institute, 1990.

Eltis, Sos. *Revising Wilde: Society and Subversion in the Plays of Oscar Wilde.* Oxford: Oxford UP, 1996.

Esch, Deborah. "Promissory Notes: The Prescription of the Future in *The Princess Casamassima.*" *American Literary History* 1.2 (1989): 317–38.

"Exhibitors' Meeting at Birmingham: The Censorship Question." *Bioscope,* 11 July 1912, 95.

The Extraordinary Life and Trial of Madame Rachel at the Central Criminal Court, Old Bailey, London, On the 22, 23, 24, and 25 September, 1868: The Report Copied Verbatim from The Times. London, 1868.

Favor, Lesli J. "The Foreign and the Female in Arthur Conan Doyle: Beneath the

Candy Coating." *English Literature in Transition, 1880–1920* 43.4 (2000): 398–409.

Fawcett, E. Douglas. *Hartmann the Anarchist: or, The Doom of the Great City*. 1893. New York: Arno P, 1975.

Field, Audrey. *Picture Palace: A Social History of the Cinema*. London: Gentry, 1974.

Felski, Rita. *The Gender of Modernity*. Cambridge, MA: Harvard UP, 1995.

Fillingham, Lydia Alix. "'The Colorless Skein of Life': Threats to the Private Sphere in Conan Doyle's *A Study in Scarlet*." *ELH* 56.3 (Autumn 1989): 667–88.

Flint, Kate. *The Victorians and the Visual Imagination*. Cambridge: Cambridge UP, 2000.

Foucault, Michel. *Discipline and Punish: The Birth of the Prison*. Trans. Alan Sheridan. New York: Pantheon, 1977.

Foucault, Michel. *The History of Sexuality: An Introduction*. Vol. 1. Trans. Robert Hurley. New York: Vintage, 1990.

Foucault, Michel. "Omnes et Singulatim: Towards a Critique of 'Political Reason.'" *The Essential Works of Foucault, 1954–1984*. Ed. Paul Rabinow and Nikolas Rose. New York: New P, 2003. 180–201.

Fraser, Hilary, Stephanie Green, and Judith Johnston. *Gender and the Victorian Periodical*. Cambridge: Cambridge UP, 2003.

Freedman, Jonathan. *Professions of Taste: Henry James, British Aestheticism, and Commodity Culture*. Stanford: Stanford UP, 1990.

Freud, Sigmund. *Three Essays on the Theory of Sexuality*. 1905. Trans. James Strachey. New York: Basic, 1975.

Furniss, Harry. "English—By the Americans." *Bioscope,* 20 March 1913, 869–75.

Furniss, Harry. *Our Lady Cinema*. 1914. Facsimile of the first edition. New York: Garland, 1978.

Furniss, Harry. "Wanted—A Censor." *Bioscope,* 9 January 1913, 81–85.

Furniss, Harry. "Where Are the English Films?" *Bioscope,* 13 March 1913, 791–95.

"The Future of the Moving Picture: Views of a Pioneer." Interview with George Howard Cricks. *Rinking World and Picture Theatre News,* 25 December 1909, 12.

Gagnier, Regenia. *Idylls of the Marketplace: Oscar Wilde and the Victorian Public*. Stanford: Stanford UP, 1986.

Gagnier, Regenia. *Subjectivities: A History of Self-Representation in Britain, 1832–1920*. Oxford: Oxford UP, 1991.

Galton, Francis. *Finger Prints*. London: Macmillan, 1892.

Gardner, FitzRoy. "Some Sidelights on Crime." *Strand Magazine* 28 (1904): 455–62.

Garnett, Olive. *Tea and Anarchy! The Bloomsbury Diary of Olive Garnett 1890–1893*. Ed. Barry C. Johnson. London: Bartletts P, 1989.

Gaskell, Elizabeth. *Mary Barton*. 1848. Ed. Jennifer Foster. Peterborough, ON: Broadview, 2000.

Geear. "The Cinema and Crime." *Film Censor,* 13 November 1912, 3.

Gifford, Denis. *The British Film Catalogue: A Reference Guide*. 3rd ed. *Volume 1, Fiction Film 1895–1994*. London: Fitzroy Dearborn, 2001.

Gissing, George. *The Odd Women*. 1893. Ed. Arlene Young. Peterborough, ON: Broadview, 1998.

Glasier, John Bruce. *William Morris and the Early Days of the Socialist Movement.* 1921. Bristol: Thommes, 1994.

Glover, David. "Aliens, Anarchists and Detectives: Legislating the Immigrant Body." *New Formations* 32 (1997): 22–33.

Goodlad, Lauren M. E. *Victorian Literature and the Victorian State.* Baltimore: Johns Hopkins UP, 2003.

Goring, Charles. *The English Convict: A Statistical Study.* London: T. Fisher Unwin, 1913.

Graham, Wendy. *Henry James's Thwarted Love.* Stanford, CA: Stanford UP, 1999.

Grand, Sarah. *The Heavenly Twins.* 1893. Ann Arbor: U of Michigan P, 1992.

Grand, Sarah. "The New Aspect of the Woman Question." 1894. Rpt. Nelson 141–46.

Grass, Sean. *The Self in the Cell: Narrating the Victorian Prisoner.* New York: Routledge, 2003.

Gray, Frances. *Women, Crime and Language.* Houndsmills, Hampshire: Palgrave, 2003.

Greene, Douglas G. Introduction. *The Detections of Miss Cusack.* By L. T. Meade and Robert Eustace. vii–xiii.

Greenslade, William. *Degeneration, Culture, and the Novel, 1880–1940.* Cambridge: Cambridge UP, 1994.

Greer, Tom. *A Modern Daedalus.* 1885. New York: Arno P, 1975.

Guimond, James and Katherine Kearney Maynard. "Kaczynski, Conrad, and Terrorism." *Conradiana* 31.1 (Spring 1999): 1–11.

Gunning, Tom. "The Cinema of Attractions: Early Film, Its Spectator and the Avant-Garde." *Wide Angle* 8 (1986): 63–70. Rpt. Elsaesser and Barker 56–62.

Gunning, Tom. *D. W. Griffith and the Origins of American Narrative Film.* Urbana: U of Illinois P, 1991.

Gunning, Tom. "In Your Face: Physiognomy, Photography, and the Gnostic Mission of Early Film." *Modernism/Modernity* 4.1 (1997): 1–29.

Gunning, Tom. "Tracing the Individual Body: Photography, Detectives, and Early Cinema." Charney and Schwartz 15–45.

Gunning, Tom. "The Whole Town's Gawking: Early Cinema and the Visual Experience of Modernity." *Yale Journal of Criticism* 7.2 (1994): 189–201.

Guy, Josephine M. "'The Soul of Man under Socialism': A (Con)Textual History." Bristow 59–85.

Guy, Josephine, and Ian Small. *Oscar Wilde's Profession.* Oxford: Oxford UP, 2000.

Habermas, Jürgen. *The Structural Transformation of the Public Sphere.* 1962. Trans. Thomas Burger. Cambridge: MIT P, 1989.

Hall, Jasmine Yong. "Ordering the Sensational: Sherlock Holmes and the Female Gothic." *Studies in Short Fiction* 28.3 (1991): 295–303.

Halloran, Jennifer A. "*The Sorceress of the Strand:* Gender, Race, and Criminal Witchcraft." *English Literature in Transition, 1880–1920* 45.2 (2002): 176–95.

Hamer, Emily. "Fighting for Freedom: Suffragette Violence against Their State." *No Angels: Women Who Commit Violence.* Ed. Alice Meyers and Sarah Wight. London: HarperCollins, 1996. 72–84.

Hampson, Robert G. "'If You Read Lombroso': Conrad and Criminal Anthropology." *The Ugo Mursia Memorial Lectures: Papers from the International Conrad*

Conference. University of Pisa, September 7th–11th 1983. Ed. Mario Currelli. Milan: Mursia, 1988.

Hansen, Miriam. *Babel and Babylon: Spectatorship in American Silent Film.* Cambridge: Harvard UP, 1991.

Hardy, Thomas. *A Laodicean.* 1881. Oxford: Oxford UP, 1991.

Hardy, Thomas. *Tess of the d'Urbervilles.* 1891. Peterborough, ON: Broadview, 1996.

Haslam, Jason. "Being Jane Warton: Lady Constance Lytton and the Disruption of Privilege." Haslam and Wright 25–56.

Haslam, Jason, and Julia M. Wright, eds. *Captivating Subjects: Writing Confinement, Citizenship, and Nationhood in the Nineteenth Century.* Toronto: U of Toronto P, 2005.

Hatton, Joseph. *By Order of the Czar.* 3 vols. London: Hutchinson, 1890.

Haweis, Mrs. H. R. [Mary]. *The Art of Beauty.* New York: Harper and Brothers, 1878.

Hay, Frederick. *Beautiful For Ever: A Farce in One Act.* London: T. H. Lacy, 1868.

Hayes, Kevin J., ed. *Henry James: The Contemporary Reviews.* Cambridge: Cambridge UP, 1996.

Hemyng, Bracebridge. "Prostitution in London." Mayhew 473–91.

Hennessy, Rosemary, and Rajeswari Mohan. "The Construction of Woman in Three Popular Texts of Empire: Towards a Critique of Materialist Feminism." *Textual Practice* 3.3 (1989): 323–59.

"High Court of Justice." *Times,* 23 March 1881, 5.

Hiley, Nicholas. "The British Cinema Auditorium." *Film and the First World War.* Ed. Karel Dibbets and Bert Hogenkamp. Amsterdam: Amsterdam UP, 1995. 160–70.

Hiley, Nicholas. "Fifteen Questions about the Early Film Audience." *Uncharted Territory: Essays on Early Nonfiction Film.* Ed. Daan Hertogs and Nico de Klerk. Amsterdam: Stichting Nederlands Filmmuseum, 1997. 105–18.

Hoare, Philip. *Wilde's Last Stand: Decadence, Conspiracy, and the First World War.* London: Duckworth, 1997.

Houen, Alex. "*The Secret Agent:* Anarchism and the Thermodynamics of Law." *ELH* 65.4 (1998): 995–1016.

Houen, Alex. *Terrorism and Modern Literature, from Joseph Conrad to Ciaran Carson.* Oxford: Oxford UP, 2002.

Howe, Irving. *Politics and the Novel.* New York: Horizon, 1957.

Hueffer, Ford Madox. *Ancient Lights and Certain New Reflections: Being the Memories of a Young Man.* London: Chapman and Hall, 1911.

Hughes, Linda K., and Michael Lund. *The Victorian Serial.* Charlottesville: UP of Virginia, 1991.

Hurley, Kelly. *The Gothic Body: Sexuality, Materialism, and Degeneration at the Fin de Siècle.* Cambridge: Cambridge UP, 1996.

Hurley, Kelly. "Hereditary Taint and Cultural Contagion: The Social Etiology of Fin-de-Siecle Degeneration Theory." *Nineteenth Century Contexts* 14.2 (1990): 193–214.

Huyssen, Andreas. *After the Great Divide: Modernism, Mass Culture, Postmodernism.* Bloomington: Indiana UP, 1986.

"Insanity or Crime?—The Dublin Theatre Outrage." *Film Censor,* 24 July 1912, 4.

"Insolvent Debtors' Court, Jan. 17." *Times,* 18 January 1862, 9.

"Irish Rush to Duck the Suffragettes." *New York Times,* 20 July 1912, 1.

"Is Sensational Taste Too Pronounced?" *Picture Theatre News,* 11 January 1911, 4.

Jacobs, Robert G. "Comrade Ossipon's Favorite Saint: Lombroso and Conrad." *Nineteenth-Century Fiction* 23:1 (1968): 74–84.

Jacobson, Marcia. *Henry James and the Mass Market.* University, AL: U of Alabama P, 1983.

James, Henry. *Letters.* Vol. 3 (1883–1895). Ed. Leon Edel. London: Macmillan, 1981.

James, Henry. *A Little Tour in France.* 1884. *Henry James: The Collected Travel Writings: The Continent.* Ed. Richard Howard. New York: Library of America, 1993. 1–277.

James, Henry. *The Princess Casamassima.* 1886. Ed. Derek Brewer. London: Penguin, 1987.

James, Henry. *The Princess Casamassima.* 1909. Ed. Leon Edel. London: Bodley Head, 1972.

James, Henry. *Roderick Hudson.* 1875. London: Thomas Nelson and Sons, 1876.

Jameson, Fredric. *A Singular Modernity: Essay on the Ontology of the Present.* London: Verso, 2002.

Jann, Rosemary. *The Adventures of Sherlock Holmes: Detecting Social Order.* New York: Twayne, 1995.

Jann, Rosemary. "Sherlock Holmes Codes the Social Body." *ELH* 57.3 (1990): 685–708.

Joll, James. *The Anarchists.* 2nd ed. London: Methuen, 1979.

Jones, Glyn. *Beautiful For Ever: A Play for Women.* London: S. French, 1978.

Joyce, Simon. *Capital Offenses: Geographies of Class and Crime in Victorian London.* Charlottesville: U of Virginia P, 2003.

Joyce, Simon. "Sexual Politics and the Aesthetics of Crime: Oscar Wilde in the Nineties." *ELH* 69.2 (2002): 501–23.

Jusová, Iveta. *The New Woman and the Empire.* Columbus: Ohio State UP, 2005.

Keep, Christopher. "The Cultural Work of the Type-Writer Girl." *Victorian Studies* 40.3 (1997): 401–26.

Kestner, Joseph. *Sherlock's Men: Masculinity, Conan Doyle, and Cultural History.* Aldershot, UK: Ashgate, 1997.

King, Andrew and John Plunkett, eds. *Victorian Print Media.* Oxford: Oxford UP, 2005.

Kipling, Rudyard. "Mrs Bathurst" (1904). *Rudyard Kipling.* Ed. Daniel Karlin. Oxford: Oxford UP, 1999. 276–92.

Knelman, Judith. *Twisting in the Wind: The Murderess and the English Press.* Toronto: U of Toronto P, 1998.

Koven, Seth. *Slumming: Sexual and Social Politics in Victorian London.* Princeton: Princeton UP, 2004.

Krafft-Ebing, Richard Von. *Psychopathia Sexualis, with Especial Reference to the Antipathic Sexual Instinct; A Medico-Forensic Study.* 1886. Trans. Franklin S. Klaf. New York: Stein and Day, 1965.

Kuklick, Henrika. "Tribal Exemplars: Images of Political Authority in British Anthropology, 1885–1945." Stocking, *Functionalism* 59–82.

Lasner, Mark Samuels, and Vincent Brome. "A BBC Interview with Mrs. Helen Rossetti Angeli." *Journal of Pre-Raphaelite Studies* 2.2 (1982): 7–19.

"The Late Madame Rachel." *Times,* 18 October 1880, 11.

Law, Graham. *Serializing Fiction in the Victorian Press.* Houndsmills, Hampshire: Palgrave, 2000.

Ledger, Sally. "In Darkest England: The Terror of Degeneration in *Fin-de-Siecle* Britain." *Literature and History* 4.2 (1995): 71–86.

Ledger, Sally. *The New Woman: Fiction and Feminism at the fin de siècle.* Manchester: Manchester UP, 1997.

Lee, Vernon. *Miss Brown.* 1884. New York: Garland, 1978.

Leps, Marie-Christine. *Apprehending the Criminal: The Production of Deviance in Nineteenth-Century Discourse.* Durham: Duke UP, 1992.

Lindner, Christoph. *Fictions of Commodity Culture: From the Victorian to the Postmodern.* Aldershot, UK: Ashgate, 2003.

Lombroso, Cesare, and William Ferrero. *The Female Offender.* With an introduction by W. Douglas Morrison. London: T. Fisher Unwin, 1895.

"London, Monday, January 26, 1885." *Times,* 26 January 1885, 9.

London in the Sixties (With a Few Digressions). By "One of the Old Brigade." London: Everett, 1908.

Longhurst, Derek. "Sherlock Holmes: Adventures of an English Gentleman 1887–1894." *Gender, Genre and Narrative Pleasure.* Ed. Derek Longhurst. London: Unwin Hyman, 1989. 51–66.

Low, Rachael. *The History of the British Film, 1906–1914.* London: George Allen & Unwin, 1949.

Low, Rachael, and Roger Manvell. *The History of the British Film, 1896–1906.* London: George Allen and Unwin, 1948.

Lysack, Krista. "Goblin Markets: Victorian Women Shoppers at Liberty's Oriental Bazaar." *Nineteenth-Century Contexts* 27.2 (2005): 139–65.

Madame Rachel. *Beautiful For Ever!* London: Madame Rachel, 47A New Bond Street, 1863.

Maixner, Paul, ed. *Robert Louis Stevenson: The Critical Heritage.* London: Routledge, 1981.

Mangum, Teresa. *Married, Middlebrow, and Militant: Sarah Grand and the New Woman Novel.* Ann Arbor: U of Michigan P, 1998.

"Marlborough-Street." *Times,* 20 December 1865, 11.

Marlow-Mann, Alex. "British Series and Serials in the Silent Era." *Young and Innocent? The Cinema in Britain 1896–1930.* Ed. Andrew Higson. Exeter: U of Exeter P, 2002. 147–61.

Marx, Karl. *Selected Writings.* Indianapolis: Hackett, 1994.

May, Philip. *Love: The Reward.* 3 vols. London: Remington, 1885.

Mayhew, Henry. *London Labour and the London Poor.* 1861–62. Ed. Victor Neuberg. London: Penguin, 1985.

McClintock, Anne. *Imperial Leather: Race, Gender, and Sexuality in the Colonial Contest.* New York: Routledge, 1995.

McGurl, Mark. "Social Geometries: Taking Place in Henry James." *Representations* 68 (1999): 59–83.

McLaughlin, Joseph. *Writing the Urban Jungle: Reading Empire in London from Doyle to Eliot*. Charlottesville: U of Virginia P, 2000.

Meade, L. T. *A Girl of the People*. 1890. New York: Hurst, n.d.

Meade, L. T. "A Young Blue-Stocking." *Ludgate Monthly* (February 1892): 235–41.

Meade, L. T., and Robert Eustace. "At the Edge of the Crater." *The Brotherhood of the Seven Kings. Strand Magazine* (January 1898): 86–98.

Meade, L. T., and Robert Eustace. "The Blood-Red Cross." *The Sorceress of the Strand. Strand Magazine* (November 1902): 505–18.

Meade, L. T., and Robert Eustace. "The Bloodhound." *The Brotherhood of the Seven Kings. Strand Magazine* (September 1898): 304–17.

Meade, L. T., and Robert Eustace. "The Bloodstone." *The Sorceress of the Strand. Strand Magazine* (February 1903): 198–212.

Meade, L. T., and Robert Eustace. *The Detections of Miss Cusack*. 1899–1901. Ed. Douglas G. Greene and Jack Adrian. Shelburne, ON: Battered Silicon Dispatch Box, 1998.

Meade, L. T., and Robert Eustace. "The Face of the Abbot." *The Sorceress of the Strand. Strand Magazine* (December 1902): 644–57.

Meade, L. T., and Robert Eustace. "The Luck of Pitsey Hall." *The Brotherhood of the Seven Kings. Strand Magazine* (April 1898): 379–92.

Meade, L. T., and Robert Eustace. "Madame Sara." *The Sorceress of the Strand. Strand Magazine* (October 1902): 387–401.

Meade, L. T., and Robert Eustace. "The Talk of the Town," *The Sorceress of the Strand. Strand Magazine* (January 1903): 67–80.

Meade, L. T., and Robert Eustace. "The Teeth of the Wolf." *The Sorceress of the Strand. Strand Magazine* (March 1903): 279–90.

Meade, L. T., and Robert Eustace. "The Winged Assassin." *The Brotherhood of the Seven Kings. Strand Magazine* (February 1898): 137–50.

Meisel, Martin. *Realizations: Narrative, Pictorial, and Theatrical Arts in Nineteenth-Century England*. Princeton: Princeton UP, 1983.

Meissner, Collin. "*The Princess Casamassima:* A Dirty Intellectual Fog." *Henry James Review* 19.1 (1998): 53–71.

Melchiori, Barbara Arnett. *Terrorism in the Late Victorian Novel*. London: Croom Helm, 1985.

Meredith, Isabel [Olivia and Helen Rossetti]. *A Girl among the Anarchists*. 1903. Lincoln: U of Nebraska P, 1992.

Miller, Andrew H. *Novels behind Glass: Commodity Culture and Victorian Narrative*. Cambridge: Cambridge UP, 1995.

Miller, D. A. *The Novel and the Police*. Berkeley: U of California P, 1988.

Miller, Elizabeth Carolyn. "Trouble with She-Dicks: Private Eyes and Public Women in *The Adventures of Loveday Brooke, Lady Detective*." *Victorian Literature and Culture* 33.1 (2005): 47–65.

Missiroli, Mario and Olivia Rossetti Agresti. *The Organisation of the Arts and Professions in the Fascist Guild State*. Rome: Laboremus, 1938.

Mitchell, Sally. *The New Girl: Girls' Culture in England, 1880–1915*. New York: Columbia UP, 1995.

Mitchell, W. J. T. *Picture Theory: Essays on Verbal and Visual Representation*. Chicago: U of Chicago P, 1994.

Monaghan, Garrett. "Performing the Passions: Comic Themes in the Films of George Albert Smith." Burton and Porter 24–32.

Morris, Virginia B. *Double Jeopardy: Women Who Kill in Victorian Fiction*. Lexington: UP of Kentucky, 1990.

Morrison, William Douglas. *Crime and Its Causes*. London: Swan Sonnenschein, 1891.

de la Motte, Brunhild. "Radicalism—Feminism—Socialism: The Case of the Women Novelists." *The Rise of Socialist Fiction, 1880–1914*. Ed. H. Gustav Klaus. New York: St. Martin's, 1987. 28–48.

Müller, F. Henrietta. "Miss Müller and Woman Suffrage." *Times*, 5 July 1884, 12.

Mulvey, Laura. "Visual Pleasure and Narrative Cinema." *Screen* 16.4 (1975): 6–18.

Mulry, David. "Popular Accounts of the Greenwich Bombing and Conrad's *The Secret Agent*." *Rocky Mountain Review of Language and Literature* 54.2 (2000): 43–64.

Murphy, Robert, ed. *The British Cinema Book*. 2nd ed. London: British Film Institute, 2001.

Nead, Lynda. *The Female Nude: Art, Obscenity, and Sexuality*. London: Routledge, 1992.

Nelson, Carolyn Christensen, ed. *A New Woman Reader: Fiction, Articles, Drama of the 1890s*. Peterborough, ON: Broadview, 2001.

Newton, Michael. "Four Notes on *The Secret Agent*." *Conradian* 32.1 (Spring 2007): 129–46.

Nicoll, David. *The Greenwich Mystery: Letters from the Dead*. London: David Nicoll, 1898.

Nollen, Scott Allen. *Sir Arthur Conan Doyle at the Cinema*. Jefferson, NC: McFarland, 1996.

Nord, Deborah Epstein. *Walking the Victorian Streets: Women, Representation, and the City*. Ithaca, NY: Cornell UP, 1995.

Nordau, Max. *Degeneration*. 1895. Lincoln: U of Nebraska P, 1993.

Norman, Henry. "*Three-Fingered Kate: The Case of the Chemical Fumes*." *Pictures* (17 August 1912): 16–20.

Oliver, Hermia. *The International Anarchist Movement in Late Victorian London*. London: Croom Helm, 1983.

Onslow, Barbara. "The Inside Story: Crime, Convicts and Careers for Women." *Victorian Crime, Madness and Sensation*. Eds. Andrew Maunder and Grace Moore. Aldershot, UK: Ashgate, 2004. 105–18.

Orczy, Emma. *Lady Molly of Scotland Yard*. 1910. New York: Akadine, 1999.

Orel, Harold, ed. *Critical Essays on Sir Arthur Conan Doyle*. New York: G. K. Hall, 1992.

Otis, Laura. "The Empire Bites Back: Sherlock Holmes as an Imperial Immune System." *Studies in Twentieth Century Literature* 22.1 (1998): 31–60.

Ouida. *Princess Napraxine*. 1884. London: Chatto and Windus, 1906.

"Our Opinion." *Film Censor*, 10 July 1912, 1.

Parsons, Deborah L. *Streetwalking the Metropolis: Women, the City, and Modernity*. Oxford: Oxford UP, 2000.

Pearson, Karl. *Chances of Death and Other Studies in Evolution*. 2 vols. London: Edward Arnold, 1897.

Pearson, Karl. "Politics and Science." *Fortnightly Review*, September 1894. Rpt. *Chances of Death* 1:140–72.

Pearson, Karl. "Woman and Labour." *Fortnightly Review*, May 1894. Rpt. *Chances of Death* 1:226–55.

Pearson, Karl. "The Woman Question." Printed for private circulation in 1885. Rpt. *Ethic of Freethought: A Selection of Essays and Lectures*. London: T. Fisher Unwin, 1888. 370–94.

"Penny Shows Must Go!" *Bioscope*, 12 August 1909, 4.

Perry, George. *The Great British Picture Show, from the 90s to the 70s*. New York: Hill and Wang, 1974.

Phillips, Wm. M. *Nightmares of Anarchy: Language and Cultural Change, 1870–1914*. Cranbury, NJ: Associated UP, 2003.

Pick, Daniel. *Faces of Degeneration: A European Disorder, c. 1848–c. 1918*. Cambridge: Cambridge UP, 1989.

"Pictures and Juvenile Crime." *Bioscope*, 20 February 1913, 553.

Popple, Simon. "The Diffuse Beam: Cinema and Change." Christopher Williams 97–106.

"Police." *Times*, 23 March 1863, 11.

Pound, Reginald. *Mirror of the Century: The Strand Magazine 1891–1950*. Cranbury, NJ: A. S. Barnes, 1966.

Powell, Kerry. "A Verdict of Death: Oscar Wilde, Actresses and Victorian Women." *The Cambridge Companion to Oscar Wilde*. Ed. Peter Raby. Cambridge: Cambridge UP, 1997. 181–94.

Pratt, Mary Louise. *Imperial Eyes: Travel Writing and Transculturation*. New York: Routledge, 1992.

Quail, John. *The Slow Burning Fuse: The Lost History of the British Anarchists*. London: Granada, 1978.

Rabinovitz, Lauren. *For the Love of Pleasure: Women, Movies, and Culture in Turn-of-the-Century Chicago*. New Brunswick, NJ: Rutgers UP, 1998.

Radzinowicz, Leon, and Roger Hood. *The Emergence of Penal Policy in Victorian and Edwardian England*. Oxford: Clarendon, 1990.

Rappaport, Erika Diane. *Shopping for Pleasure: Women in the Making of London's West End*. Princeton: Princeton UP, 2000.

Ray, Martin. "Conrad, Nordau, and Other Degenerates: The Psychology of *The Secret Agent*." *Conradiana* 16.2 (1984): 125–40.

Reed, Frances Miriam, ed. and introduction. *Vera; or, The Nihilist*. By Oscar Wilde. Lewiston, NY: Edwin Mellen P, 1989.

Reimer, Mavis. "L. T. Meade." *Dictionary of Literary Biography*. Vol. 141, *British Children's Writers, 1880–1914*. Ed. Laura Zaidman and Caroline Hunt. Detroit: Gale Research Group, 1994. 186–98.

Rhys, Jean. *Voyage in the Dark*. *Jean Rhys: The Complete Novels*. New York: Norton, 1985. 1–115.

Richards, Thomas. *The Commodity Culture of Victorian England: Advertising and Spectacle, 1851–1914*. Stanford, CA: Stanford UP, 1990.

Richardson, Angelique, and Chris Willis, eds. *The New Woman in Fiction and in Fact: Fin-de-Siècle Feminisms*. New York: Palgrave, 2001.

Richardson, LeeAnne. *New Woman and Colonial Adventure Fiction in Victorian Britain*. Gainesville: UP of Florida, 2006.

Riddle, John M. *Eve's Herbs: A History of Contraception and Abortion in the West.* Cambridge: Harvard UP, 1997.

Rook, Clarence. "The Stir Outside the Café Royal: A Story of Miss Van Snoop, Detective." *Harmsworth Magazine,* September 1898. Rpt. *Rivals of Sherlock Holmes.* Ed. Alan K. Russell. Secaucus, NJ: Castle Books, 1978. 221–26.

Rossetti, William Michael. *Some Reminiscences of William Michael Rossetti.* 2 vols. New York: Scribner's, 1906.

Rothfield, Lawrence. *Vital Signs: Medical Realism in Nineteenth-Century Fiction.* Princeton: Princeton UP, 1992.

Rothstein, Eric. "Broaching a Cultural Logic of Modernity." *Modern Language Quarterly* 61.2 (2000): 359–94.

Roughead, William. *Rascals Revived.* London: Cassell, 1940.

Rowell, George. "The Truth about *Vera.*" *Nineteenth-Century Theatre* 21.2 (1993): 94–100.

Ruddick, James. *Death at the Priory: Love, Sex, and Murder in Victorian England.* New York: Grove, 2001.

Said, Edward. *Orientalism.* New York: Pantheon, 1978.

Sanders, Lise Shapiro. *Consuming Fantasies: Labor, Leisure, and the London Shopgirl, 1880–1920.* Columbus: Ohio State UP, 2006.

Sandison, Alan. *Robert Louis Stevenson and the Appearance of Modernism: A Future Feeling.* Houndsmills, Hampshire: Macmillan, 1996.

Sandison, Alan. "A World Made for Liars: Stevenson's *Dynamiter* and the Death of the Real." *Robert Louis Stevenson Reconsidered: New Critical Perspectives.* Ed. William B. Jones, Jr. Jefferson, NC: McFarland, 2003. 140–62.

Saveson, John E. "Conrad, *Blackwood's,* and Lombroso." *Conradiana* 6.1 (1974): 57–62.

Scanlan, Margaret. "Terrorism and the Realistic Novel: Henry James and *The Princess Casamassima.*" *Texas Studies in Literature and Language* 34.3 (1992): 380–402.

Seltzer, Mark. "*The Princess Casamassima:* Realism and the Fantasy of Surveillance." *Nineteenth-Century Fiction* 35.4 (1981): 506–34.

Shaffer, Brian W. "'The Commerce of Shady Wares': Politics and Pornography in Conrad's *The Secret Agent.*" *ELH* 62.2 (1995): 443–66.

Shaw, Bernard. *Mrs. Warren's Profession.* 1898. *Norton Anthology of English Literature.* Ed. M. H. Abrams et al. 7th ed. Vol. 2. New York: Norton, 2000. 1810–56.

Showalter, Elaine. *Sexual Anarchy: Gender and Culture at the Fin-de-Siecle.* London: Virago, 1992.

"Signora Olivia Agresti: Rossettian Voice of Anglo-Italy." *Times,* Obituaries, 16 November 1960, 15.

Simpson, H. B. "Crime and Punishment." *Contemporary Review* 70.1 (July 1896): 91–108.

Sims, George R. *Dorcas Dene: Her Life and Adventures.* London: F. V. White, 1897.

Singer, Ben. "Female Power in the Serial-Queen Melodrama: The Etiology of an Anomaly." *Camera Obscura* 22 (1990): 90–129.

Singer, Ben. *Melodrama and Modernity: Early Sensational Cinema and Its Contexts.* New York: Columbia UP, 2001.

Singer, Ben. "Modernity, Hyperstimulus, and the Rise of Popular Sensationalism." Charney and Schwartz 72–99.

Slung, Michele B., ed. *Crime on Her Mind: Fifteen Stories of Female Sleuths from the Victorian Era to the Forties*. New York: Pantheon, 1975.

Smith, Arnold. "The Ethics of Sensational Fiction." *Westminster Review* 162.2 (August 1904): 188–94.

Sobchack, Thomas. "Gypsies, Children, and Criminals: Anti-authority Themes in Early British Silent Film." *Journal of Popular Film and Television* 17.1 (1989): 15–19.

Sontag, Susan. *On Photography*. New York: Farrar, Straus and Giroux, 1978.

Sopocy, Martin. "The Role of the Intertitle in Film Exhibition, 1904–1910." Christopher Williams 123–34.

Soskice, Juliet M. *Chapters from Childhood: Reminiscences of an Artist's Granddaughter*. 1921. Wilmington, DE: Scholarly Resources, 1972.

Srebnick, Amy Gilman. *The Mysterious Death of Mary Rogers: Sex and Culture in Nineteenth-Century New York*. Oxford: Oxford UP, 1995.

Stamp, Shelley. *Movie-Struck Girls: Women and Motion Picture Culture after the Nickelodeon*. Princeton: Princeton UP, 2000.

Stanley, Liz, with Ann Morley. *The Life and Death of Emily Wilding Davison*. London: Women's P, 1988.

Stashower, Daniel. *Teller of Tales: The Life of Arthur Conan Doyle*. New York: Holt, 1999.

Stepniak. *Underground Russia: Revolutionary Profiles and Sketches from Life*. 1882. 2nd ed. New York: Scribner's, 1885.

Stevenson, Robert Louis. "The Beach of Falesá." 1892. *Fictions of Empire*. Ed. John Kucich. Boston: Houghton Mifflin, 2003. 187–245.

Stevenson, Robert Louis. *The Letters of Robert Louis Stevenson*. Vol. 5 (July 1884–August 1887). Ed. Bradford A. Booth and Ernest Mehew. New Haven: Yale UP, 1995.

Stevenson, Robert Louis. *New Arabian Nights*. 1882. New York: Scribner, 1922.

Stevenson, Robert Louis. *The Strange Case of Dr. Jekyll and Mr. Hyde*. 1886. Peterborough, ON: Broadview, 1999.

Stevenson, Robert Louis, and Fanny Van de Grift Stevenson. *The Dynamiter*. London: Longmans, 1885.

Stevenson, Robert Louis, and Fanny Van de Grift Stevenson. *The Dynamiter*. Freeport, NY: Books for Libraries P, 1971.

Stocking, George, ed. *Functionalism Historicized: Essays on British Social Anthropology*. Madison: U of Wisconsin P, 1984.

Stocking, George. *Victorian Anthropology*. New York: Free P, 1987.

Stott, Rebecca. *The Fabrication of the Late-Victorian Femme Fatale: The Kiss of Death*. London: Macmillan, 1992.

Stott, Rebecca. "The Woman in Black: Race and Gender in *The Secret Agent*." *Conradian* 17.2 (Spring 1993): 39–58.

Surrette, Leon. "Ezra Pound at St. Elizabeth's." *Precursors and Aftermaths* 2.1 (2004): 7–23.

Surridge, Lisa. *Bleak Houses: Marital Violence in Victorian Fiction*. Athens: Ohio UP, 2005.

Sypher, Eileen. "Anarchism and Gender: James's *The Princess Casamassima* and Conrad's *The Secret Agent*." *Henry James Review* 9.1 (1988): 1–16.

Sypher, Eileen. *Wisps of Violence: Producing Public and Private Politics in the Turn-of-the-Century British Novel*. London: Verso, 1993.

Taylor, Barbara. *Eve and the New Jerusalem: Socialism and Feminism in the Nineteenth Century*. Cambridge: Harvard UP, 1993.

Thirlwell, Angela. *William and Lucy: The Other Rossettis*. New Haven: Yale UP, 2003.

Thomas, Ronald R. *Detective Fiction and the Rise of Forensic Science*. Cambridge: Cambridge UP, 1999.

Thomas, Ronald R. "The Fingerprint of the Foreigner: Colonizing the Criminal Body in 1890s Detective Fiction and Criminal Anthropology." *ELH* 61.3 (1994): 655–83.

Thomas, Ronald R. "Making Darkness Visible: Capturing the Criminal and Observing the Law in Victorian Photography and Detective Fiction." Christ and Jordan 134–68.

Thompson, E. P. *William Morris: Romantic to Revolutionary*. New York: Pantheon, 1955.

Thoms, Peter. *Detection and Its Designs: Narrative and Power in Nineteenth-Century Detective Fiction*. Athens: Ohio UP, 1998.

Tickner, Lisa. *The Spectacle of Women: Imagery of the Suffrage Campaign, 1907–1914*. Chicago: U of Chicago P, 1988.

Tilley, W. H. *The Background of "The Princess Casamassima."* Gainesville: U of Florida P, 1960.

Tingle, Nicholas. "Realism, Naturalism, and Formalism: James and *The Princess Casamassima*." *American Literary Realism* 21.2 (1989): 54–66.

Townshend, The Marchioness. "Crime and the Cinema: A Comment." *Pathé's Cinema Journal,* 15 November 1913, 25.

Trench-Bonett, Dorothy. "Naming and Silence: A Study of Language and the Other in Conrad's *Heart of Darkness*." *Conradiana* 32.2 (2000): 84–95.

Trilling, Lionel. *The Liberal Imagination*. New York: Viking, 1950.

Trowbridge, W. R. H. *Daughters of Eve*. London: Chapman and Hall, 1912.

Tryphonopoulos, Demetres. "Ezra Pound and Olivia Rossetti Agresti: Their Correspondence." *Ezra Pound and Europe*. Ed. Richard Taylor and Claus Melchior. Amsterdam: Rodopi, 1993. 93–104.

Tryphonopoulos, Demetres P., and Leon Surette, eds. *'I Cease Not to Yowl': Ezra Pound's Letters to Olivia Rossetti Agresti*. Urbana: U of Illinois P, 1998.

Turvey, Gerry. "Weary Willie and Tired Tim Go into Pictures: The Comic Films of the British and Colonial Kinematograph Company." Burton and Porter 69–75.

Urry, James. "Englishmen, Celts, and Iberians: The Ethnographic Survey of the United Kingdom, 1892–1899." Stocking, *Functionalism* 83–105.

Van Alstine, Jeannette. *Charlotte Corday*. London: W. H. Allen, 1890.

Vicinus, Martha. *Independent Women: Work and Community for Single Women, 1850–1920*. Chicago: U of Chicago P, 1985.

W. C. H. [Walter Hart] *Confessions of an Anarchist*. 1906. London: Grant Richards, 1911.

Wakeman, Geoffrey. *Victorian Book Illustration: The Technical Revolution*. Norwich, UK: David & Charles, 1973.

Walkowitz, Judith. *City of Dreadful Delight: Narratives of Sexual Danger in Late-Victorian London*. Chicago: U of Chicago P, 1992.

Walkowitz, Judith. *Prostitution and Victorian Society: Women, Class, and the State*. Cambridge: Cambridge UP, 1980.

Warner, Michael. *Publics and Counterpublics*. New York: Zone, 2002.

Weedon, Alexis. "Watch This Space: Wilkie Collins and New Strategies in Victorian Publishing in the 1890s." *Victorian Identities: Social and Cultural Formations in Nineteenth-Century Literature*. Ed. Ruth Robbins and Julian Wolfreys. New York: St. Martin's, 1996. 163–83.

Wiener, Martin J. *Reconstructing the Criminal: Culture, Law, and Policy in England, 1830–1914*. Cambridge: Cambridge UP, 1990.

Weiss, Marta. "Staged Photography in the Victorian Album." *Acting the Part: Photography as Theatre*. Ed. Lori Pauli. London: Merrell, 2006. 81–99.

Whitlock, Tammy. *Crime, Gender and Consumer Culture in Nineteenth-Century England*. Aldershot, UK: Ashgate, 2005.

Whitlock, Tammy. "A 'Taint Upon Them': The Madame Rachel Case, Fraud, and Retail Trade in Nineteenth-Century England." *Victorian Review* 24.1 (1998): 29–52.

Whitworth, Michael. "Inspector Heat Inspected: *The Secret Agent* and the Meanings of Entropy." *Review of English Studies* 49.193 (1998): 40–59.

Wilde, Oscar. *The Complete Letters of Oscar Wilde*. Ed. Merlin Holland and Rupert Hart-Davis. London: Fourth Estate, 2000.

Wilde, Oscar. *Complete Works of Oscar Wilde*. New York: HarperCollins, 1966.

Wilde, Oscar. "The Decay of Lying." 1889. *Complete Works* 970–92.

Wilde, Oscar. "The Harlot House." 1885. *Complete Works* 789.

Wilde, Oscar. *The Importance of Being Earnest*. 1895. New York: Norton, 2006.

Wilde, Oscar. "Madonna Mia." 1881. *Complete Works* 732.

Wilde, Oscar. "The New Helen." 1881. *Complete Works* 733.

Wilde, Oscar. *The Picture of Dorian Gray*. 1891. New York: Longman, 2007.

Wilde, Oscar. *Salomé*. 1894. *Complete Works* 552–75.

Wilde, Oscar. "The Soul of Man under Socialism." *The Annotated Oscar Wilde*. Ed. H. Montgomery Hyde. London: Orbis, 1982. 398–417.

Wilde, Oscar. *Vera; or, The Nihilists*. 1883. *Works of Oscar Wilde*. Vol. 2. London: Methuen, 1908. 115–261.

Wilde, Oscar. *Vera; or, The Nihilist*. 1883 staged edition. Ed. Frances Miriam Reed. Lewiston, NY: Edwin Mellen P, 1989.

Williams, Christopher, ed. *Cinema: The Beginnings and the Future*. London: U of Westminster P, 1996.

Williams, Neville. *Powder and Paint: A History of the Englishwoman's Toilet, Elizabeth I–Elizabeth II*. London: Longman, 1957.

Willis, Chris. "The Female Moriarty: The Arch-Villainess in Victorian Popular Fiction." *The Devil Himself: Villainy in Detective Fiction and Film*. Ed. Stacy Gillis and Philippa Gates. Westport, CT: Greenwood P, 2002. 57–68.

Wiltse, Ed. "'So Constant an Expectation': Sherlock Holmes and Seriality." *Narrative* 6.2 (1998): 105–22.

Wyndham, Horace. *Blotted Scutcheons: Some Society Causes Célèbres*. London: Hutchinson, 1928.

Zedner, Lucia. *Women, Crime, and Custody in Victorian England*. Oxford: Clarendon, 1991.

INDEX

(1910), 117; *Three-Fingered Kate—The Pseudo-Quartette* (1912), 117–18

Express, 77

Extradition Act of 1870, 153, 188

Fabian Society, 172

Factory Girl's Honour, A (1913), 112

Fascism, Italian, 207, 250n31

Fawcett, E. Douglas; *Hartmann the Anarchist: or, The Doom of the Great City,* 241n1

Felski, Rita, 4, 227n3, 228n12, 252n2

feminism, 7, 13, 16, 18, 20, 22, 31, 50–51, 53–57, 66, 69, 71–74, 81–85, 87–88, 91, 97, 100, 107, 111–13, 122–24, 130–34, 143, 150–51, 164, 167, 169, 175, 186–87, 190, 195, 197–200, 202, 204–5, 207–10, 212, 216, 220–22, 225–26, 228n12, 232n31, 233n3, 235n17, 238n27, 241n2, 244n29, 245n29, 252n43; Anglo-feminism, 19, 92–96, 100; consumerist feminism, 83–84, 178; feminist criticism, 81–84, 107, 216, 229n14, 235n14; liberal feminism, 71; Marxist feminism, 167; pseudofeminism, 19, 70; state feminism, 69. *See also* New Woman, suffrage movement, suffragettes, women in the economic sphere, women in the political sphere, women in science and medicine

Fenians, 156, 175, 188, 190, 205–6, 211, 214, 241n4, 242n11, 246n6, 247n9, 249n30. *See also* Ireland: Irish nationalism

Figner, Vera, 190

film, 1, 6, 11–12, 17, 19–20, 22, 27, 29–30, 47, 69, 103–45, 180, 215, 223–25, 228n7, 228n9, 235n14, 236nn1–4, 236nn6–7, 237n8, 237n10, 237n13, 237n21, 238nn26–28, 238nn38–39, 239nn41–44, 239n53, 240nn56–57, 240nn59–63, 252n1; anti-authoritarianism in film, 105–6, 114–18, 122–26, 128–33, 143–45; audience composition, 105–6, 114–16, 236n3, 237n21; crime film, 3–6, 19–20, 103, 106, 111, 113–32, 143–45, 223, 236n7, 237n22, 238nn26–28, 238nn38– 39, 239nn42–44, 240n59, 240n63; film noir, 69; films of Queen Victoria's Diamond Jubilee, 142; serial queen films, 238n27. *See also* United States: U.S. films

Film Censor, 105, 119, 144

Film House Record, 117, 138, 239n49

Flaubert, Gustave; *Madame Bovary,* 88

Flint, Kate, 29–30, 33

Foiled by a Girl (1912), 113, 237n18–20

Ford, Ford Madox, 206, 242n10, 249n30

Fortnightly Review, 32

Foucault, Michel, 4–5, 54, 164

fraud, 16, 18, 73, 76, 233n5, 234n8

free love, 208, 210, 213, 250nn32–33

Freedman, Jonathan, 195, 248n18

French Revolution, 163, 178, 187, 203, 205, 210, 244n22, 246n3, 248n16, 250n34. *See also* Charlotte Corday

Freud, Sigmund, 243n18

Furniss, Harry, 142, 144, 236n4

Gagnier, Regenia, 158, 248n17

Galton, Francis, 14, 31, 92, 110

Gaskell, Elizabeth; *Mary Barton,* 15–16

Gaumont, 141, 238n26

Gilbert, Sandra, 229n14

Gissing, George; *The Odd Women,* 207

glamour, 5, 12, 67, 69, 103, 106, 108–10, 116, 133–34, 143, 180, 191, 215–16

Glasier, Bruce, 245n34

Goodlad, Lauren M. E., 5, 150, 228n6

Goring, Charles, 229n19

Grand, Sarah, 8, 57, 123–24, 216, 233n4, 235n17; *The Heavenly Twins,* 123–24

Great Exhibition, 11

Meade, L. T. (*continued*)
234n7 ("The Blood-Red Cross,"
86–87, 89, 94, 98, 233n5; "The
Bloodstone," 86, 88–89, 92, 99;
"Madame Sara," 72, 85–86,
92–94, 98; "The Talk of the
Town," 96; "The Teeth of the
Wolf," 94, 98); *A Sweet Girl
Graduate,* 233n3; "A Young
Blue-Stocking," 233n3
Meddling Policeman, The (1904), 115
medicine. *See* women in science and
medicine
Melchiori, Barbara, 156, 240n1,
241n8, 246n6, 247n10, 251n40
melodrama, 112–13, 194–95, 200, 204,
219, 238n27, 248n16
Men and Women's Club, 244n29
Meredith, Isabel. *See* Helen Rossetti,
Olivia Rossetti
Midwives' Act, 99
Militant Suffragette, The, 134, 239n52
Mill, John Stuart, 150–51, 228n6
Mill Girl, The (1913), 112
Misguided Bobby, The (1905), 115
Mitchell, W. J. T., 26, 246n1
Modjeska, Helen, 191
Moore, George; *A Drama in Muslin,*
125
Morris, William, 172, 242n11,
245nn34–36
Morrison, William Douglas, 14, 16,
97, 187, 235n23
Most, Johann, 248n14
Müller, F. Henrietta, 221
Mulvey, Laura, 11, 107–8, 235n14
murder, 4, 15–16, 39–41, 49, 54, 56,
60–69, 86, 97, 107, 132, 134,
158–59, 162–63, 173–75, 191,
200–202, 212, 224, 230n13,
231n25, 232n27, 232n34, 235n24,
239n43. *See also* assassination,
poison

Nation, 179
National Union of Women's Suffrage
Societies, 7–11, 239n47
nationalism / national identity, 53,

59–60, 74, 77–78, 81, 93–96, 100,
105, 157, 219–20, 231n16,
235n17, 236n4, 236n6, 238n39,
250n36. *See also* imperialism, state
Nechayev, Sergey, 249n27
New Imperialism, 94–95, 100. *See also*
imperialism
New Journalism, 28
Newnes, George, 28
newsreels, 133, 139–41, 240n56
New Woman, The, 3–4, 7–10, 16, 22,
81, 89, 91, 99–100, 112, 122–24,
138, 187, 190, 208, 212, 216, 220,
228n11, 233n4, 235n17, 241n2;
New Woman novel / New
woman fiction, 123, 157, 208,
210, 216, 224, 242n14. *See also*
feminism, office work, suffrage
movement, women in the economic sphere, women in the political sphere, women in science
and medicine
New Woman, The (1905), 112
New York Daily Tribune, 197
New York Times, 179, 197
New York World, 194
Nicoll, David, 242n10
Nietzscheism, 160
nihilism / nihilists, 156, 188, 190–91,
194–206, 228n10, 242n12,
244n25, 246n6, 247n8,
247nn10–11, 248n14,
248nn20–21, 249n26, 249n28,
250n30
Nordau, Max, 91, 98, 227n2, 231n15,
235n16

office work, women's, 12, 61, 81, 91,
112–13
Once Too Often (1904), 112
Orczy, Emma; *Lady Molly of Scotland
Yard,* 237n20
Orientalism, 93–95, 235n21, 251n41
Ouida; *Princess Napraxine,* 165, 244n25
Our New Policeman (1906), 115

Paget, Sydney, 45, 231n24
Pall Mall Gazette, 234n12, 251n40

Pankhurst, Emmeline, 240n57
Pankhurst, Sylvia, 142
Parsons, Albert, 241n5
Parsons, Deborah, 107, 108, 216, 228nn11–12, 235n13
passante, 26, 108, 110, 215–16
Pathé, 139, 141–42, 240n56
Patmore, Coventry, 219
Paul, R. W., 1, 114
Pearson, Karl, 32, 134, 159, 235n16, 244n29
penny dreadfuls, 2, 144
penny press, 105
photography, 27–28, 31–32, 34–35, 42, 45, 47, 67, 108, 111, 131, 180, 187, 230n12, 232n1, 246n3; mug shot, 35, 111
Pictures, The, 117–18, 120, 122, 127
Pioneer Club, The, 233n3
Pirkis, C. L., 237n20
poisoning, 93, 97–98, 202, 235n24, 236n25
police and policing, 4, 18, 20, 27, 34, 53–54, 61, 66, 88, 97, 114–16, 121, 129–31, 142, 171, 175–76, 181, 199–200, 209–10, 218, 224, 232n26, 239n44, 242n10, 251n40. *See also* women police and war- dens
political crime, 20–22, 152–53, 157, 165, 175, 186–90, 195–99, 203, 205–6, 209, 212, 216, 220–21, 242n11, 246n6, 250n36. *See also* terrorism, women revolutionaries
politics. *See* women in the political sphere
popular culture, 104–5, 182–83, 241n7. *See also* mass culture
Porter, Edwin, 114, 239n41
Pound, Ezra, 250n31
Prescott, Marie, 191–93, 247n13, 249n24
Prevention of Cruelty to Children Acts, 13
prison, 73–74, 98, 131, 163–65, 171–73, 200–201, 234n6, 239n43, 239n47, 244nn23–24, 244n26, 248n14, 249n26

private sphere, 7, 16, 27, 51, 57, 144, 209–10. *See also* domestic sphere
prostitution, 15–16, 21, 77, 83–84, 167, 184–85, 229n21; procura- tion, 75, 77, 234n12
public sphere, 8–12, 14, 16, 49–51, 57, 62, 66, 69, 71, 74, 77, 80–84, 96, 107, 111–13, 144, 189, 210, 222, 236n3, 240n61; proletarian public sphere, 236n3
Punch, 9–12, 73, 89–90, 230n8
Purcell, E., 215

Queen of Criminals, 238n27

race, 27, 31–35, 38–39, 41, 60, 64, 78, 92–96, 100, 116–17, 159, 231n20, 231n23, 232n33, 246n39, 250n36, 251n36
Rachel's Sin (1911), 239n43
Ranelagh, Lord, 76, 78–79
Rappaport, Erika, 228nn12–13, 233n3, 235n13, 246n37
realism, 4, 15, 27, 29, 47, 139, 214, 217, 219, 224
Revolting Daughters Controversy, 232n30
revolutionaries. *See* anarchism, ni- hilism, socialism, women revolu- tionaries
Rhys, Jean; *Voyage in the Dark,* 121–22
Richardson, Mary, 221, 252n43
Rook, Clarence, 237n20
Rossetti, Arthur, 249n29
Rossetti, Christina, 93, 125, 206; "Goblin Market," 93, 125
Rossetti, Dante Gabriel, 206, 250n31
Rossetti, Helen, 21–22, 55, 186, 189, 206–14, 218, 221, 225, 242n10, 249n29, 249n30, 250n31, 250n36; *A Girl among the Anarchists,* 21–22, 186, 189, 197, 206–14, 216, 218, 220–21, 224, 242n10, 250n36, 251n36
Rossetti, Lucy, 206, 249n30
Rossetti, Olivia, 21–22, 55, 186, 189, 206–14, 218, 221, 225, 242n10, 249nn29–30, 250n31,

87, 150, 153–56, 230nn4–5, 230n10, 231n24

Subject for a Rogues' Gallery, A (1904), 110–11

suffrage movement, 7–11, 51, 57, 69, 95, 100, 112, 132–33, 137–43, 187, 221, 233n3, 239n47, 239n49, 239n51, 239n53, 240n57, 252n43. *See also* feminism, suffragettes, women in the political sphere

Suffragette Derby of 1913 (1913), 140–41, 240n58

Suffragette Film (1908), 140

Suffragette in the Barber Shop (1898), 133, 239n48

Suffragette Riot at Westminster (1910), 142

suffragettes, 12, 20, 57, 106, 132–43, 221, 239n47, 239n53, 246n6, 250n30; militant suffragette terror, 20, 57, 106, 132–34, 138–40, 142–43, 186, 221, 246n6

Suffragettes and the Hobble Skirt (1910), 133

Suffragettes' Downfall; Or, Who Said Rats? (1911), 137–38

Sweet Suffragettes (1906), 133

Symonds, John Addington, 251n40

terrorism / terrorists, 2, 6–7, 16–17, 20–22, 131–32, 149–57, 160–62, 165, 170, 175, 183–84, 186, 188–91, 197–98, 205–6, 209–15, 217–24, 228n10, 241n2, 241n4, 242nn10–11, 244n25, 246n6, 247n9, 250n35, 251n40. *See also* assassination, dynamite, political crime, suffragettes: militant suffragette terror

Terry, Ellen, 191

theater, 108, 190–94, 238n28, 247n8, 247nn13–14, 248n15. *See also* actresses

theft, 16, 20, 25, 54, 59–62, 87–88, 96–97, 106, 115–18, 121–23, 126, 128–31, 134, 144, 156, 218, 239n44

Thomas, Ronald, 26, 34, 227n5,

229n20, 230n1, 231n19, 243n16

Three-Fingered Kate. See *Exploits of Three-Fingered Kate*

Times (London), 73, 77–79, 86, 188, 211–12, 215, 217, 221, 234n6, 234n8, 235n18, 235n21, 242n12, 247n7, 247n9, 250n35

Topinard, Paul, 187, 189

Torch, 206, 242n10, 248n20, 249nn29–30, 250n30, 251n36

Trafalgar Square Riot (1913), 141–42

Tube of Death, The (1913), 131–32, 239n45

"typewriter" girls. See office work, women's

Uncle Josh at the Moving Pictures Show (1902), 227n1

United States, 77–78, 152, 188, 191, 197, 217, 230n4, 234n12, 241n5, 247n13; U.S. films / film industry, 105, 107, 110, 134, 224, 227n1, 236nn3–4, 236n6, 237n8, 237n10, 238n27, 238n39, 239n41, 240n57, 240n61

Unwin, Raymond, 172

Velázquez, Diego; *The Toilet of Venus* (aka *The Rokeby Venus*), 221, 252n43

visuality, 18, 26–35, 38–42, 45–51, 57–59, 62, 64, 67–72, 81, 87, 93, 103, 106–15, 133, 135, 139–42, 182, 191, 221–25, 228n6, 229n15, 230n2, 230n9, 230nn11–12, 232n1, 235n14, 236n3, 237n10, 240n61. *See also* image

Walkowitz, Judith, 4, 14–15, 82, 84, 228nn11–12, 229n21, 235n13, 244n29, 246n40

Warner, Michael, 13–14

Westminster Review, 1, 227n2

When Women Join the Force (1910), 112

Whitlock, Tammy, 76, 86, 123, 228n12, 234n9

Wife's Revenge, A; Or, The Gambler's End (1904), 132

Wilde, Oscar, 15–16, 21–22, 55, 186, 189–207, 210, 214, 221, 231n21, 247n10, 247nn12–14, 248nn14–15, 248nn17–18, 248n21, 249nn22–25, 249n27; *The Duchess of Padua*, 191; "The Harlot House," 16; *The Importance of Being Earnest*, 202, 205; *The Picture of Dorian Gray*, 92, 194; *Salomé*, 15, 191; "The Soul of Man under Socialism," 195–96; *Vera; Or, the Nihilist* (stage production), 191–94, 197, 247nn13–14, 248nn14–15, 249nn22–24; *Vera; Or, the Nihilists* (drama), 21–22, 186, 189–207, 210, 214, 216, 220–21, 224, 247n10, 248n15, 249nn24–27

"woman question," 7, 73, 167. *See also* feminism, suffrage movement

Woman's Treachery, A (1910), 131–32, 239nn42–43

women in the economic sphere, 56–57, 72–86, 88–89, 93–96, 100, 176–82, 232n31, 234n8, 246n38. *See also* Married Women's Property Acts, office work, shopgirls, shops

women in the political sphere, 22, 62–63, 68, 72–75, 137–39, 165–70, 186–91, 195–222, 233n3, 239n53. *See also* suffrage movement, suffragettes, women revolutionaries

women in science and medicine, 73, 81, 96–100, 235n22

women police and wardens, 112, 163–64, 244n23

women revolutionaries, 21–22, 165–71, 173–74, 178, 186–222, 246n1, 247nn8–11, 249n24, 249n26, 249nn28–30, 250n31, 250nn33–34, 250n36, 251n38, 251n41. *See also* suffragettes

Women's Rights (1898), 134–37, 239n41, 239n53

Women's Social and Political Union, 7, 186, 221, 239n47

women's suffrage. *See* suffrage movement

working class. *See* class

Yellow Book, 89, 91

Zasulich, Vera, 190, 247n11

Printed and bound by CPI Group (UK) Ltd, Croydon, CR0 4YY

09/06/2025

14685645-0002